DATE DUE

MY 27 '94			
DE 1 8 '98			
AG 5 '04			

DEMCO 38-296

Library Index
and
Guide

*An index to the tables of contents, issues, and topics
in the 20-volume library set.*

The Dushkin Publishing Group, Inc.

Taking Sides® is a registered trademark of
The Dushkin Publishing Group, Inc.

Manufactured in the United States of America

Library of Congress Cataloging-in-Publication Data

Main entry under title:
    Taking sides: library index and guide.
        1. Social problems—Indexes. 2. Taking sides—Indexes.
          Z7164.S66T35
          [HN17.5]   016.301—dc20
          ISBN: 1–56134–308–0   93–38744

PREFACE

The **Taking Sides Library** is an easy-to-access source of lively and thought-provoking controversial issues from a wide range of disciplines. These controversies can be used as the basis for term papers, brief writing assignments, in-class debates or discussions, speech contests—any situation where a stimulating and critical examination of a topic is required.

The **Taking Sides Library** is composed of 20 debate-style readers. Each reader is designed to introduce students to a mix of long-standing and contemporary controversies within a field of study. For each issue in the Taking Sides volumes, a question is asked (e.g., *Should Capital Punishment Be Abolished?*), and an affirmative and a negative response are supplied (e.g., YES: Jack Greenberg, from "Against the American System of Capital Punishment" / NO: Ernest van den Haag, from "The Ultimate Punishment: A Defense"). The **Taking Sides Library** has a total of 734 pro and con essays that debate 367 important issues.

The purpose of the debate format is to stimulate interest in the subject matter and to encourage the application of critical thinking skills. In addition, the Taking Sides format helps students to understand and appreciate the nature and value of evidence in forming opinions. The pro and con selections reflect a variety of ideological viewpoints and have been selected for their liveliness and substance and because of their value in a debate framework. The selections are written by scholars and commentators who are respected and accomplished in their fields.

Each issue in each of the volumes in the **Taking Sides Library** has an issue *introduction*, which sets the stage for the debate, provides some background information on each author, and generally puts the issue into context. Each issue concludes with a *postscript*, which briefly summarizes the debate, gives the reader paths for further investigation, and suggests additional readings that might be helpful. Each volume in the **Taking Sides Library** concludes with a list of *contributors* (with a brief biography of each contributor) and an *index*. (See Explanatory Chart on next page for a sample page from each of these elements.)

How to Use This *Library Index and Guide*

This *Library Index and Guide* is designed to be a quick and easy reference to the issues in each of the Taking Sides volumes. It has four sections:

- Reference Key
- Tables of Contents
- Issue List
- Topic Index

EXPLANATORY CHART

Issue Introduction	Postscript

ISSUE 16

POSTSCRIPT

Does the United States Need Socialized Medicine?

Does the United States Need Socialized Medicine?

YES: Nancy Watzman, from "Socialized Medicine Now—Without the Wait," *The Washington Monthly* (October 1991)

NO: John C. Goodman, from "An Expensive Way to Die," *National Review* (April 16, 1990)

ISSUE SUMMARY

YES: Policy analyst Nancy Watzman argues that the Canadian model of universal medical insurance can be adapted and improved in order to provide superior and less expensive care for all Americans.
NO: John C. Goodman, president of the National Center for Policy Analysis, maintains that Americans get more and better health care more promptly than do individuals in countries with compulsory schemes of national health insurance.

Since World War II, more Nobel Prizes in physiology and medicine have been awarded to physicians and medical scientists working in the United States than in the rest of the world. It is widely acknowledged that the training and education of medical personnel in the United States is the best in the world. The latest medical technology is more widely available in the United States than anywhere else. It is no surprise that when wealthy people in other countries have a disease that is difficult to treat, they often seek treatment in one of the renowned medical clinics or research hospitals in the United States.

By contrast, it is estimated that more than 30 million Americans have no medical coverage and another 100 million are underinsured. This is true despite the fact that roughly $750 billion a year is currently spent on health care in the United States. One-third of this amount is spent directly by the federal government. In 1991, the total expenditure for health care amounted to more than 14 percent of the gross national product, nearly 10 times the amount spent in the United States 40 years ago, and every year the total grows higher.

There are two overriding political issues involved in health care reform: coverage and cost. In 1965, the national government recognized and tried to

280

If the American health care system is the patient, perhaps it is time for a complete check-up. There are those who argue that the system is in very good health and should be left alone. They may concede that strong medicine may be necessary in dealing with specific problems, as was the case with the creation of Medicare and Medicaid, but if such radical treatments as socialized medicine are prescribed for the system as a whole, the cure could be worse than the disease.

Former secretary of Health, Education, and Welfare Joseph A. Califano, Jr., believes that the system is not well, but in *America's Health Care Revolution: Who Lives? Who Dies? Who Pays?* (Random House, 1986), Califano argues that the movement to a sound health care system must be accomplished largely in the private sector. More critically, Charles J. Dougherty's *American Health Care: Realities, Rights, and Reforms* (Oxford University Press, 1988) is a sober examination of the moral right to health care, to which Americans do not always have ready access, and Dougherty proposes changes in the delivery system.

Others argue that radical surgery is necessary. One criticism is that the health care industry has lost the ability to control costs and that the present payment system must change. This view is argued in Dan C. Coddington, David J. Keen, Keith D. Moore, and Richard L. Clarke, *The Crisis in Health Care* (Jossey Bass, 1990). Similarly, Thomas H. Ainsworth, *Live or Die* (Macmillan, 1983), attacks escalating costs, restricted access, overspecialization, and technological overkill. Robert H. Blank, *Rationing Medicine* (Columbia University Press, 1988), examines the moral and economic implications of expensive procedures such as organ transplants, the treatment of seriously ill newborn babies, reproductive technologies, and fetal health. *Setting Limits* (Simon & Schuster, 1987) is a provocative examination of these issues by Daniel Callahan, director of the Hastings Center, that focuses upon moral issues in American society.

Some critics believe that medical costs have gotten out of hand, in part because expensive equipment and drugs tempt doctors and hospitals to prescribe unnecessary treatments and in part because modern medical technology can extend the life of a sick premature infant or a terminally ill person, but at costs that society simply cannot afford to pay. Given the finite limits that we must impose on medical costs, how do we choose what we are—and are not—prepared to pay for?

295

The Reference Key provides an explanation for the abbreviations used for the Taking Sides titles. The Tables of Contents section reproduces the detailed table of contents from each Taking Sides volume. The Issue List is an alphabetical listing of every issue, and each issue is cross-referenced to the Taking Sides volume in which it appears. In the Topic Index, each issue in the 20 volumes that compose the **Taking Sides Library** has been indexed according to its main topic(s) and is cross-referenced to the Taking Sides volume in which it appears. (See the sample entries at the top of the Issue List and the Topic Index.)

Once you have located an issue of interest in the Issue List or Topic Index, you can easily turn to the Tables of Contents section, locate the table of

Contributors

Index

AUTHORS

HERBERT E. ALEXANDER is the director of the Citizens Research Foundation in Los Angeles, California, and a professor of political science at the University of Southern California.

ROBERT L. BARTLEY, the recipient of the 1980 Pulitzer Prize for editorial writing, is the editor and vice president of the *Wall Street Journal*, with primary responsibility for the editorial page. He is a member of the Council on Foreign Relations and the American Political Science Association, and he holds honorary doctor of laws degrees from Macalester College and Babson College.

WALTER BERNS received his Ph.D. from the University of Chicago in 1953. He taught at the University of Toronto, Cornell University, and Yale University before becoming the John M. Olin Professor of Government at Georgetown University in Washington, D.C. He is also the author of more than 40 articles and 7 books, including *Taking the Constitution Seriously* (Simon & Schuster, 1987). He has held a Guggenheim Fellowship, a Fulbright Fellowship, and a Rockefeller Fellowship, among other honors.

HARRY A. BLACKMUN has been an associate justice of the U.S. Supreme Court since his appointment by former president Nixon in 1970. He wrote the Court's decision in the landmark *Roe v. Wade* case.

DAVID BOLLIER is a journalist and a consultant specializing in politics, law, the media, and consumer affairs. He graduated from Yale Law School in 1985, and he is the coauthor, with Henry S. Cohn, of *The Great Hartford Circus Fire* (Yale University Press, 1991).

ROBERT H. BORK, a former U.S. Court of Appeals judge for the District of Columbia Circuit, is the John M. Olin Scholar in Legal Studies at the American Enterprise Institute in Washington, D.C., a privately funded public policy research organization.

STANLEY C. BRUBAKER is a professor of political science in the Department of Government at Colgate University in Hamilton, New York, and the director of Colgate University's Washington Study Group.

STEPHEN L. CARTER is a professor of law at Yale University Law School and the author of *Reflections of an Affirmative Action*

campaign finance reform, 20; need for radical reform of Congress and, 79–80, 85–86; controversy over, and PACs, 48–55
Campaign Reform Act of 1971, 20
Canada, socialized medicine in, 282, 283, 284–285, 286–287, 288, 290–291, 292–293
capital punishment, 169; controversy over, 174–185
Carey v. Population Services, International, 306
Carter, Jimmy, 106
Carter, Stephen L., argument of, against affirmative action, 190–193
Case for Open Debate, The, 216
CBS, 61, 63
censorship, 67
Chaplinsky v. New Hampshire, 207, 212
Charles, Earl, 182, 184–185
Charter Commission, 34
Chile, 67, 71
Chomsky, Noam, on elitism in media, 66–71
Chris Craft Corp., 8
Chrysler Corporation, federal loans to, and corporate grass-roots lobbying, 8–9
churches, controversy over "wall of separation" between church and state and, 314–326
Civil Aeronautics Board (CAB), 115–116
civil liberties, 222, 223
civil rights, controversy over affirmative action and, 190–200
Civil Rights Act, 136, 195, 197
Civil War, 196
Clark, Kenneth, 191–192
Claybrook, Joan, on governmental regulation, 121–129

cocaine, *see* drugs
Columbia University, 206
committees, need for radical reform of Congress and number of, 82–83, 84
Common Cause, 11–12, 48, 51
Commonwealth of Pennsylvania and Williams v. Operating Engineers, Local 542, 198
communism, 68, 70
community-based corrections, 167, 168
"compelling point," health of the mother issue in abortion and, 307
Congress, 136, 146, 233; debate over ending system of divided government at federal level, 98–100; PACs and, 48–55; controversy over need for radical reform of, 78–93
"conservative" approach, to material poverty, and welfare, 247–248
conspiracy theory, of assassination attempt on Pope John Paul II, 68, 70, 71
Constitution: affirmative action and, 194–200; controversy over "original intent" of, 134–148
Consumer Product Safety Commission (CPSC), 128–129
consumption, national debt and, 267, 269, 270
consumption tax, on legalization of drugs, 226, 229
Corporate Average Fuel Economy (CAFE), 117–118
corporations: debate over domination of government by, 4–26; information services of, 69–70; PACs and, 48, 49, 50, 53, 54
corruption: police, and drug trafficking, 222, 227–228; need for radical reform in Congress and,

contents for the Taking Sides volume in which your issue appears, and read a brief description of the issue. In this way, the *Library Index and Guide* quickly gives you access to information on a controversial issue and allows you to accurately target the most appropriate volume (or volumes) for your needs.

We hope that you will find this *Library Index and Guide* to be a valuable reference tool. Please let us know how it can be improved.

Mimi Egan
Program Manager

CONTENTS

Preface   i

Reference Key   1

Tables of Contents   4

American History, Volume I, Fifth Edition   4
American History, Volume II, Fifth Edition   11
Bioethical Issues, Fifth Edition   18
Business Ethics and Society, Second Edition   26
Crime and Criminology, Third Edition   34
Drugs and Society, First Edition   41
Economic Issues, Sixth Edition   48
Educational Issues, Seventh Edition   55
Environmental Issues, Fifth Edition   62
Family and Personal Relationships, First Edition   69
Health and Society, First Edition   76
Human Sexuality, Fourth Edition   82
Legal Issues, Fifth Edition   90
Mass Media and Society, Second Edition   96
Moral Issues, Fourth Edition   103
Political Issues, Eighth Edition   111
Psychological Issues, Seventh Edition   118
Race and Ethnicity, First Edition   125
Social Issues, Seventh Edition   132
World Politics, Fifth Edition   139

Issue List   146

Topic Index   156

REFERENCE KEY

Use the following key to determine the *Taking Sides* volume references used in this index:

AH1   *Taking Sides: Clashing Views on Controversial Issues in American History, Volume I*, Fifth Edition

AH2   *Taking Sides: Clashing Views on Controversial Issues in American History, Volume II*, Fifth Edition

Bio   *Taking Sides: Clashing Views on Controversial Bioethical Issues*, Fifth Edition

BE   *Taking Sides: Clashing Views on Controversial Issues in Business Ethics and Society*, Second Edition

CR   *Taking Sides: Clashing Views on Controversial Issues in Crime and Criminology*, Third Edition

Dru   *Taking Sides: Clashing Views on Controversial Issues in Drugs and Society*, First Edition

Eco   *Taking Sides: Clashing Views on Controversial Economic Issues*, Sixth Edition

Edu   *Taking Sides: Clashing Views on Controversial Educational Issues*, Seventh Edition

Env   *Taking Sides: Clashing Views on Controversial Environmental Issues*, Fifth Edition

Fam   *Taking Sides: Clashing Views on Controversial Issues in Family and Personal Relationships*, First Edition

Hea   *Taking Sides: Clashing Views on Controversial Issues in Health and Society*, First Edition

HS   *Taking Sides: Clashing Views on Controversial Issues in Human Sexuality*, Fourth Edition

Leg   *Taking Sides: Clashing Views on Controversial Legal Issues*, Fifth Edition

MM   *Taking Sides: Clashing Views on Controversial Issues in Mass Media and Society*, Second Edition

Mor   *Taking Sides: Clashing Views on Controversial Moral Issues*, Fourth Edition

Pol   *Taking Sides: Clashing Views on Controversial Political Issues*, Eighth Edition

Psy   *Taking Sides: Clashing Views on Controversial Psychological Issues*, Seventh Edition

RER   *Taking Sides: Clashing Views on Controversial Issues in Race and Ethnicity*, First Edition

Soc   *Taking Sides: Clashing Views on Controversial Social Issues*, Seventh Edition

WP   *Taking Sides: Clashing Views on Controversial Issues in World Politics*, Fifth Edition

AMERICAN HISTORY,
Volume I, Fifth Edition

ISSUE 1. **Was Colonial Culture Uniquely American?**   **2**

YES: Gary B. Nash, from *Race, Class, and Politics: Essays on American Colonial and Revolutionary Society*   **4**

NO: David Hackett Fischer, from *Albion's Seed: Four British Folkways in America*   **11**

Professor of history Gary B. Nash argues that colonial American culture emerged from a convergence of three broad cultural traditions—European, Native American, and African—which produced a unique triracial society in the New World. Professor of history David Hackett Fischer contends that the cultural traditions of colonial America and the United States were derived from English folkways transported by migrants from four different regions in the British Isles.

ISSUE 2. **Was Race a Central Factor in the Colonists' Attitudes Toward Native Americans?**   **22**

YES: Alden T. Vaughan, from "From White Man to Redskin: Changing Anglo-American Perceptions of the American Indian," *The American Historical Review*   **24**

NO: Karen Ordahl Kupperman, from *Settling With the Indians: The Meeting of English and Indian Cultures in America, 1580–1640*   **31**

Professor of history Alden T. Vaughan presents the Native American as a victim of color symbolism, racial differences, and nonconformity to European culture. Professor of history Karen Ordahl Kupperman insists that the English colonists' efforts to exercise unrestricted power over Native Americans, not racism, provided the catalyst for conflict between these two groups in early America.

ISSUE 3. **Was the Salem Witchcraft Hysteria Caused by a Fear of Women?**   **42**

YES: Carol F. Karlsen, from *The Devil in the Shape of a Woman: Witchcraft in Colonial New England*   **44**

NO: Kai T. Erikson, from *Wayward Puritans: A Study in the Sociology of Deviance*   **54**

Associate professor of history Carol F. Karlsen contends that the belief that women were evil existed implicitly at the core of Puritan culture and that it explains why alleged witches, as threats to the desired order of society, were generally seen as women. Professor of sociology Kai T. Erikson argues that the Salem witchcraft hysteria was a product of the Puritan colonists' efforts to restore a common sense of mission, which they believed had eroded over the first 60 years of settlement.

ISSUE 4.   Did Capitalist Values Motivate the American Colonists?   62

YES: James T. Lemon, from *The Best Poor Man's Country: A Geographical Study of Early Southeastern Pennsylvania*   64

NO: James A. Henretta, from "Families and Farms: *Mentalité* in Pre–Industrial America," *William and Mary Quarterly*   74

Professor of geography James T. Lemon argues that the liberal, middle-class, white settlers of southeastern Pennsylvania placed individual freedom and material gain at a higher priority than that of the public interest. Professor of American history James A. Henretta claims that the colonial family determined the character of agrarian life because it was the primary economic and social unit.

ISSUE 5.   Did American Slaves Develop a Distinct African American Culture in the Eighteenth Century?   86

YES: Allan Kulikoff, from *Tobacco and Slaves: The Development of Southern Cultures in the Chesapeake, 1680–1800*   88

NO: Jean Butenhoff Lee, from "The Problem of Slave Community in the Eighteenth-Century Chesapeake," *William and Mary Quarterly*   97

Professor of history Allan Kulikoff claims that Chesapeake slaves developed their own social institutions and a distinct indigenous culture in the years between 1740 and 1790. Associate professor of history Jean Butenhoff Lee emphasizes the difficult and often unsuccessful efforts of slaves to create a stable family and community life in eighteenth-century Maryland.

ISSUE 6.   Was the Great Awakening a Key to the American Revolution?   108

YES: Patricia U. Bonomi, from *Under the Cope of Heaven: Religion, Society, and Politics in Colonial America*   110

NO: Jon Butler, from "Enthusiasm Described and Decried: The Great Awakening as Interpretative Fiction," *Journal of American History*   117

Professor of history Patricia U. Bonomi asserts that the Great Awakening, by fostering challenges to established authority and by encouraging people to act on individual conscience, represented a rehearsal for the colonists' political assault on English rule that began in the 1760s. Professor of American history Jon Butler challenges the validity of the term *Great Awakening* and argues that a link between the eighteenth-century colonial religious revivals and the American Revolution was virtually nonexistent.

ISSUE 7.   Was the American Revolution a Conservative Movement?   130

YES: Carl N. Degler, from *Out of Our Past: The Forces That Shaped Modern America*, 3rd ed.   132

NO: Gordon S. Wood, from *The Radicalism of the American Revolution*   142

Pulitzer Prize–winning author Carl N. Degler argues that upper-middle-class colonists led a conservative American Revolution that left untouched the prewar economic and social class structure of an upwardly mobile people. Prize-winning historian Gordon S. Wood argues that the American Revolution was a far-reaching, radical event that produced a unique democratic society in which ordinary people could make money, pursue happiness, and be self-governing.

ISSUE 8.   Were the Founding Fathers Democratic Reformers?   148

YES: John P. Roche, from "The Founding Fathers: A Reform Caucus in Action," *American Political Science Review*   150

NO: Michael Parenti, from *Democracy for the Few*, 5th ed.   162

Political scientist John P. Roche believes that the Founding Fathers were not only revolutionaries but also superb democratic politicians who created a Constitution that supported the needs of the nation and at the same time was acceptable to the people. Political scientist Michael Parenti argues that the Constitution was framed by financially successful planters, merchants, and creditors in order to protect the rights of property rather than the rights and liberties of individuals.

ISSUE 9. **Did President Jefferson Outfederalize the Federalists?** **174**

YES: Richard Hofstadter, from *The American Political Tradition and the Men Who Made It* **176**

NO: Forrest McDonald, from *The Presidency of Thomas Jefferson* **188**

Pulitzer Prize–winning historian Richard Hofstadter (1916–1970) argues that Thomas Jefferson was a moderate, practical politician who followed a course of action that eventually co-opted the major policies of the Federalists. Professor of history Forrest McDonald believes that President Jefferson attempted to replace Hamiltonian Federalist principles with a republican ideology and that he wanted to restore America's agrarian heritage.

ISSUE 10. **Did the Election of 1828 Represent a Democratic Revolt of the People?** **202**

YES: Robert V. Remini, from "Election of 1828," in Arthur M. Schlesinger, Jr., ed., *The Coming to Power: Critical Presidential Elections in American History* **204**

NO: Richard P. McCormick, from "New Perspectives on Jacksonian Politics," *The American Historical Review* **209**

Professor of history Robert V. Remini argues that the 1828 presidential election symbolized the people's arrival at political responsibility and began a genuine, nationally organized, two-party system that came of age in the 1830s. Professor of history Richard P. McCormick maintains that voting statistics demonstrate that a genuine political revolution did not take place until the presidential election of 1840, when fairly well balanced political parties had been organized in virtually every state.

ISSUE 11. **Was Antebellum Reform Motivated Primarily by Humanitarian Goals?** **218**

YES: Alice Felt Tyler, from *Freedom's Ferment: Phases of American Social History from the Colonial Period to the Outbreak of the Civil War* **220**

NO: David J. Rothman, from *The Discovery of the Asylum: Social Order and Disorder in the New Republic* **228**

Professor of history Alice Felt Tyler argues that American reformers in the antebellum period were products of evangelical religion and frontier democracy who accepted the mission of perfecting human institutions. Professor of history David J. Rothman contends that antebellum reformers established orphan asylums and reformatories primarily to enforce strict discipline and to inculcate respect for authority and order among those seeking refuge in these institutions.

ISSUE 12. Did Slaves Exercise Religious Autonomy? 238

YES: Albert J. Raboteau, from "Slave Autonomy and Religion,"
Journal of Religious Thought 240

NO: John B. Boles, from "Introduction," in John B. Boles, ed.,
*Masters and Slaves in the House of the Lord: Race and Religion in the
American South, 1740–1870* 251

Professor of history Albert J. Raboteau claims that the religious activities of American slaves were characterized by institutional and personal independence, which undermined the ability of the masters to exercise effective control over their chattel property. Professor of history John B. Boles recognizes that slaves often worshiped apart from their masters, but he asserts that the primary religious experience of Southern slaves occurred within a biracial setting in churches dominated by whites.

**ISSUE 13. Was U.S. Foreign Policy in the Early Nineteenth
             Century Imperialistic?** 264

YES: Ramón Eduardo Ruiz, from "Manifest Destiny and the
Mexican War," in Howard H. Quint et al., eds., *Main Problems in
American History, vol. 1,* 5th ed. 266

NO: Robert Hugh Ferrell, from *American Diplomacy, A History,* 2d
ed. 274

Professor of history Ramón Eduardo Ruiz argues that for the purpose of conquering Mexico's northern territories, the United States waged an aggressive war against Mexico from which Mexico never recovered. Professor of diplomatic history Robert Hugh Ferrell believes that although the American government waged an aggressive war in Mexico, it remained the Manifest Destiny of the United States to possess Texas, New Mexico, and California.

**ISSUE 14. Were Southern Slaveholding Women Covert
             Abolitionists?** 286

YES: Suzanne Lebsock, from *The Free Women of Petersburg: Status
and Culture in a Southern Town, 1784–1860* 288

NO: Elizabeth Fox-Genovese, from *Within the Plantation
Household: Black and White Women of the Old South* 295

Professor of history Suzanne Lebsock believes that slaveholding women, operating from a distinct value system based on personalism, subverted the institution of slavery by protecting favored bond servants and even by freeing slaves through their wills. Professor of Southern history Elizabeth Fox-Genovese insists that although slaveholding women in the South might

have complained occasionally about slavery, their racism and the privileges associated with owning slaves prevented them from joining the ranks of the abolitionists.

ISSUE 15. Was the Confederacy Defeated Because of Its "Loss of Will"?   306

YES: Richard E. Beringer, Herman Hattaway, Archer Jones, and William N. Still, Jr., from *Why the South Lost the Civil War*   308

NO: James M. McPherson, from *Battle Cry of Freedom: The Civil War Era*   318

Professors Richard E. Beringer, Herman Hattaway, Archer Jones, and William N. Still, Jr., believe that the Confederacy lacked the will to win the Civil War because of an inability to fashion a viable Southern nationalism, increasing religious doubts about their cause, and guilt over slavery. Pulitzer Prize–winning historian James M. McPherson maintains that either side might have emerged victorious in the Civil War but that the Union success was contingent upon winning three major campaigns between 1862 and 1864.

ISSUE 16. Was Abraham Lincoln America's Greatest President?   326

YES: Stephen B. Oates, from *Abraham Lincoln: The Man Behind the Myths*   328

NO: M. E. Bradford, from *Remembering Who We Are: Observations of a Southern Conservative*   338

Professor of history Stephen B. Oates insists that Abraham Lincoln's greatness as president of the United States stemmed from a moral vision that had as its goal the protection and expansion of popular government. Professor of English literature M. E. Bradford characterizes Lincoln as a cynical politician whose abuse of authority as president and commander in chief during the Civil War marked a serious departure from the republican goals of the Founding Fathers and established the prototype for the "imperial presidency" of the twentieth century.

ISSUE 17. Was Reconstruction a "Splendid Failure"?   348

YES: Eric Foner, from "The New View of Reconstruction," *American Heritage*   350

NO: Thomas Holt, from *Black Over White: Negro Political Leadership in South Carolina During Reconstruction*   360

Professor of history Eric Foner believes that although Reconstruction did not achieve radical goals, it was a "splendid failure" because it offered African Americans in the South a temporary vision of a free society. Professor of American history Thomas Holt concludes that in South Carolina, where African Americans wielded significant political clout, Reconstruction failed to produce critical economic reforms for working-class blacks because of social and cultural divisions within the black community.

AMERICAN HISTORY,
Volume II, Fifth Edition

ISSUE 1. Was Reconstruction a "Splendid Failure"?   2

YES: Eric Foner, from "The New View of Reconstruction," *American Heritage*   4

NO: Thomas Holt, from *Black Over White: Negro Political Leadership in South Carolina During Reconstruction*   14

Professor of history Eric Foner believes that although Reconstruction did not achieve radical goals, it was a "splendid failure" because it offered African Americans in the South a temporary vision of a free society. Professor of American history Thomas Holt concludes that in South Carolina, where African Americans wielded significant political clout, Reconstruction failed to produce critical economic reforms for working-class blacks because of social and cultural divisions within the black community.

ISSUE 2. Were Nineteenth-Century Entrepreneurs Robber Barons?   24

YES: John Tipple, from "Big Businessmen and a New Economy," in H. Wayne Morgan, ed., *The Gilded Age*   26

NO: Alfred D. Chandler, Jr., from "The Beginnings of 'Big Business' in American Industry," *Business History Review*   36

Professor John Tipple characterizes big businessmen of the late nineteenth century as destructive forces whose power and greed undermined the nation's traditional institutions and values. Professor Alfred D. Chandler, Jr., concludes that American entrepreneurs were marketing innovators whose creation of great industrial corporations strengthened the country's economy by sparking the growth of a national urban market.

ISSUE 3. Was the American Labor Movement Radical?   50

YES: Bruce Laurie, from *Artisans Into Workers: Labor in Nineteenth-Century America*   52

NO: Carl N. Degler, from *Out of Our Past: The Forces That Shaped Modern America*, 3rd ed.   62

Professor of history Bruce Laurie argues that the Knights of Labor was a radical labor organization composed of skilled and unskilled workers that favored using governmental remedies to improve working conditions. Professor of history Carl N. Degler maintains that the American labor movement accepted capitalism and reacted conservatively to the radical organizational changes brought about in the economic system by big business.

ISSUE 4.   Were the Immigrants' Old World Cultures Destroyed as They Adjusted to American Life?   72

YES: Oscar Handlin, from *The Uprooted: The Epic Story of the Great Migrations That Made the American People,* 2d ed.   74

NO: John Bodnar, from *The Transplanted: A History of Immigrants in Urban America*   82

Pulitzer Prize–winning historian Oscar Handlin argues that the immigrants were alienated from their Old World cultures as they adjusted to an unfamiliar and hostile environment. Associate professor of history John Bodnar maintains that various immigrant groups retained, modified, and transformed their Old World cultures in response to urban/industrial America in the years between 1880 and 1920.

ISSUE 5.   Did the Westward Movement Transform the Traditional Roles of Women in the Late Nineteenth Century?   96

YES: Sandra L. Myres, from *Westering Women and the Frontier Experience 1800–1915*   98

NO: Christine Stansell, from "Women on the Great Plains 1865-1890," *Women's Studies*   110

Professor of history Sandra L. Myres (1933–1991) argues that first- and second-generation women, though not revolutionary, often moved outside the home and worked as teachers, missionaries, doctors, lawyers, ranchers, miners, and businesspeople. According to Professor Christine Stansell, women on the Great Plains were not able to create a network of female friendships and consequently endured lonely lives and loveless marriages.

ISSUE 6. Was City Government in Late Nineteenth-Century America a "Conspicuous Failure"?   120

YES: Ernest S. Griffith, from *A History of American City Government: The Conspicuous Failure, 1870–1900*   122

NO: Jon C. Teaford, from *The Unheralded Triumph: City Government in America, 1860–1900*   131

Professor of political science and political economy Ernest S. Griffith (1896–1981) focuses upon illegal and unethical operations of the political machine and concludes that the governments controlled by the bosses represented a betrayal of the public trust. Professor of history Jon C. Teaford argues that scholars traditionally have overlooked the remarkable success municipal governments in the late nineteenth century achieved in dealing with the challenges presented by rapid urbanization.

ISSUE 7. Did the Progressives Fail?   142

YES: Richard M. Abrams, from "The Failure of Progressivism," in Richard Abrams and Lawrence Levine, eds., *The Shaping of the Twentieth Century,* 2d ed.   144

NO: Arthur S. Link and Richard L. McCormick, from *Progressivism*   154

Professor of history Richard M. Abrams maintains that progressivism was a failure because it tried to impose a uniform set of values upon a culturally diverse people and never seriously confronted the inequalities that still exist in American society. Professors of history Arthur S. Link and Richard L. McCormick argue that the Progressives were a diverse group of reformers who confronted and ameliorated the worst abuses that emerged in urban industrial America during the early 1900s.

ISSUE 8. Was Early Twentieth-Century American Foreign Policy in the Caribbean Basin Dominated by Economic Concerns?   168

YES: Walter LaFeber, from *Inevitable Revolutions: The United States in Central America*   170

NO: David Healy, from *Drive to Hegemony: The United States in the Caribbean, 1898–1917*   179

Professor of history Walter LaFeber argues that the United States developed a foreign policy that deliberately made the Caribbean nations its economic dependents from the early nineteenth century on. Professor of history David Healy maintains that the two basic goals of American foreign policy in the Caribbean were to provide security against the German threat and to develop the economies of the Latin American nations, whose peoples were considered to be racially inferior.

**ISSUE 9. Was the Ku Klux Klan of the 1920s an Extremist
Movement?**   192

YES: David H. Bennett, from *The Party of Fear: From Nativist
Movements to the New Right in American History*   194

NO: Stanley Coben, from *Rebellion Against Victorianism: The
Impetus for Cultural Change in 1920s America*   204

Professor of history David H. Bennett argues that the Ku Klux Klan of the 1920s was a traditional nativist organization supported mainly by fundamentalist Protestants who were opposed to the changing social and moral values associated with the Catholic and Jewish immigrants. Professor of history Stanley Coben believes that local Klansmen were not a fringe group of fundamentalists but were solid, middle-class citizens who were concerned about the decline in moral standards in their communities.

**ISSUE 10. Was the New Deal an Effective Answer to the Great
Depression?**   216

YES: William E. Leuchtenburg, from "The Achievement of the
New Deal," in Harvard Sitkoff, ed., *Fifty Years Later: The New Deal
Evaluated*   218

NO: Gary Dean Best, from *Pride, Prejudice, and Politics: Roosevelt
Versus Recovery, 1933–1938*   229

Professor of history William E. Leuchtenburg contends that the New Deal extended the power of the national government in order to humanize the worst features of American capitalism. Professor of history Gary Dean Best argues that Roosevelt established an antibusiness environment with the creation of the New Deal regulatory programs, which retarded the nation's economic recovery from the Great Depression until World War II.

ISSUE 11. Did World War II Liberate American Women?   **244**

YES: Sherna Berger Gluck, from *Rosie the Riveter Revisited: Women, the War, and Social Change*   **246**

NO: Elaine Tyler May, from *Homeward Bound: American Families in the Cold War Era*   **255**

Sherna Berger Gluck, a lecturer in oral history, recognizes that although most women lost their industrial jobs after World War II, their wartime experiences transformed their concept of themselves as women and produced rising expectations that fueled the new women's consciousness movement. Professor of American studies Elaine Tyler May insists that World War II underscored women's tasks as homemakers, consumers, and mothers and reinforced sex segregation in the American work force.

ISSUE 12. Was It Necessary to Drop the Atomic Bomb to End World War II?   **266**

YES: McGeorge Bundy, from *Danger and Survival*   **268**

NO: Martin J. Sherwin, from *A World Destroyed: Hiroshima and the Origins of the Arms Race*   **277**

Professor of history McGeorge Bundy maintains that President Truman wisely dropped the atomic bomb in order to end the war as quickly as possible. Professor of history Martin J. Sherwin argues that American policymakers ruled out all other options and dropped the atomic bomb, an understandable but unnecessary act.

ISSUE 13. Was Dwight Eisenhower a Great President?   **286**

YES: Stephen E. Ambrose, from *Eisenhower: The President, vol. 2*   **288**

NO: Arthur M. Schlesinger, Jr., from *The Cycles of American History*   **296**

Professor of history Stephen E. Ambrose maintains that Eisenhower was a greater president than his predecessors and successors because he balanced the budget, stopped inflation, and kept the peace. Professor of the humanities Arthur M. Schlesinger, Jr., argues that Eisenhower failed as a president because he refused to tackle the moral and environmental issues at home and because he established a foreign policy that relied on covert CIA activities and threats of nuclear arms.

ISSUE 14. Did the Great Society Fail?   308

YES: Charles Murray, from "The Legacy of the 60's," *Commentary*   310

NO: Joseph A. Califano, Jr., from "How Great Was the Great
Society?" in Barbara C. Jordan and Elspeth D. Rostow, eds., *The
Great Society: A Twenty Year Critique*   317

Social critic Charles Murray argues that not only did the Great Society's retraining, anticrime, and welfare programs not work, but they actually contributed to the worsening plight of U.S. inner cities. Joseph A. Califano, Jr., a former aide to President Lyndon Johnson, maintains that the Great Society programs brought about positive revolutionary changes in the areas of civil rights, education, health care, the environment, and consumer protection.

**ISSUE 15. Could the United States Have Prevented the Fall of
South Vietnam?**   326

YES: Guenter Lewy, from *America in Vietnam*   328

NO: George C. Herring, from "America and Vietnam: The
Unending War," *Foreign Affairs*   337

Guenter Lewy believes that the South Vietnamese government might not have lost the war if the United States had followed "a strategy of surprise and massed strength at decisive points" against North Vietnam. George C. Herring argues that the policymakers exaggerated the strategic importance of Vietnam and deluded themselves about America's power.

**ISSUE 16. Was Martin Luther King, Jr.'s Leadership Essential to
the Success of the Civil Rights Movement?**   344

YES: August Meier, from "On the Role of Martin Luther King,"
in August Meier and Elliott Rudwick, eds., *Along the Color Line:
Explorations in the Black Experience*   346

NO: Clayborne Carson, from "Martin Luther King, Jr.:
Charismatic Leadership in a Mass Struggle," *Journal of American
History*   355

Professor of history August Meier depicts King as a "conservative militant" whose ability to communicate black aspirations to whites and to serve as a bridge between the radical and conservative wings of the civil rights movement made him the critical link in the chain of nonviolent direct action campaigns of the 1960s. Associate professor of history Clayborne Carson concludes that the civil rights struggle would have followed a similar course of development even if King had never lived because its successes depended upon mass activism, not the actions of a single leader.

ISSUE 17. Did President Reagan Win the Cold War?   362

YES: John Lewis Gaddis, from *The United States and the End of the Cold War: Implications, Reconsiderations, Provocations*   364

NO: Daniel Deudney and G. John Ikenberry, from "Who Won the Cold War?" *Foreign Policy*   374

Professor of history John Lewis Gaddis argues that President Reagan combined a policy of militancy and operational pragmatism to bring about the most significant improvement in Soviet-American relations since the end of World War II. Professors Daniel Deudney and G. John Ikenberry believe that the cold war ended only when Soviet president Gorbachev accepted western liberal values and the need for global cooperation.

BIOETHICAL ISSUES,
Fifth Edition

ISSUE 1. Should Courts Be Permitted to Order Women to Use
Long-Acting Contraceptives?   **2**

YES: Jim Persels, from "The Norplant Condition: Protecting the
Unborn or Violating Fundamental Rights?" *The Journal of Legal
Medicine*   **4**

NO: American Medical Association, from "Board of Trustees
Report: Requirements or Incentives by Government for the Use of
Long-Acting Contraceptives," *Journal of the American Medical
Association*   **14**

Law student Jim Persels believes that the use of long-acting but reversible contraceptive technologies as requirements for probation for women convicted of child abuse or drug use serves to guard the unborn while simultaneously limiting the intrusion on the individual's privacy rights and the state's burden of supervision. The American Medical Association's board of trustees opposes the use of long-acting contraceptives either as a condition of probation or as an incentive to women to get off welfare because such demands threaten a person's fundamental right to refuse medical treatment, to procreate, and to be protected from cruel and unusual punishment.

ISSUE 2.   Is There a Moral Right to Abortion?   **22**

YES: Beverly Wildung Harrison, from *Our Right to Choose: Toward
a New Ethics of Abortion*   **24**

NO: Sidney Callahan, from "Abortion and the Sexual Agenda: A
Case for Prolife Feminism," *Commonweal*   **29**

Professor of Christian ethics Beverly Wildung Harrison argues that women ought to decide whether or not to bear children on the basis of their own moral preparedness to become responsible mothers. Psychologist Sidney Callahan asserts that a woman's moral obligation to continue a pregnancy arises from both her status as a member of the human community and her unique life-giving female reproductive power.

ISSUE 3.   Should Thawing Unused Frozen Embryos Be Permitted?   40

YES: American Medical Association, from "Board of Trustees Report: Frozen Pre-Embryos," *Journal of the American Medical Association*   42

NO: David T. Ozar, from "The Case Against Thawing Unused Frozen Embryos," *Hastings Center Report*   50

The American Medical Association's board of trustees concludes that the man and woman who provided the sperm and egg should decide about the disposition of an unused frozen embryo and that they may legally and ethically decide to thaw and dispose of it. Philosopher David T. Ozar argues that the responsible parties have a moral obligation to preserve frozen embryos until they are implanted in a woman's womb or can no longer survive implantation.

ISSUE 4.   Should Commercial Surrogate Motherhood Be Banned?   60

YES: Thomas A. Shannon, from *Surrogate Motherhood: The Ethics of Using Human Beings*   62

NO: Carmel Shalev, from *Birth Power*   71

Professor of religious studies Thomas A. Shannon maintains that surrogacy continues social devaluing of women and encourages women and children to be treated as commodities rather than as persons worthy of respect. Attorney Carmel Shalev argues that women as autonomous and responsible individuals ought to be free to enter legally binding contracts and that the real issue is not commercialism but power to control reproduction.

ISSUE 5.   Is It Ethical to Withhold the Truth from Dying Patients?   84

YES: Bernard C. Meyer, from "Truth and the Physician," in E. Fuller Torrey, ed., *Ethical Issues in Medicine*   86

NO: Sissela Bok, from *Lying: Moral Choice in Public and Private Life*   96

Physician Bernard C. Meyer argues that physicians must use discretion in communicating bad news to patients. Adherence to a rigid formula of truth telling fails to appreciate the differences in patients' readiness to hear and understand the information. Philosopher Sissela Bok challenges the traditional physician's view by arguing that the harm resulting from disclosure is less

than they think and is outweighed by the benefits, including the important one of giving the patient the right to choose among treatments.

ISSUE 6.   Is Physician-Assisted Suicide Ethical?   108

YES: **Sidney H. Wanzer et al.,** from "The Physician's Responsibility Toward Hopelessly Ill Patients: A Second Look," *The New England Journal of Medicine*   110

NO: **David Orentlicher,** from "Physician Participation in Assisted Suicide," *Journal of the American Medical Association*   114

Physician Sidney H. Wanzer and a group of nine other physicians believe that it is not immoral for a physician to assist in the rational suicide of a terminally ill person. Physician and lawyer David Orentlicher argues that treatment designed to bring on death, by definition, does not heal and is therefore fundamentally inconsistent with the physician's role.

ISSUE 7.   Is It Ever Morally Right to Withhold Food and Water from Dying Patients?   120

YES: **Joanne Lynn and James F. Childress,** from "Must Patients Always Be Given Food and Water?" *Hastings Center Report*   122

NO: **Gilbert Meilaender,** from "On Removing Food and Water: Against the Stream," *Hastings Center Report*   131

Physician Joanne Lynn and professor of religious studies James F. Childress claim that nutrition and hydration are not morally different from other life-sustaining medical treatments that may be withheld or withdrawn, according to the patient's best interest. Professor of religion Gilbert Meilaender asserts that removing the ordinary human care of feeding aims to kill and is morally wrong.

ISSUE 8.   Are There Limits to Confidentiality?   140

YES: **Mark Siegler,** from "Confidentiality in Medicine: A Decrepit Concept," *The New England Journal of Medicine*   142

NO: **Michael H. Kottow,** from "Medical Confidentiality: An Intransigent and Absolute Obligation," *Journal of Medical Ethics*   147

Physician Mark Siegler argues that confidentiality is necessarily compromised in order to ensure complete and proper medical treatment. Physician Michael H. Kottow argues that any kind of breach of patient confidentiality causes harms that are more serious than hypothetical benefits.

ISSUE 9.   Do Physicians Have an Ethical Duty to Treat AIDS
           Patients?   158

YES: Albert R. Jonsen, from "The Duty to Treat Patients With
AIDS and HIV Infection," in Lawrence C. Gostin, ed., *AIDS and the
Health Care System*   160

NO: James W. Tegtmeier, from "Ethics and AIDS: A Summary of
the Law and a Critical Analysis of the Individual Physician's
Ethical Duty to Treat," *American Journal of Law and Medicine*   172

Philosopher Albert R. Jonsen asserts that refusing treatment in specific cases, because it is inconvenient, risky, or burdensome, casts a shadow on the most precious value of medicine—its commitment to service. Attorney James W. Tegtmeier asserts that it is improper to assert that physicians have an ethical duty to treat individuals with AIDS because the grounds for imposing such a duty are too weak to support that conclusion.

ISSUE 10.   Should HIV-Infected Health Care Workers Be
            Restricted from Performing Some Procedures?   182

YES: Gordon G. Keyes, from "Health-Care Professionals With
AIDS: The Risk of Transmission Balanced Against the Interests of
Professionals and Institutions," *Journal of College and University Law*   184

NO: Norman Daniels, from "HIV-Infected Professionals, Patient
Rights, and the 'Switching Dilemma,'" *Journal of the American
Medical Association*   190

Professor of dentistry and lawyer Gordon G. Keyes asserts that HIV-infected health care professionals should not perform invasive procedures because they are ethically obligated to perform only procedures for which they have obtained full consent and which pose no risk of transmission. Philosopher Norman Daniels contends that a focus on HIV-infected health care professionals, where patients switch to uninfected practitioners, will result in everyone being worse off; the benefits that would result from cooperating around more effective infection control strategies will be lost.

ISSUE 11.   Should Doctors Be Able to Refuse Demands for
            "Futile" Treatment?   198

YES: Steven H. Miles, from "Informed Demand for
'Non-Beneficial' Medical Treatment," *The New England Journal of
Medicine*   200

NO: Felicia Ackerman, from "The Significance of a Wish,"
Hastings Center Report   205

Physician Steven H. Miles believes that physicians' duty to follow patients' wishes ends when the requests are inconsistent with what medical care can reasonably be expected to achieve, when they violate community standards of care, and when they consume an unfair share of collective resources. Philosopher Felicia Ackerman contends that it is ethically inappropriate for physicians to decide what kind of life is worth prolonging and that decisions involving personal values should be made by the patient or family.

ISSUE 12. Should Animal Experimentation Be Permitted?   212

YES: Jerod M. Loeb, William R. Hendee, Steven J. Smith, and M. Roy Schwarz, from "Human vs. Animal Rights: In Defense of Animal Research," *Journal of the American Medical Association*   214

NO: Tom Regan, from "Ill-Gotten Gains," in Donald Van DeVeer and Tom Regan, eds., *Health Care Ethics: An Introduction*   222

Jerod M. Loeb, William R. Hendee, Steven J. Smith, and M. Roy Schwarz, representing the American Medical Society's Group on Science and Technology, assert that concern for animals, admirable in itself, cannot impede the development of methods to improve the welfare of humans. Philosopher Tom Regan argues that conducting research on animals exacts the grave moral price of failing to show proper respect for animals' inherent value, whatever the benefits of the research.

ISSUE 13. Is It Unethical to Implant Animal Parts in Humans?   230

YES: Peter Singer, from "Xenotransplantation and Speciesism," *Transplantation Proceedings*   232

NO: Arthur L. Caplan, from "Is Xenografting Morally Wrong?" *Transplantation Proceedings*   239

Philosopher Peter Singer objects to using animals as a source for organ donation because doing so disregards the interests of nonhuman animals by ranking them as less worthy of our concern and respect than any member of our own species, no matter how limited in capacities and potential. Philosopher Arthur L. Caplan argues that it is moral to use animals as sources of organs because the scarcity of organs and tissues from human sources is real, growing, and unlikely to be solved by any other alternative approaches in the near future.

ISSUE 14. Is It Ethical for Scientists to Use Data from the Nazi Experiments? 248

YES: R. S. Pozos, from "Scientific Inquiry and Ethics: The Dachau Data," in Arthur L. Caplan, ed., *When Medicine Went Mad: Bioethics and the Holocaust* 250

NO: Robert L. Berger, from "Nazi Science: Comments on the Validation of the Dachau Human Hypothermia Experiments," in Arthur L. Caplan, ed., *When Medicine Went Mad: Bioethics and the Holocaust* 259

Physiologist and hypothermia researcher R. S. Pozos believes that data from the freezing experiments conducted by the Nazis at Dachau were scientifically valid and may be cited, although he reserves the decision about their ethical acceptability to individual conscience. Cardiac surgeon Robert L. Berger declares that there is conclusive evidence that the data from the Dachau experiments were seriously flawed, making the ethical discussion inappropriate and harmful.

ISSUE 15. Should Research With Aborted Fetal Tissue Be Banned? 270

YES: James Tunstead Burtchaell, from "University Policy on Experimental Use of Aborted Fetal Tissue," *IRB: A Review of Human Subjects Research* 272

NO: Benjamin Freedman, from "The Ethics of Using Human Fetal Tissue," *IRB: A Review of Human Subjects Research* 281

Theologian James Tunstead Burtchaell declares that experimentation with fetal tissue is unethical because of the lack of informed consent and because it would place researchers in moral complicity with abortion. Philosopher Benjamin Freedman disputes these arguments, declaring that it would be wrong for the state to prohibit the use of aborted fetal tissue because there is no consensus on the moral status of the fetus and because the practice does not violate norms of consent.

ISSUE 16. Should Newborns Without Brains Be Used as Organ Donors? 292

YES: Michael R. Harrison, from "Organ Procurement for Children: The Anencephalic Fetus as Donor," *The Lancet* 294

NO: John D. Arras and Shlomo Shinnar, from "Anencephalic Newborns as Organ Donors: A Critique," *Journal of the American Medical Association* 301

Pediatric surgeon Michael R. Harrison believes that if anencephalic newborns were treated as brain-dead rather than as brain-absent, their organs could be transplanted and their families could be offered the consolation that their loss provided life for another child. Philosopher John D. Arras and pediatric neurologist Shlomo Shinnar argue that the current principles of the strict definition of brain death are sound public policy and good ethics.

ISSUE 17. Should There Be a Market in Body Parts?   306

YES: Lori B. Andrews, from "My Body, My Property," *Hastings Center Report*   308

NO: Thomas H. Murray, from "Gifts of the Body and the Needs of Strangers," *Hastings Center Report*   316

Attorney Lori B. Andrews believes that donors, recipients, and society will benefit from a market in body parts so long as owners—and no one else—retain control over their bodies. Ethicist Thomas H. Murray argues that the gift relationship should govern transfer of body parts because it honors important human values, which are diminished by market relationships.

ISSUE 18. Should Health Care for the Elderly Be Limited?   326

YES: Daniel Callahan, from "Limiting Health Care for the Old?" *The Nation*   328

NO: Amitai Etzioni, from "Spare the Old, Save the Young," *The Nation*   333

Philosopher Daniel Callahan believes that since health care resources are scarce, people who have lived a full natural life span should be offered care that relieves suffering but not expensive life-prolonging technologies. Sociologist Amitai Etzioni argues that rationing health care for the elderly would encourage conflict between generations and would invite restrictions on health care for other groups.

ISSUE 19. Should the United States Follow the Canadian Model of a National Health Program?   340

YES: Steffie Woolhandler and David U. Himmelstein, from "A National Health Program: Northern Light at the End of the Tunnel," *Journal of the American Medical Association*   342

NO: Ronald Bronow, from "A National Health Program: Abyss at the End of the Tunnel—The Position of Physicians Who Care," *Journal of the American Medical Association*   347

Physicians Steffie Woolhandler and David U. Himmelstein propose a sweeping reform of health care financing, following the Canadian model of a single-source system of payment, to ensure equity of access and efficiency. Physician Ronald Bronow, on behalf of an organization called Physicians Who Care, believes that problems of underfinancing and rationing in the Canadian system would be magnified in the American setting.

ISSUE 20. Will the Human Genome Project Lead to Abuses in Genetic Engineering? 354

YES: **Evelyn Fox Keller,** from "Nature, Nurture, and the Human Genome Project," in Daniel J. Kevles and Leroy Hood, eds., *The Code of Codes: Scientific and Social Issues in the Human Genome Project* 356

NO: **Daniel J. Kevles and Leroy Hood,** from "Preface" and "Reflections," in Daniel J. Kevles and Leroy Hood, eds., *The Code of Codes: Scientific and Social Issues in the Human Genome Project* 365

Professor of history and philosophy of science Evelyn Fox Keller warns that the Human Genome Project's beneficent focus on "disease-causing genes" may lead to a "eugenics of normality," in which inherently ambiguous standards of normality and individual responsibility may be abused. Professor of humanities Daniel J. Kevles and professor of biology Leroy Hood discount fears of a resurgence of negative eugenics because enlightened public opinion and contemporary political democracies, as well as technological difficulties, would make it unlikely.

BUSINESS ETHICS,
Second Edition

ISSUE 1. Is Capitalism Viable for the Future?   **2**

YES: Russell Kirk, from "Is Capitalism Still Viable?" *Journal of
Business Ethics*   **4**

NO: Michael Harrington, from "Is Capitalism Still Viable?"
Journal of Business Ethics   **9**

Russell Kirk, distinguished scholar at the Heritage Foundation, clarifies the meaning of *capitalism* and argues that this form of economic pattern will survive in the United States. Michael Harrington, a political theorist and prominent socialist, argues that American capitalism is in crisis and is not viable in the long run.

**ISSUE 2. Can Corporate Codes of Ethics Promote Ethical
            Behavior?**   **16**

YES: Cecily A. Raiborn and Dinah Payne, from "Corporate
Codes of Conduct: A Collective Conscience and Continuum,"
Journal of Business Ethics   **18**

NO: LaRue Tone Hosmer, from *The Ethics of Management*   **27**

Associate professor of accounting Cecily A. Raiborn and assistant professor of management Dinah Payne argue that a code of ethics conveys the culture of a corporation and can play a positive role in the firm's fulfillment of its fiduciary duties. Professor of corporate strategies LaRue Tone Hosmer argues that codes of ethics are really only for show and are ineffective in bringing about more ethical behavior on the part of employees.

**ISSUE 3. Should the "Pay-for-Performance" System Be
            Overhauled?**   **32**

YES: Dana Wechsler Linden and Vicki Contavespi, from
"Incentivize Me, Please," *Forbes*   **34**

NO: Kevin J. Murphy, from "Top Executives Are Worth Every
Nickel They Get," *Harvard Business Review*   **41**

Dana Wechsler Linden and Vicki Contavespi, associate editor and reporter for *Forbes* magazine, respectively, believe that many chief executive officers (CEOs) are overcompensated and that accountability for such rewards must be enforced to avoid general cynicism about the way corporations do business. Associate professor of economics Kevin J. Murphy argues that high executive compensation is consistently correlated with increased value for the shareholders and that most CEOs are actually undercompensated for their efforts in increasing the overall value of the corporation.

ISSUE 4. Do Employees Have a Moral Right to Meaningful Work?   54

YES: Patricia H. Werhane, from *Persons, Rights and Corporations*   56

NO: Ian Maitland, from "Rights in the Workplace: A Nozickian Argument," *Journal of Business Ethics*   61

Professor of business ethics Patricia H. Werhane claims that employees have economic rights that are derived from basic moral rights, including the right to a safe workplace, the right to fair pay, the right to participate in employment decisions, and the right to work that seems to be worthwhile. Professor of philosophy Ian Maitland argues that the enforced collective establishment of possibly unwanted workers' "rights" may come at the expense of each worker's freedom to choose compensatory income instead.

ISSUE 5. Are Programs of Preferential Treatment Unjustifiable?   68

YES: Lisa H. Newton, from "Reverse Discrimination as Unjustified," *Ethics*   70

NO: Richard Wasserstrom, from "A Defense of Programs of Preferential Treatment," *National Forum: The Phi Kappa Phi Journal*   75

Professor of philosophy Lisa H. Newton argues that programs of preferential treatment represent reverse discrimination and are therefore antimerit and unjust. These programs replace fair procedures with political positioning and open preferential avenues to minorities. Professor of philosophy Richard Wasserstrom maintains that society is not fair and merit based to begin with. He argues that there is no inconsistency in objecting to racist and sexist discrimination while favoring preferential treatment; the social realities of numbers and power do not make discrimination against the majority any more objectionable than discrimination against minorities.

ISSUE 6. Do Employers Have an Obligation to Provide Parental Leave Policies for Their Employees?　　82

YES: Margaret E. Meiers, from "Down With the Wait-and-See Approach," *Management Review*　　84

NO: Doug Bandow, from "Home Alone: Should Congress Play With Family Leave?" *Business and Society Review*　　90

Margaret E. Meiers, a senior associate of an organization that advises on the career development of women, considers the social and economic costs of effectively firing every working woman who has a child and training a replacement. She argues that parental leave may be less costly to corporations than its alternatives. Doug Bandow, senior fellow at the Cato Institute, argues that employers should not be asked to bear the costs of parental leave and that the prospect of such costs will make them less willing to hire women who might eventually choose to start a family.

ISSUE 7. Can Whistle-Blowing Be Clearly Justified?　　98

YES: Richard T. DeGeorge, from *Business Ethics*, 2d ed.　　100

NO: Alan F. Westin, from "What Can and Should Be Done to Protect Whistle Blowers in Industry?" in Alan F. Westin, ed., *Whistle Blowing: Loyalty and Dissent in the Corporation*　　105

Professor of philosophy Richard T. DeGeorge argues that "blowing the whistle" is often morally permissible and occasionally morally required. He presents the conditions that he thinks would justify a conclusion that an employee had an obligation to become a whistle-blower. Professor of public law and government Alan F. Westin points out that evaluations of whistle-blowers must take certain negative possibilities into account. Whistle-blowing may not be all selflessness and nobility: it might just be a mistake or a vendetta.

ISSUE 8. Is Drug Testing an Unwarranted Invasion of Employee Privacy?　　110

YES: John Hoerr, Katherine M. Hafner, Gail DeGeorge, Anne R. Field, and Laura Zinn, from "Privacy," *Business Week*　　112

NO: Janice Castro, Jonathan Beaty, Barbara Dolan, and Jeanne McDowell, from "Battling the Enemy Within," *Time*　　119

John Hoerr and staff for *Business Week* survey the range of issues now generally categorized under the heading of "privacy in the work place." Corporate policies that require drug testing, AIDS tests, lie detector tests, computer surveillance, and genetic screening are themselves being tested, in the courts, as invasions of privacy. Janice Castro and staff for *Time* chronicle the growing awareness of the damaging effects and high costs of employee drug use in the public and the private sectors. This awareness, they claim, has sparked a growing movement for policies of mandatory testing.

ISSUE 9. Is Litigation the Best Way to Compensate Asbestos Workers for Disease and Risk?   132

YES: Paul Brodeur, from *Outrageous Misconduct*   134

NO: Suzanne L. Oliver and Leslie Spencer, from "Who Will the Monster Devour Next?" *Forbes*   142

Paul Brodeur, a staff writer for *The New Yorker* magazine, reports that asbestos workers who develop asbestos-related diseases should bring litigation against the manufacturers of the products with which they worked to ensure that they get the compensation they deserve. Suzanne L. Oliver and Leslie Spencer, staff writers for *Forbes* magazine, point out that the threat of endless litigation, rendered less endurable by deceptive legal tricks used by plaintiffs' lawyers to attract clients, is driving many innocent companies to bankruptcy.

ISSUE 10. Is Advertising Fundamentally Deceptive?   152

YES: Roger Crisp, from "Persuasive Advertising, Autonomy, and the Creation of Desire," *Journal of Business Ethics*   154

NO: John O'Toole, from *The Trouble with Advertising*   162

Philosopher Roger Crisp argues that persuasive advertising removes the possibility of real decision-making by manipulating consumers without their knowledge, and for no good reason, and thus destroys personal autonomy. John O'Toole, president of the American Association of Advertising Agencies, argues that advertising is only salesmanship functioning in the paid space and time of mass media and is no more coercive than an ordinary salesperson.

ISSUE 11. Product Liability: Was Ford to Blame in the Pinto Case?   174

YES: W. Michael Hoffman, from "The Ford Pinto," *Department of Philosophy, Bentley College*   176

NO: Ford Motor Company, from "Closing Argument by Mr. James Neal," Brief for the Defense, *State of Indiana v. Ford Motor Company*, U.S. District Court, South Bend, Indiana.   **182**

Professor of business ethics W. Michael Hoffman describes the controversial accusations that Ford Motor Company deliberately put an unsafe car on the road—the Pinto—causing hundreds of people to suffer burns, death, and horrible disfigurement. James Neal, chief attorney for Ford Motor Company during the Pinto litigation, argues to the jury that Ford cannot be held responsible for deaths that were caused by others—such as the driver of the van that struck the victims—and that there is no proof of criminal intent or negligence on the part of Ford.

ISSUE 12. Should Tobacco Advertising Be Banned?   **192**

YES: Mark Green, from "Luring Kids to Light Up," *Business and Society Review*   **194**

NO: John Luik, from "Government Paternalism and Citizen Rationality: The Justifiability of Banning Tobacco Advertising," *International Journal of Advertising*   **199**

Mark Green, the Commissioner of Consumer Affairs in New York City, attacks a popular cigarette advertising campaign that seems to be aimed directly at children and claims that such unconscionable methods of advertising should be prevented. Professor of philosophy John Luik argues that restricting the freedom of commercial speech cannot be justified unless it is shown to be absolutely necessary to avoid certain harm, which has not been done in the case of tobacco advertising.

ISSUE 13. Are Federal "Marketing Orders" Unfair?   **210**

YES: Carolyn Lochhead, from "Fruit Fight: Independent Growers Challenge Agribusiness Giants," *Insight*   **212**

NO: Farmers for an Orderly Market, from *Democratic Self-Determination: An Alternative to Subsidies*   **220**

Carolyn Lochhead, a news reporter for *Insight* magazine, reports as questionable the activities of agribusiness cartels, who determine the amount of produce that independent fruit growers may sell, which has the effect of ensuring greater market share for the large corporations. The Farmers for an Orderly Market, a coalition of citrus growers, including Sunkist Growers, Inc., formed to counter the arguments being made by dissident citrus marketers, support the tradition of Federal marketing orders as the only way to ensure a 12-month supply of high-quality fruit and solvency for the fruit farmer.

ISSUE 14. Can Hostile Takeovers Be Justified?   232

YES: Craig Lehman, from "Takeovers and Takeover Defenses: Some Utilities of the Free Market," in Tom L. Beauchamp and Norman E. Bowie, eds., *Ethical Theory and Business*, 3rd ed.   234

NO: Lisa H. Newton, from "The Hostile Takeover: An Opposition View," in Tom L. Beauchamp and Norman E. Bowie, eds., *Ethical Theory and Business*, 3rd ed.   241

Craig Lehman, an educational software developer, argues that hostile takeovers are useful in the ecology of American business because they contribute to the efficient allocation of capital, weed out weak management, maximize the interests of the shareholders, and provide opportunities for new entrepreneurial managers. Professor of philosophy Lisa H. Newton responds that hostile takeovers destroy American enterprise by liquidating the investments of generations to provide ready cash for a few millionaires. As a result, employees and communities suffer and the future of American business is severely compromised.

ISSUE 15. Does Insider Trading Serve a Useful Purpose?   250

YES: Henry G. Manne, from "In Defense of Insider Trading," *Harvard Business Review*   252

NO: Allen M. Parkman, Barbara C. George, and Maria Boss, from "Owners or Traders: Who Are the Real Victims of Insider Trading?" *Journal of Business Ethics*   260

Professor of law Henry G. Manne argues that insider trading—the use of inside knowledge by corporate insiders to trade the corporation's stock—is the best reward for entrepreneurial services. Professors Allen M. Parkman, Barbara C. George, and Maria Boss argue that too much of the uproar about insider trading focuses on the wrong parties (i.e., the outside traders), when it is actually the insiders' employers—the ongoing shareholders—who are likely to be hurt. They conclude that inside trading should be treated as embezzlement or theft.

ISSUE 16. Should Industry Be Held Accountable for Acid Rain?   268

YES: George Reiger, from "What Can Be Done About Acid Rain?" *Field and Stream*   270

NO: William M. Brown, from "Maybe Acid Rain Isn't the Villain," *Fortune*   275

Environmentalist George Reiger claims that acidified rain and ozone caused by high levels of fossil fuel air pollution is causing irreparable damage to the Earth's lakes and forests. The research has been done, he argues, and now public action is needed to stop the pollution. William M. Brown, director of technical studies at the Hudson Institute, concedes that our forests are having problems, but the causes are much more complex than industrial pollution alone, including cyclic diseases and anti–forest fire policies. Given the high cost of stopping sulfur emissions, premature or misdirected legislation should be avoided.

ISSUE 17. Can Current Pollution Strategies Improve Air Quality?   282

YES: John G. McDonald, from "Gasoline and Clean Air: Good News, Better News, and a Warning," *Vital Speeches of the Day*   284

NO: Hilary F. French, from "Communication: A Global Agenda for Clean Air," *Energy Policy*   291

Oil company executive John G. McDonald argues that automotive technology will continue to improve and will produce more efficient engines and better fuels, which will eventually bring the pollution from automobile exhaust under control. Energy policy analyst Hilary F. French claims that energy use, transportation, and industrial policies must undergo major changes if air pollution is to be controlled.

ISSUE 18. Should Eastern European Nations Be Encouraged to Develop Free Market Institutions?   300

YES: Gail E. Schares, Ken Olsen, Lynne Reaves, and Elizabeth Weiner, from "Reawakening: A Market Economy Takes Root in Eastern Europe," *Business Week*   302

NO: John Kenneth Galbraith, from "Which Capitalism For Eastern Europe?" *Harper's Magazine*   308

Gail E. Schares and staff for *Business Week* support the individual initiative of the entrepreneurs who continue to build for themselves a market economy in post-Communist Europe. Economist John Kenneth Galbraith suggests that caution is in order, since the free market advocated by the economic right is not one that would ever be tolerated in America, and it might turn Eastern Europe's fragile economies into international catastrophes.

ISSUE 19. Did Nestlé Act Irresponsibly in Marketing Infant Formula to the Third World?   312

YES: Doug Clement, from "Infant Formula Malnutrition: Threat to the Third World," *The Christian Century*   314

NO: Maggie McComas, Geoffrey Fookes, and George Taucher, from "The Dilemma of Third World Nutrition: Nestlé and the Role of Infant Formula," *Paper prepared for Nestlé, S. A.*   323

Doug Clement, coordinator of the National Infant Formula Action (INFACT) coalition, argues that infant formula distribution in the Third World has been a disaster for the health of the infants. INFACT brought this issue to world attention and called for the boycott of Nestlé products to protest the formula promotions. Maggie McComas et al. present Nestlé's response to its attackers and the company's view of its present and future role in protecting infant nutrition in the Third World.

ISSUE 20. Is Bribery Ever Justified?   336

YES: Michael Philips, from "Bribery," *Ethics*   338

NO: Thomas L. Carson, from "Bribery and Implicit Agreements: A Reply to Philips," *Journal of Business Ethics*   349

Professor of philosophy Michael Philips argues that not every payment that seems to be a bribe is, in fact, a bribe. He claims that although it is often difficult to distinguish a true bribe from other payments, there may be no *prima facie* reason to refuse the offer of a bribe. Professor of philosophy Thomas L. Carson argues that every acceptance of a bribe involves the violation of an implicit or explicit promise or understanding connected with one's office, and that Philips has failed in his attempts to show that acceptance of a bribe can sometimes be morally permissible.

CRIME AND CRIMINOLOGY,
Third Edition

ISSUE 1. Is Crime Functional?   **2**

YES: Emile Durkheim, from *Rules of Sociological Method*   **4**

NO: Jeffrey H. Reiman, from *The Rich Get Richer and the Poor Get
Prison: Ideology, Class, and Criminal Justice,* 2d ed.   **9**

Classic sociologist Emile Durkheim (1858–1917) theorizes that crime exists in all societies because it reaffirms moral boundaries and at times assists needed social changes. Professor of philosophy Jeffrey H. Reiman asserts that crime is functional not because it promotes social solidarity but because it provides an ideology to justify the status quo.

ISSUE 2. Are General Theories of Crime Possible?   **14**

YES: Charles R. Tittle, from "The Assumption That General
Theories Are Not Possible," in Robert F. Meier, ed., *Theoretical
Methods in Criminology*   **16**

NO: W. Byron Groves and Graeme Newman, from "Against
General Theory in Comparative Research," *International Journal of
Comparative and Applied Criminal Justice*   **22**

Criminologist Charles R. Tittle links the advancement of science with general theory building and insists that criminology will remain stagnant if it continues to neglect general theory. Professors W. Byron Groves and Graeme Newman challenge Tittle and declare that his ideas are neither feasible nor desirable for criminology.

ISSUE 3. Is Criminal Behavior Biologically Determined?   **30**

YES: C. R. Jeffery, from "Criminology as an Interdisciplinary
Behavioral Science," *Criminology*   **32**

NO: Tony Platt and Paul Takagi, from "Biosocial Criminology: A
Critique," *Crime and Social Justice*   **39**

Criminologist C. R. Jeffery argues that physiological and chemical imbalances are frequently precipitants of criminal behavior. Therefore, research into causes and possible cures might be better placed in the hands of medical researchers. *Crime and Social Justice* editors Tony Platt and Paul Takagi characterize Jeffery's proposals as ridiculous and dangerous and contend that his ideas suffer from a poor understanding of biology, history, and criminology.

ISSUE 4.   Is Street Crime More Serious Than White-Collar Crime?   46

YES: James Q. Wilson and Richard J. Herrnstein, from *Crime and Human Nature*   48

NO: Jeffrey H. Reiman, from *The Rich Get Richer and the Poor Get Prison: Ideology, Class, and Criminal Justice,* 2d ed.   59

Professor James Q. Wilson and psychologist Richard J. Herrnstein argue that the focus of crime study ought to be on persons who "hit, rape, murder, steal, and threaten." Professor of philosophy Jeffrey H. Reiman contends that a focus on street crimes is little more than a cover-up for more serious crimes such as pollution, medical malpractice, and dangerous working conditions that go uncorrected.

ISSUE 5.   Is Punishment Good Crime Control?   78

YES: Stanley C. Brubaker, from "In Praise of Punishment," *The Public Interest*   80

NO: M. Kay Harris, from "Moving into the New Millennium: Toward a Feminist Vision of Justice," in Harold E. Pepinsky and Richard Quinney, eds., *Criminology as Peacemaking*   89

Political scientist Stanley Brubaker, drawing inspiration from Frederick Douglass, argues that just as praise motivates achievement and is fundamental for a civilized society, so punishment is necessary to condemn wrongdoing. Feminist criminologist and peace movement activist M. Kay Harris counters that punishment is a failure. What is needed is a reformulation of the criminal justice system so that a new vision of justice, one based on both reason and kindness, can be brought about.

ISSUE 6.   Is Criminal Justice Free of Systemic Racism?   96

YES: William Wilbanks, from *The Myth of a Racist Criminal Justice System*   98

NO: Michael J. Lynch and E. Britt Patterson, from "Racial Discrimination in the Criminal Justice System: Evidence from Four Jurisdictions," in Brian D. MacLean and Dragan Milovanovic, eds., *Racism, Empiricism, and Criminal Justice*   104

Criminologist William Wilbanks raises several important issues in his defense of the U.S. criminal justice system. While acknowledging that there are racist police officers, district attorneys, and judges, he contends that, overall, criminal justice is fair. Professors of criminology Michael J. Lynch and E. Britt Patterson directly challenge Wilbanks. For Lynch and Patterson, how Wilbanks looks at racial discrimination in criminal justice processes is flawed because Wilbanks only treats discrimination as a phenomenon that is related to being either black or white. In their view, a more accurate assessment of racial discrimination can only be made by using a more appropriate race variable: white/nonwhite. They summarize a study that seems to show systemic racism in several courts.

ISSUE 7.   Juvenile Justice: Are Kids "Getting Away With Murder"?   112

YES: Alfred S. Regnery, from "Getting Away With Murder: Why the Juvenile Justice System Needs an Overhaul," *Policy Review*   114

NO: Stephen J. Brodt and J. Steven Smith, from "Public Policy and the Serious Juvenile Offender," *Criminal Justice Policy Review*   121

Former Office of Juvenile Justice and Delinquency Prevention administrator Alfred S. Regnery says that children commit one-third of all crimes yet are not held accountable for their acts. He calls for a return to the doctrine of deterrence because the old rehabilitation philosophy has clearly failed. Criminologists Stephen J. Brodt and J. Steven Smith reject Regnery's view of juvenile delinquency as well as the solutions he proposes, assert that claims of juveniles getting away with murder are greatly exaggerated, and argue that rehabilitation remains a workable ideal.

ISSUE 8.   Should Plea Bargaining Continue to Be an Accepted Practice?   132

YES: Samuel Walker, from *Sense and Nonsense About Crime: A Policy Guide,* 2d ed.   134

NO: Ralph Adam Fine, from *Escape of the Guilty: A Trial Judge Speaks Out Against Crime*   139

Professor of criminal justice Samuel Walker, while acknowledging that plea bargaining is an imperfect component of the criminal justice system, still feels that it is an integral part of both the courtroom work group and the manufacturing and maintenance of justice. Judge Ralph Adam Fine argues that criminals are hardly punished for even the most heinous crimes due to plea bargaining and, citing some of the same studies that Walker draws from, concludes that elimination of plea bargaining increases justice.

ISSUE 9.   Should Capital Punishment Be Abolished?   144

YES: Jack Greenberg, from "Against the American System of Capital Punishment," *Harvard Law Review*   146

NO: Ernest van den Haag, from "The Ultimate Punishment: A Defense," *Harvard Law Review*   150

Law professor Jack Greenberg maintains that capital punishment is unfairly administered and ineffective, both as a deterrent and as a punishment. Professor Ernest van den Haag challenges those who claim that capital punishment is barbaric and unfair and insists that capital punishment does deter criminals and is just retribution for terrible crimes.

ISSUE 10.   Is Research on Criminal Careers Helpful?   160

YES: Alfred Blumstein and Jacqueline Cohen, from "Characterizing Criminal Careers," *Science*   162

NO: Michael Gottfredson and Travis Hirschi, from "Science, Public Policy, and the Career Paradigm," *Criminology*   177

Professors Alfred Blumstein and Jacqueline Cohen declare that traditional criminological knowledge of the correlates of crime, such as low income and race, is not helpful. Based on Blumstein's extensive research over the past 15 years, they claim criminal career studies are far more helpful. Professor of management and policy Michael Gottfredson and professor of sociology Travis Hirschi continue their running debate with Blumstein and his followers. They charge that research on criminal careers is pretentious, ignores counterevidence, is conceptually and methodologically unsound, and will lead "public policy . . . in the wrong direction."

ISSUE 11. Can Traditional Criminology Make Sense Out of
            Domestic Violence?   192

YES: Lawrence W. Sherman, from "The Influence of Criminology
on Criminal Law: Evaluating Arrests for Misdemeanor Domestic
Violence," *The Journal of Criminal Law and Criminology*   194

NO: Cynthia Grant Bowman, from "The Arrest Experiments: A
Feminist Critique," *The Journal of Criminal Law and Criminology* 200

Professor of criminology and president of the Crime Control Institute
Lawrence W. Sherman worries that political concerns may weaken experimental studies of domestic violence control. He insists that, if used
judiciously, studies of arrests for misdemeanor domestic assault can be fundamental for understanding and reducing domestic violence. Law professor
Cynthia Grant Bowman counters that traditional criminology, until recently,
ignored domestic violence. And current research is badly flawed since it
is usually conducted from the perspective of the abuser, ignores feminist
thinking, and does not address vital social factors.

ISSUE 12. Do Ignition Interlocks Reduce Drunk Driving
            Arrests?   208

YES: Barbara J. Morse and Delbert S. Elliott, from "Effects of
Ignition Interlock Devices on DUI Recidivism: Findings from a
Longitudinal Study in Hamilton County, Ohio," *Crime and
Delinquency*   210

NO: Richard A. Ball and J. Robert Lilly, from "The Potential Use
of Home Incarceration for Drunken Drivers," *Crime and Delinquency* 219

To determine the effectiveness of ignition interlock devices as a means for
reducing drunk driving arrests, researchers Barbara J. Morse and Delbert
S. Elliott carefully studied two groups of defendants arrested for DUI. One
group was comprised of DUI defendants sentenced to using ignition interlock
devices; the other group was made up of DUI defendants who had had their
licenses suspended or revoked. After comparing subsequent DUI charges at
three different points in time, they found that interlock users were far less
likely to be rearrested. Professor of sociology Richard A. Ball and professor of
sociology and criminal justice J. Robert Lilly discount the value of interlock
devices and recommend instead home incarceration for drinking drivers.

ISSUE 13. Should Elderly Offenders Get Lighter Sentences?   236

YES: Robert Sherwin, from "Employing Life Expectancy as a
Guideline in Sentencing Criminal Offenders: Toward a Humanistic
Proposal for Change," *Prison Journal*   238

NO: James R. Acker, from "On Confusing Justice With Mercy: A
Reply to Professor Sherwin," *Prison Journal*   242

Professor of sociology Robert Sherwin insists that a long prison sentence for someone over 60 is often a death sentence, and thus unfair as compared to giving the same sentence to a younger offender. He argues that since the current system encourages shorter sentences for juveniles, why not do the same for elderly offenders? Assistant professor of criminal justice James R. Acker likes the idea of shorter sentences for the elderly, but only out of mercy. It is not justice, he insists, to having sliding sentences based on age for offenders who commit the same crime. Nor would it be practical.

ISSUE 14. Will Gun Control Reduce Crime?   246

YES: Josh Sugarmann, from "The NRA Is Right: But We Still
Need to Ban Handguns," *Washington Monthly*   248

NO: James D. Wright, from "Second Thoughts About Gun
Control," *Public Interest*   254

Josh Sugarmann, formerly with the National Coalition to Ban Handguns, identifies several problems with legalized handguns, including what he describes as unacceptably high rates of suicides with guns, family homicides, and accidents. Sociologist James D. Wright argues that banning small handguns would not reduce crime and sets forth what he classifies as the many legitimate uses of "Saturday night specials."

ISSUE 15. Are Private Prisons a Good Idea?   264

YES: Charles H. Logan, from *Private Prisons: Cons and Pros*   266

NO: John J. DiIulio, Jr., from "The Duty to Govern: A Critical
Perspective on the Private Management of Prisons and Jails," in
Douglas C. McDonald, ed., *Private Prisons and the Public Interest*   275

Criminologist Charles Logan contends that many aspects of criminal justice, including components of corrections, are currently being handled by private companies. Citing halfway houses, Immigration and Naturalization Service (INS) detention centers, and many juvenile training schools, among other correctional categories, he argues that the advantages of privatization far outweigh the disadvantages. He bristles at critics who, he says, unfairly dismiss private prisons. Controversial political scientist John J. DiIulio, Jr., dismisses private prisons as simply old wine in new bottles. He feels that both morally and practically private prisons are doomed to failure. Privatizing trash collection may be one thing for governments to consider, he says, but not the management of incarcerated human beings, which ought to be left solely in the hands of government.

ISSUE 16. Is the Victims' Rights Movement Succeeding?   **286**

YES: Frank Carrington and George Nicholson, from "Follow-up Issue on Victims' Rights," *Pepperdine Law Review*   **288**

NO: Robert Elias, from *The Politics of Victimization: Victims, Victimology, and Human Rights*   **294**

Frank Carrington, attorney and executive director of the Victims Assistance Legal Organization, and municipal court judge George Nicholson are convinced that the victims' movement "has arrived," and, after reviewing its progress within various court systems and committees, they conclude that the movement has been a success in spite of some remaining hurdles. Political scientist Robert Elias contends that the victims' movement has hurt both victims and defendants in several unexpected ways, and he sees it as only helping certain people within the criminal justice system that may not have any real interest in either victims or their rights.

ISSUE 17. Will Drug Legalization Help the Criminal Justice System?   **302**

YES: Arnold S. Trebach, from *"Law Enforcement News* Interview With Trebach," *Law Enforcement News*   **304**

NO: John Kaplan, from "Taking Drugs Seriously," *Public Interest*   **311**

Law professor Arnold S. Trebach insists that the war against illegal drugs is lost and says that the only sensible path remaining is immediately to make many drugs legal. Law professor John Kaplan argues that legalization is not the answer and that the lesser evil is to step up the fight against hard-core drug use and sales in order to reduce crime.

ISSUE 18. Are Human Rights Basic to Justice?   **320**

YES: Rhoda E. Howard, from "Human Rights and the Necessity for Cultural Change," *Focus on Law Studies*   **322**

NO: Vinay Lal, from "The Imperialism of Human Rights," *Focus on Law Studies*   **326**

Sociology professor Rhoda E. Howard argues that human rights are both universal and basic for justice. Although she makes some allowances for "weak cultural relativism," she nevertheless insists that justice largely depends on a general acceptance of basic rights. Vinay Lal, a professor of humanities, dismisses human rights as a tool used by Western nations to legitimize brutal tactics that maintain their power over weaker nations and regions. Focusing primarily on the international level, Professor Lal proposes that, in practice, human rights have been used as little more than a cover for injustice.

DRUGS AND SOCIETY,
First Edition

ISSUE 1.   Should Drugs Be Legalized?   2

YES: Ethan A. Nadelmann, from "America's Drug Problem: A
Case for Decriminalization," *Bulletin of the American Academy of Arts
and Sciences*   4

NO: James Q. Wilson, from "Against the Legalization of Drugs,"
Commentary   15

Professor Ethan A. Nadelmann feels that current drug control policies are costly and ineffective in combating drug problems, and he argues that more emphasis should be put on drug education, prevention, and treatment instead of on drug prohibition. Criminologist James Q. Wilson argues that legalizing drugs is fundamentally unprincipled and inappropriate, and he feels that legalization would increase drug use and addiction and pose great risks to society.

**ISSUE 2.   Should Medical Patients Be Permitted to Use
           Marijuana?**   28

YES: Mae Nutt, from "In the Matter of Marijuana Rescheduling
Petition," U.S. Department of Justice, Drug Enforcement
Administration   30

NO: John C. Lawn, from "Their Government Tells Them All to
Get Lost," *The Federal Register*   41

Speaking as a mother, Mae Nutt describes the physical and emotional relief that marijuana provided her son while he was undergoing cancer treatment and argues that patients should be allowed to use marijuana while in treatment. John C. Lawn, director of the Drug Enforcement Administration, contends that medical patients should not be permitted to use marijuana because there is a lack of reliable scientific evidence showing marijuana's safety and its usefulness in the treatment of medical conditions.

ISSUE 3. Does Drug Testing Violate Civil Rights?   50

YES: Leonard H. Glantz, from "A Nation of Suspects: Drug Testing and the Fourth Amendment," *American Journal of Public Health*   52

NO: Robert L. DuPont, from "Mandatory Random Testing Needs to Be Undertaken at the Worksite," in Ruth C. Engs, ed., *Controversies in the Addiction's Field, Volume One*   62

Professor of health law Leonard H. Glantz argues that random drug testing violates civil liberties and sacrifices citizens' Fourth Amendment rights for the sake of the war on drugs. Physician and psychiatrist Robert L. DuPont contends that the dangers of illicit drug use warrant mandatory random drug testing.

ISSUE 4. Should the Drinking Age Remain at 21?   70

YES: Richard J. Goeman, from "Why We Need a Minimum-Purchase Age of 21," in Ruth C. Engs, ed., *Controversies in the Addiction's Field, Volume One*   72

NO: David J. Hanson, from "The Drinking Age Should Be Lowered," in Ruth C. Engs, ed., *Controversies in the Addiction's Field, Volume One*   78

Research associate Richard J. Goeman points out that consumption of alcohol among young adults accounts for a disproportionate number of automobile accidents, fatalities, and other alcohol-related problems. He argues that maintaining the current minimum drinking age is necessary to prevent further alcohol-related problems. David J. Hanson, a professor of sociology, argues that minimum-age drinking laws are unnecessary because they fail to prevent underage drinking and alcohol-related problems.

ISSUE 5. Is the War on Drugs Misdirected?   88

YES: James F. Mosher and Karen L. Yanagisako, from "Public Health, Not Social Warfare: A Public Health Approach to Illegal Drug Policy," *Journal of Public Health Policy*   90

NO: Office of National Drug Control Policy, from *National Drug Control Strategy: A Nation Responds to Drug Use*   100

Public health specialists James F. Mosher and Karen L. Yanagisako argue that drug problems should come under the province of public health and not the criminal justice system. They believe that too much emphasis is placed on controlling illegal drugs and not enough on legal drugs, like alcohol and tobacco. The Office of National Drug Control Policy feels that not only should

drug users be prosecuted but that efforts should be directed toward disrupting and dismantling multinational criminal organizations.

ISSUE 6.   Should Needle Exchange Programs Be Promoted?   **108**

YES: Merrill Singer, Ray Irizarry, and Jean J. Schensul, from "Needle Access as an AIDS Prevention Strategy for IV Drug Users: A Research Perspective," *Human Organization*   **110**

NO: Office of National Drug Control Policy, from "Needle Exchange Programs: Are They Effective?" *ONDCP Bulletin No. 7*   **124**

Professors Merrill Singer and Jean J. Schensul and drug treatment specialist Ray Irizarry believe that the tremendous rise in the incidence of AIDS necessitates exploring needle exchange programs for intravenous drug users as a prevention strategy. The Office of National Drug Control Policy sees needle exchange programs as an admission of defeat and a retreat from the ongoing battle against drug use.

ISSUE 7.   Should Drug Use by Pregnant Women Be Considered Child Abuse?   **134**

YES: Paul A. Logli, from "Drugs in the Womb: The Newest Battlefield in the War on Drugs," *Criminal Justice Ethics*   **136**

NO: Alida V. Merlo, from "Prosecuting Pregnant Drug Users," in Arnold S. Trebach and Kevin B. Zeese, eds., *New Frontiers in Drug Policy*   **143**

Paul A. Logli, a prosecuting attorney, argues that pregnant women who use drugs should be prosecuted because they risk harming their unborn children. Professor of criminal justice Alida V. Merlo asserts that the prosecution of pregnant drug users is unfair and discriminatory because such prosecution primarily affects poor, minority women who lack access to quality prenatal care and drug treatment facilities.

ISSUE 8.   Is Passive Smoking Harmful to Nonsmokers?   **156**

YES: Richard G. Schlaadt, from *Tobacco and Health*   **158**

NO: Gary L. Huber, Robert E. Brockie, and Vijay K. Mahajan, from "Passive Smoking: How Great a Hazard?" *Consumers' Research*   **165**

Richard G. Schlaadt, director of the University of Oregon Substance Abuse Program, concludes that the evidence regarding passive smoking shows that it poses a great risk to nonsmokers. Physicians Gary L. Huber, Robert E. Brockie, and Vijay K. Mahajan contend that claims about the adverse effects of passive smoking are not based on scientific fact, because the level of exposure to secondhand smoke cannot be measured.

ISSUE 9. Can Caffeine Be Bad for Your Health?   **176**

YES: Janis A. Work, from "Are Java Junkies Poor Sports?" *The Physician and Sportsmedicine*   **178**

NO: Diederick E. Grobbee, Eric B. Rimm, Edward Giovannucci, Graham Colditz, Meir Stampfer, and Walter Willett, from "Coffee, Caffeine, and Cardiovascular Disease in Men," *The New England Journal of Medicine*   **183**

Free-lance writer Janis A. Work argues that the consumption of caffeine, even at low levels, can have adverse physical effects. Dr. Diederick E. Grobbee and associates from the Department of Epidemiology and Nutrition at Harvard University's School of Public Health report on a study in which caffeine use did not increase the risk for cardiovascular disease.

ISSUE 10. Is Alcoholism Hereditary?   **190**

YES: Secretary of Health and Human Services, from *Seventh Special Report to the U.S. Congress on Alcohol and Health,* U.S. Department of Health and Human Services   **192**

NO: Stanton Peele and Archie Brodsky, from *The Truth About Addiction and Recovery: The Life Process Program for Outgrowing Destructive Habits*   **200**

The U.S. Department of Health and Human Services maintains that heredity is the major risk factor contributing to alcoholism. Social and clinical psychologist Stanton Peele and health care activist Archie Brodsky argue that research studies claiming a genetic basis for alcoholism ignore personal values and environment as factors contributing to alcoholism.

ISSUE 11. Do Drug Education Programs Prevent Drug Abuse?   **210**

YES: Falcon Baker, from *Saving Our Kids from Deliquency, Drugs, and Despair*   **212**

NO: Harry H. Avis, from *Drugs and Life*   **217**

Falcon Baker, a director of delinquency programs, argues that drug education is a viable avenue for dealing with drug problems. Professor of psychology Harry H. Avis highlights many of the inadequacies of drug education and argues that schools are unfairly being asked to address problems that exist in all of society.

ISSUE 12. Should Tobacco Advertising Be Prohibited?   226

YES: Don Cahalan, from *An Ounce of Prevention: Strategies for Solving Tobacco, Alcohol, and Drug Problems*   228

NO: John Luik, from "Government Paternalism and Citizen Rationality: The Justifiability of Banning Tobacco Advertising," *International Journal of Advertising*   236

Don Cahalan, an emeritus professor of public health, discusses the link between tobacco companies advertising to certain audiences and the increase in tobacco use among these populations and argues that such advertising should be restricted. Professor of philosophy John Luik argues that individual autonomy is solely responsible for the desire to smoke and that prohibiting tobacco advertisements infringes on freedom of speech.

ISSUE 13. Is the "Disease" of Alcoholism a Myth?   246

YES: Herbert Fingarette, from "Alcoholism: The Mythical Disease," *The Public Interest*   248

NO: William Madsen, from "Thin Thinking About Heavy Drinking," *The Public Interest*   259

Professor of philosophy Herbert Fingarette asserts that proof for labeling alcoholism a disease is lacking and that identifying alcoholism as a disease is a great disservice to heavy drinkers. Professor of anthropology William Madsen claims that research showing that alcoholics can be moderate drinkers is faulty and that promoting the idea may prove fatal to the problem drinker.

ISSUE 14. Should Alcohol Advertising Be Limited?   266

YES: Patricia Taylor, from Statement Before the Subcommittee on Transportation and Hazardous Materials, Committee on Energy and Commerce, U.S. House of Representatives   268

NO: Harold Shoup and Christine Dobday, from "Alcohol Advertising Restrictions Without Due Cause," in Ruth C. Engs, ed., *Controversies in the Addiction's Field, Volume One*   274

Patricia Taylor, director of the Alcohol Policies Project of the Center for Science in the Public Interest, argues that banning alcohol advertisements aimed at youths and minorities will help eliminate alcohol-related problems. Harold Shoup and Christine Dobday, executives of the American Association of Advertising Agencies, contend that research does not support singling out advertising as a major controlling cause of alcohol abuse.

ISSUE 15. Are Drug Addicts Always in Control of Their Addiction? 280

YES: Jeffrey A. Schaler, from "Drugs and Free Will," *Society* 282

NO: Craig Nakken, from *The Addictive Personality: Understanding Compulsion in Our Lives* 290

Psychotherapist Jeffrey A. Schaler contends that addicts always have control over their addiction and that they must therefore assume responsibility for their behaviors. Addiction, he says, is a matter of the addict's free volition. Lecturer and certified chemical dependency therapist Craig Nakken argues that once an addictive personality has been established, the addict has no control over his or her addiction.

ISSUE 16. Do Alcoholics Have to Maintain a Lifetime of Abstinence? 298

YES: Ray Hoskins, from *Rational Madness: The Paradox of Addiction* 300

NO: Harry H. Avis, from "Beyond AA: Rational, Secular Recovery," in Arnold S. Trebach and Kevin B. Zeese, eds., *New Frontiers in Drug Policy* 307

Ray Hoskins, an alcoholism and drug abuse counselor, advocates total abstinence for the successful treatment of addiction, and he argues that controlling addiction through moderation is impractical. Harry H. Avis, a professor of psychology, criticizes the 12-step model of Alcoholics Anonymous and other self-help groups because it is not applicable to many addicts, and he argues that alternatives to lifelong recovery need to be explored in helping people deal with their addictions.

ISSUE 17. Are the Dangers of Steroids Exaggerated? 316

YES: Virginia S. Cowart, from "Support Lags for Research on Steroid Effects," *Journal of the American Medical Association* 318

NO: National Institute on Drug Abuse, from "Anabolic Steroids: A Threat to Body and Mind," a NIDA Research Report Series, U.S. Department of Health and Human Services 323

Medical writer Virginia S. Cowart asserts that the long-term consequences of anabolic steroid use has yet to be determined because this type of research has not been scientifically conducted. The National Institute on Drug Abuse identifies many short-term physical and psychological problems and potential long-term problems linked to the unregulated use of anabolic steroids.

ECONOMIC ISSUES,
Sixth Edition

ISSUE 1. Are Profits the Only Business of Business?   **2**

YES: Milton Friedman, from "The Social Responsibility of
Business Is to Increase Its Profits," *The New York Times Magazine*   **4**

NO: Christopher D. Stone, from "Corporate Accountability in
Law and Morals," in Oliver F. Williams and John W. Houck, eds.,
The Judeo-Christian Vision and the Modern Corporation   **10**

Free-market economist Milton Friedman contends that the sole responsibility
of business is to increase its profits. Philosopher Christopher D. Stone insists
that the time for corporate social responsibility has come and considerations
other than profit making sometimes take precedence in a business.

ISSUE 2. Should American Farmers Be Forced to Face Market
Competition?   **22**

YES: Dick Armey, from "Moscow on the Mississippi: America's
Soviet-Style Farm Policy," *Policy Review*   **24**

NO: Andrew Larkin, from "Ethics, Economics, and Agricultural
Policy: Considerations for the 1990 Farm Bill," *Journal of Economic
Issues*   **32**

Former economics professor and current congressman Dick Armey (R-Texas)
asserts that government farm programs are costly, reduce productivity, decrease competitiveness, and only hurt those they are intended to help. Economics professor Andrew Larkin argues that lawmakers need to radically
rethink U.S. farm policy so as to address the consequences of low farm prices
and high farm costs that cause both farmers and the environment to suffer.

ISSUE 3. Is National Service at Odds With American National
Interest?   **40**

YES: Doug Bandow, from "National Service: Unnecessary and
Un-American," *Orbis: A Journal of World Affairs*   **42**

NO: Charles Moskos, from "Rebuttal: Necessary and American,"
Orbis: A Journal of World Affairs   **49**

Doug Bandow, a former special assistant to President Reagan, argues that the Nunn-McCurdy proposal on national service represents an objectionable intrusion of the state into the affairs of individual members of society—an intrusion that will weaken our future military preparedness. Professor of sociology Charles Moskos, who advises the conservative-leaning Democratic Leadership Conference, characterizes this proposal as "bold legislation" and "a GI Bill without the GI."

ISSUE 4. **Are Women Paid Less Than Men Because Their Working Conditions Are More Favorable?** 56

YES: **Randall K. Filer,** from "Occupational Segregation, Compensating Differentials, and Comparable Worth," in Robert T. Michael et al., eds., *Pay Equity: Empirical Inquiries* 58

NO: **Jerry A. Jacobs and Ronnie J. Steinberg,** from "Compensating Differentials and the Male-Female Wage Gap: Evidence from the New York State Comparable Worth Study," *Social Forces* 66

Associate professor of economics Randall K. Filer maintains that comparable worth policies are unnecessary since wage differentials simply reflect differences in workers' preferences for jobs with varying degrees of pleasantness. Associate professors of sociology Jerry A. Jacobs and Ronnie J. Steinberg argue that empirical evidence proves that wage differentials cannot be explained by worker employment choices.

ISSUE 5. **Are Rent Controls the Cause of America's Homelessness?** 80

YES: **William Tucker,** from "How Housing Regulations Cause Homelessness," *The Public Interest* 82

NO: **Richard P. Appelbaum, Michael Dolny, Peter Dreier, and John I. Gilderbloom,** from "Scapegoating Rent Control: Masking the Causes of Homelessness," *Journal of the American Planning Association* 91

Journalist William Tucker analyzes the problem of homelessness across the United States and suggests that rent controls and homelessness are correlated. Sociologist Richard P. Appelbaum and his research associates submit that Tucker's statistical analysis is flawed and that he ignores the real causes of homelessness: poverty, the lack of affordable housing, and inadequate support services for those who suffer from mental illness and alcoholism.

ISSUE 6.   Do Hostile Takeovers Harm Society?   100

YES: Lisa Newton, from "The Hostile Takeover: An Opposition
View," in Tom L. Beauchamp and Norman E. Bowie, eds., *Ethical
Theory and Business*, 3rd ed.   102

NO: Robert Almeder and David Carey, from "In Defense of
Sharks: Moral Issues in Hostile Liquidating Takeovers," *Journal of
Business Ethics*   112

Professor of philosophy Lisa Newton warns that hostile corporate takeovers
are *"not* business as usual"; rather, they are an "assault with a deadly
weapon." Philosophers Robert Almeder and David Carey charge that Newton's arguments are "seriously flawed" and that it is the use of "shark
repellents" that is immoral.

ISSUE 7.   Is Mass Transit the Answer to Improving U.S. Energy
           Efficiency?   126

YES: Peter W. G. Newman and Jeffrey R. Kenworthy, from
"Gasoline Consumption and Cities: A Comparison of U.S. Cities
With a Global Survey," *Journal of the American Planning Association*   128

NO: Peter Gordon and Harry W. Richardson, from "Gasoline
Consumption and Cities: A Reply," *Journal of the American Planning
Association*   142

Environmental scientists Peter W. G. Newman and Jeffrey R. Kenworthy
conclude that land use and transportation priorities are more important than
price, income, and vehicle efficiency in the determination of urban gasoline consumption patterns. Urban economists Peter Gordon and Harry W.
Richardson allege that Newman and Kenworthy "ignore a mountain of research that contradicts their view" and draw very troubling conclusions.

ISSUE 8.   Is Choice a Panacea for the Ills of Public Education?   150

YES: John E. Chubb and Terry M. Moe, from "America's Public
Schools: Choice *Is* a Panacea," *The Brookings Review*   152

NO: Bill Honig, from "Why Privatizing Public Education Is a Bad
Idea," *The Brookings Review*   163

Political scientists John E. Chubb and Terry M. Moe believe that the United
States must free public schools from "political and bureaucratic control" and
instead rely upon "markets and parental choice" in the quest for quality
education. Public school superintendent Bill Honig replies that privatizing
public schools through a system of choice is both unnecessary, given the

school reforms of the 1980s, and dangerous, in light of the expected market consequences.

ISSUE 9.   Did Reaganomics Fail?   170

YES: Samuel Bowles, David M. Gordon, and Thomas E. Weisskopf, from "Right-Wing Economics Backfired," *Challenge*   172

NO: Paul Craig Roberts, from "What Everyone 'Knows' About Reaganomics," *Commentary*   179

Economists Samuel Bowles, David M. Gordon, and Thomas E. Weisskopf believe that the economic policies of the Reagan administration failed to reverse the long-term deterioration of the U.S. economy due to the inability of Reaganomics to escape the contradictions of right-wing economics. The policies created an economic environment that hindered rather than stimulated investment. Paul Craig Roberts, an economist and former government policymaker, believes that Reaganomics was a success: it was not the cause of increased government budget deficits; careful analysis of the data suggests that the United States does not save or invest too little; it created an improved investment environment; and some 20 million jobs were created during the Reagan era.

ISSUE 10.   Do Federal Budget Deficits Matter?   190

YES: Alan Greenspan, from "Deficits Do Matter," *Challenge*   192

NO: Robert Eisner, from "Our Real Deficits," *Journal of the American Planning Association*   197

Federal Reserve chairman Alan Greenspan believes that federal government budget deficits, in the long run, hurt the economy. The deficits crowd out or reduce net private domestic investment, which means a reduction in the rate of growth in the nation's capital stock. This, in turn, means less capital per worker and a reduction in labor productivity, the result of which is that the output of goods and services is smaller and persons are worse off. Economics professor Robert Eisner believes that if the budget position of the government is measured appropriately, then, in "a fundamental, long-run sense, . . . the total budget is now in balance." The real problems of the U.S. economy are not budget deficits but a lack of expenditures on "human capital and in public investment."

ISSUE 11. Should the Federal Reserve Target Zero Inflation?　　206

YES: W. Lee Hoskins, from "The Case for Price Stability,"
Economic Commentary, Federal Reserve Bank of Cleveland　　208

NO: Michael Meeropol, from "Zero Inflation: Prescription for
Recession," *Challenge*　　217

Former Cleveland Federal Reserve Bank president W. Lee Hoskins supports House Joint Resolution 409, which calls for the Federal Reserve to pursue policies to eliminate inflation. Hoskins believes zero inflation would "help markets avoid distortions and imbalances, stabilize the business cycle, and promote the highest sustainable growth in our economy." Economics professor Michael Meeropol opposes House Joint Resolution 409. He believes that a move to zero inflation will not reduce unemployment and reduce the risk of inflation, it will not produce a higher possible rate of saving and investment, and it may increase income inequality by redistributing income to high-income people from low-income people.

ISSUE 12. Does the United States Save Enough?　　224

YES: Fred Block, from "Bad Data Drive Out Good: The Decline of
Personal Savings Reexamined," *Journal of Post Keynesian Economics*　　226

NO: William D. Nordhaus, from "What's Wrong With a
Declining National Saving Rate?" *Challenge*　　236

Sociology professor Fred Block argues that savings should be calculated using the Federal Reserve's flow of funds data rather than the conventional National Income and Product Accounts data, and that the former data indicate that savings are adequate. Economics professor William D. Nordhaus believes that increased amounts of saving and investment are necessary if the United States is to avoid a substantial decrease in its standard of living.

ISSUE 13. Should the Capital Gains Tax Be Lowered?　　244

YES: Robert W. Kasten, Jr., from "Lower Capital Gains Rate Will
Gain Revenue," *Congressional Record*　　246

NO: John Miller, from "Helping the Rich Help Themselves,"
Dollars and Sense　　250

Senator Robert W. Kasten, Jr. (R-Wisconsin) wants to reduce the tax rate on capital gains because such a reduction will increase government revenues, stimulate the economy and the job market, and bring the U.S. economy more in line with "European and Asian competitors." Professor of economics John Miller is against a cut in the tax rate on capital gains because he believes that the benefits will primarily go to the rich and that it will not stimulate

investment. Instead, he proposes an increase in the tax rate on short-term capital gains.

ISSUE 14. Is Workfare a Good Substitute for Welfare?   256

YES: Lawrence M. Mead, from Statement Before the Subcommittee on Trade, Productivity, and Economic Growth, Joint Economic Committee, U.S. Congress   258

NO: Morton H. Sklar, from Statement Before the Subcommittee on Trade, Productivity, and Economic Growth, Joint Economic Committee, U.S. Congress   267

Associate professor of politics Lawrence M. Mead, an advocate of the work ethic, urges Congress to make work a fundamental condition of receiving welfare assistance. Attorney Morton H. Sklar rejects Mead's contention that work must be a key ingredient in any welfare system. His experience suggests that a work requirement is inappropriate for many welfare recipients and not cost-effective for those who would be asked to work.

ISSUE 15. Should the United States Protect Domestic Industries from Foreign Competition?   278

YES: Robert Kuttner, from "The Free Trade Fallacy," *The New Republic*   280

NO: Michael Kinsley, from "Keep Free Trade Free," *The New Republic*   287

Columnist Robert Kuttner alleges that David Ricardo's eighteenth-century view of the world does not "describe the global economy as it actually works" in the twentieth century. He says that, today, "comparative advantage" is determined by exploitative wage rates and government action; it is not determined by free markets. Social critic Michael Kinsley replies that we do not decrease American living standards when we import the products made by cheap foreign labor. He claims protectionism today, just as it did in the eighteenth century, weakens our economy and only "helps to put off the day of reckoning."

ISSUE 16. Is Japan a Threat to America's Economic and National Security?   292

YES: Stephen D. Cohen, from "United States–Japanese Trade Relations," *Proceedings of the Academy of Political Science*   294

NO: Philip H. Trezise, from "Japan, the Enemy?" *The Brookings Review*   306

Professor of international economic relations Stephen D. Cohen concludes that a continuation of our "inferior industrial performance relative to Japan" is a threat to both the "economic [and] national security interests of the United States." Philip H. Trezise, a senior fellow of the Brookings Institution, replies that "on any rational calculation, economic competition from Japan does not threaten America's national security" or its long-run economic vitality.

**ISSUE 17. Does Global Warming Require Immediate
          Government Action?**   318

YES: Cynthia Pollock Shea, from "Protecting Life on Earth: Steps
to Save the Ozone Layer," *Worldwatch Paper 87*   320

NO: Lester B. Lave, from "The Greenhouse Effect: What
Government Actions Are Needed?" *Journal of Policy Analysis and
Management*   330

Cynthia Pollock Shea, a senior researcher with the Worldwatch Institute, pleads with governments and industries to initiate a "crash program" designed to halt emissions of chemicals that deplete the ozone, such as chlorofluorocarbons, before irreparable damage is done to world agriculture, marine life, and human health. Professor of economics Lester B. Lave warns against drastic solutions that could themselves be harmful or, at a minimum, "costly if the greenhouse consequences are more benign than predicted."

**ISSUE 18. Should a New Military-Industrial Complex Be
          Developed?**   340

YES: Mackubin T. Owens, from "Expand the Military-Industrial
Complex? Yes—Preparedness Requires It," *Orbis: A Journal of World
Affairs*   342

NO: William J. Long, from "Expand the Military-Industrial
Complex? No—It's Unnecessary and Inefficient," *Orbis: A Journal of
World Affairs*   349

Mackubin T. Owens, a professor of defense economics, warns that the industrial base would be "hard-pressed to support our military needs" without substantial lead time, and, therefore, a strategic trade and investments policy should be "enacted as soon as possible." Associate professor of international affairs William J. Long attacks Owens's military-industrial complex and proclaims that "defense protectionism, like other forms of protectionism, is unnecessary, ineffective, and even dangerous."

EDUCATIONAL ISSUES,
Seventh Edition

ISSUE 1.   Should Schooling Be Based on Social Experiences?   **2**

YES: John Dewey, from *Experience and Education*   **4**

NO: Robert M. Hutchins, from *The Conflict in Education*   **12**

Noted philosopher John Dewey suggests a reconsideration of the traditional approaches to schooling, giving fuller attention to the social development of the learner and the quality of his or her total experience. Robert M. Hutchins, former chancellor of the University of Chicago, argues for a liberal arts education geared to the development of intellectual powers.

ISSUE 2.   Should Schools Determine What Is Learned?   **18**

YES: Clifton Fadiman, from "The Case for Basic Education," in
James D. Koerner, ed., *The Case for Basic Education*   **20**

NO: John Holt, from *Escape from Childhood*   **27**

Writer and editor Clifton Fadiman argues for standardized subject matter, which rescues the learner from triviality and capriciousness. Educator John Holt feels that an imposed curriculum damages the individual and usurps a basic human right to select one's own path of development.

ISSUE 3.   Should Behaviorism Shape Educational Practices?   **34**

YES: B. F. Skinner, from *Beyond Freedom and Dignity*   **36**

NO: Carl R. Rogers, from *Freedom to Learn*   **42**

Noted psychologist and proponent of behaviorism B. F. Skinner critiques the concept of "inner freedom" and links learning and motivation to the influence of external forces. Noted psychologist and educator Carl R. Rogers offers the "humanistic" alternative to behaviorism, insisting on the reality of subjective forces in human motivation.

ISSUE 4.   Should Values Be Developed Rather Than Transmitted?   50

YES: Lawrence Kohlberg, from "The Cognitive-Developmental Approach to Moral Education," *Phi Delta Kappan*   52

NO: Edward A. Wynne, from "The Great Tradition in Education: Transmitting Moral Values," *Educational Leadership*   61

Professor of education Lawrence Kohlberg outlines his theory that, following Dewey and Piaget, links values to cognitive growth. Professor of education Edward A. Wynne feels that the schools, under the influence of Kohlberg and others, have abandoned our educational traditions.

ISSUE 5.   Is Church-State Separation Being Threatened?   70

YES: R. Freeman Butts, from "A History and Civics Lesson for All of Us," *Educational Leadership*   72

NO: Robert L. Cord, from "Church-State Separation and the Public Schools: A Re-evaluation," *Educational Leadership*   78

Professor of education R. Freeman Butts warns that current efforts to redefine the relationship between religion and schooling are eroding the Constitution's intent. Professor of political science Robert L. Cord offers a more accommodating interpretation of this intent.

ISSUE 6.   Does a Common Curriculum Promote Equality?   88

YES: Mortimer J. Adler, from "The Paideia Proposal: Rediscovering the Essence of Education," *The American School Board Journal*   90

NO: Floretta Dukes McKenzie, from "The Yellow Brick Road of Education," *Harvard Educational Review*   97

Mortimer J. Adler, director of the Institute for Philosophical Research, contends that equality of educational opportunity can be attained in qualitative terms by establishing uniform curricular objectives for all. Former public schools superintendent Floretta Dukes McKenzie points out Adler's faulty assumptions about the learning process and his lack of attention to the realities of contemporary society.

ISSUE 7.   Will Reforming School Funding Remove "Savage Inequalities"?   104

YES: Ruth Sidel, from "Separate and Unequal," *The Nation*   106

NO: Peter Schrag, from "Savage Equalities: The Case Against Jonathan Kozol," *The New Republic*   110

Sociology professor Ruth Sidel examines Jonathan Kozol's controversial book *Savage Inequalities* and finds his argument for the equalization of funding compelling. Journalist Peter Schrag argues that Kozol's analysis is sometimes simplistic and often impractical.

ISSUE 8.   Should National Goals Guide School Performance?   116

YES: Denis P. Doyle, from "America 2000," *Phi Delta Kappan*   118

NO: Evans Clinchy, from "America 2000: Reform, Revolution, or Just More Smoke and Mirrors?" *Phi Delta Kappan*   126

Hudson Institute scholar Denis P. Doyle lauds "America 2000" as a history-making initiative in federal policy. Evans Clinchy, a scholar at the Institute for Responsive Education, finds a major internal contradiction in the document and calls for serious rethinking.

ISSUE 9.   Can "Choice" Lead the Way to Educational Reform?   140

YES: John E. Chubb and Terry M. Moe, from "America's Public Schools: Choice *Is* a Panacea," *The Brookings Review*   142

NO: Frances C. Fowler, from "The Shocking Ideological Integrity of Chubb and Moe," *Journal of Education*   154

Political science researchers John E. Chubb and Terry M. Moe, authors of the much-discussed *Politics, Markets, and America's Schools,* make the case for choice as a means of true reform. Frances C. Fowler of Miami University in Oxford, Ohio, analyzes the premises underlying the proposals of Chubb and Moe and finds an antidemocratic tone.

ISSUE 10. Will the "Edison Project" Prompt Major Reforms?   164

YES: Geoffrey Morris, from "Whittling at the Wall," *National Review*   166

NO: Jonathan Kozol, from "Whittle and the Privateers," *The Nation*   169

Geoffrey Morris, executive editor of *National Review*, describes and lauds Chris Whittle's new plan for a nationwide network of for-profit, private secondary schools. Social activist Jonathan Kozol sees the plan, called the Edison Project, as corporate exploitation and a threat to public schooling.

ISSUE 11. Is Home Schooling a Viable Alternative?　　176

YES: David Guterson, from "When Schools Fail Children: An English Teacher Educates His Kids at Home," *Harper's Magazine*　　178

NO: Jennie F. Rakestraw and Donald A. Rakestraw, from "Home Schooling: A Question of Quality, an Issue of Rights," *The Educational Forum*　　188

David Guterson, a public school teacher, explains why he and his wife educate their own children at home. Jennie F. Rakestraw and Donald A. Rakestraw, assistant professors at Georgia Southern College, examine the history and legal status of home schooling and raise questions about the balance of power between parents and society.

ISSUE 12. Can Schools Prevent Urban Dropouts?　　196

YES: Larry Cuban, from "At-Risk Students: What Teachers and Principals Can Do," *Educational Leadership*　　198

NO: Paul Woodring, from "A New Approach to the Dropout Problem," *Phi Delta Kappan*　　203

Professor of education and former school superintendent Larry Cuban offers some basic assumptions and specific guidelines for dealing with the urban dropout problem. Paul Woodring, an emeritus professor of educational psychology, attacks the conventional wisdom and turns his attention outside the school.

ISSUE 13. Should Literacy Be Based on Traditional Culture?　　208

YES: E. D. Hirsch, Jr., from "Restoring Cultural Literacy in the Early Grades," *Educational Leadership*　　210

NO: James A. Banks, from "Multicultural Literacy and Curriculum Reform," *Educational Horizons*　　219

Professor of English E. D. Hirsch, Jr., insists that higher levels of literacy must be achieved through a renewed emphasis on traditional information and a common culture. Professor of education James A. Banks argues that the nation's demographic makeup necessitates a curriculum reshaped along multicultural lines.

ISSUE 14. Do Black Students Need an Afrocentric Curriculum?   228

YES: Molefi Kete Asante, from "The Afrocentric Idea in
Education," *Journal of Negro Education*   230

NO: Arthur M. Schlesinger, Jr., from "The Disuniting of
America," *American Educator*   240

Black studies professor Molefi Kete Asante puts forth his argument for providing black students with an Afrocentric frame of reference, which will also enhance their self-esteem. Noted historian Arthur M. Schlesinger, Jr., documents his concerns about the recent spread of Afrocentric programs, the multiculturalization of the curriculum, and the use of history as therapy.

ISSUE 15. Should Bilingual Education Programs Be
          Abandoned?   252

YES: Diane Ravitch, from "Politicization and the Schools: The
Case of Bilingual Education," *Proceedings of the American
Philosophical Society*   254

NO: Donaldo Macedo, from "English Only: The Tongue-Tying of
America," *Journal of Education*   263

History of education professor Diane Ravitch finds inadequate evidence of success in bilingual education programs and expresses concern over the effort's politicization. Donaldo Macedo, an associate professor of linguistics, deplores the incessant attack on bilingual education by Ravitch and other conservatives and explores pedagogical and political implications of abandoning such programs.

ISSUE 16. Does Tracking Create Educational Inequality?   274

YES: Jeannie Oakes, from "Keeping Track, Part 1: The Policy and
Practice of Curriculum Inequality," *Phi Delta Kappan*   276

NO: Charles Nevi, from "In Defense of Tracking," *Educational
Leadership*   286

Associate professor Jeannie Oakes argues that tracking exaggerates initial differences among students and contributes to mediocre schooling for many who are placed in middle or lower tracks. Charles Nevi, the director of curriculum and instruction for the Puyallup School District, feels that tracking accommodates individual differences while making "high status knowledge" available to all.

ISSUE 17. Is Mainstreaming Beneficial to All?   292

YES: Dean C. Corrigan, from "Political and Moral Contexts That
Produced Public Law 94-142," *Journal of Teacher Education*   294

NO: Susan Ohanian, from "P.L. 94-142: Mainstream or
Quicksand?" *Phi Delta Kappan*   300

Dean of education Dean C. Corrigan traces the roots of the Education for All
Handicapped Children Act and concludes that mainstreaming can restore a
sense of social purpose to the schools. Susan Ohanian, a free-lance writer and
former teacher, provides case study evidence of dysfunctions in the execution
of the federal mandate for mainstreaming.

ISSUE 18. Do "Discipline Programs" Promote Ethical Behavior?   310

YES: Lee Canter, from "Assertive Discipline—More Than Names
on the Board and Marbles in a Jar," *Phi Delta Kappan*   312

NO: John F. Covaleskie, from "Discipline and Morality: Beyond
Rules and Consequences," *The Educational Forum*   319

Lee Canter, developer of the Assertive Discipline program, argues for the
value of a positive approach to behavior management. John F. Covaleskie of
Syracuse University criticizes the behavioral approach and claims that it fails
to shape character.

ISSUE 19. Are Current Sex Education Programs Lacking in
            Moral Guidance?   328

YES: Kevin Ryan, from "Sex, Morals, and Schools," *Theory into
Practice*   330

NO: Peter Scales, from "Overcoming Future Barriers to Sexuality
Education," *Theory into Practice*   336

Professor of education Kevin Ryan argues for movement toward a firmer
moral grounding of sex education programs. Peter Scales, a leading advocate
of sexuality education, feels that current objections to these programs are
unwarranted.

ISSUE 20. Should Schools of Education Be Abolished?   **344**

YES: Rita Kramer, from *Ed School Follies: The Miseducation of America's Teachers*   **346**

NO: Donald J. Stedman, from "Re-inventing the Schools of Education: A Marshall Plan for Teacher Education," *Vital Speeches of the Day*   **354**

Researcher Rita Kramer reports on her nationwide observations of teacher training institutions, concluding that they are not doing what they should do. School of education dean Donald J. Stedman feels that these programs are necessary and can be retooled to reach maximum effectiveness.

ENVIRONMENTAL ISSUES,
Fifth Edition

ISSUE 1. Did the United Nations Earth Summit Produce
Useful Results?   2

YES: Peter M. Haas, Marc A. Levy, and Edward A. Parson, from
"Appraising the Earth Summit: How Should We Judge UNCED's
Success?" *Environment*   4

NO: William F. Jasper, from "ECO '92: Launching Pad for
International Global Governance," *The New American*   13

Political science and public policy professors Peter M. Haas, Marc A. Levy,
and Edward A. Parson acknowledge the failure of the Earth Summit to resolve many issues but are optimistic about the many resulting initiatives that
may help solve the intertwined problems of environment and development.
Conservative journal editor William F. Jasper sees the results of the summit
as unnecessary threats to national sovereignty.

ISSUE 2. Does Wilderness Have Intrinsic Value?   24

YES: Robert K. Olson, from "Wilderness International: The New
Horizon," *Wilderness*   26

NO: William Tucker, from "Is Nature Too Good for Us?" *Harper's
Magazine*   31

Wilderness activist Robert K. Olson contends that global change and resource
depletion have transformed wilderness preservation from a value in its own
right to an international imperative. William Tucker, a writer and social critic,
asserts that wilderness areas are elitist preserves designed to keep people out.

ISSUE 3. Should the Endangered Species Act Be Reauthorized?   44

YES: Endangered Species Coalition, from *The Endangered Species
Act: A Commitment Worth Keeping*   46

NO: Suzanne Winckler, from "Stopgap Measures," *The Atlantic
Monthly*   58

A coalition of 50 environmental, conservation, and wildlife organizations argues that, despite limited funding, the Endangered Species Act has succeeded in saving many species from extinction with minimal disruption of commerce. Natural history author Suzanne Winckler contends that we should protect critical ecosystems rather than near-extinct species.

ISSUE 4.   Is Population Control the Key to Preventing Environmental Deterioration?   66

YES: Paul R. Ehrlich and John P. Holdren, from "Impact of Population Growth," *Science,* a publication of the American Association for the Advancement of Science   68

NO: Barry Commoner, Michael Corr, and Paul J. Stamler, from "The Causes of Pollution," *Environment*   76

Environmental scientists Paul R. Ehrlich and John P. Holdren argue that population increase is the principal cause of environmental degradation. Environmental scientists Barry Commoner, Michael Corr, and Paul J. Stamler contend that technological change rather than population growth has been the chief cause of environmental stress.

ISSUE 5.   Should Risk Assessment Methods Be Used to Set Environmental Priorities?   90

YES: William K. Reilly, from "Why I Propose a National Debate on Risk," *EPA Journal*   92

NO: David Durenberger, Lawrie Mott, and Mark Sagoff, from "A Dissenting Voice," *EPA Journal*   97

U.S. EPA administrator William K. Reilly argues that relying on risk assessments will improve the scientific rigor of the choices made by his agency. U.S. senator David Durenberger, environmental scientist Lawrie Mott, and philosopher Mark Sagoff raise serious questions about the accuracy of risk analysis and its failure to factor in the values that are important to the public.

ISSUE 6.   Will the "Greening" of Multinational Corporations Lead to Environmental Improvements?   106

YES: Nazli Choucri, from "The Global Environment and Multinational Corporations," *Technology Review*   108

NO: Jack Doyle, from "Hold the Applause: A Case Study of Corporate Environmentalism," *The Ecologist*   116

Political science professor Nazli Choucri claims global concerns about the environment make preservation of the planet's natural resources sound business practice as well as excellent public relations. Environmental writer Jack Doyle questions the efficacy of corporate environmentalism based on a comparison of the claims and actions of the Du Pont chemical company.

ISSUE 7. Should Energy Policy Focus on Reducing the Use of Fossil Fuels?   **126**

YES: **Dwight Holing,** from "America's Energy Plan: Missing in Action," *The Amicus Journal*   **128**

NO: **L. G. Rawl,** from "U.S. Energy Policy: Perception and Reality," *Vital Speeches of the Day*   **134**

Energy analyst and author Dwight Holing argues against an energy policy that favors increased oil exploration and supports one that relies on improved efficiency and renewable resources. Exxon chairperson L. G. Rawl claims that the goal should not be to minimize energy use but rather to promote the development of all available energy sources.

ISSUE 8. Can Current Pollution Strategies Improve Air Quality?   **142**

YES: **John G. McDonald,** from "Gasoline and Clean Air: Good News, Better News, and a Warning," *Vital Speeches of the Day*   **144**

NO: **Hilary F. French,** from "Communication: A Global Agenda for Clean Air," *Energy Policy*   **151**

Oil company executive John G. McDonald argues that air pollution from automobiles can be controlled by using cleaner fuels and continuing to improve the automobile engine. Energy policy analyst Hilary F. French claims that adequate control of air pollutants requires major efforts to reorient energy use, transportation, and industrial production toward pollution prevention.

ISSUE 9. Are the Effects of Acid Rain Serious Enough to Justify Strict Enforcement of Clean Air Legislation?   **158**

YES: **Thomas H. Moore,** from "Acid Rain: New Approach to Old Problem," *Editorial Research Reports*   **160**

NO: **William Anderson,** from "Acid Test," *Reason*   **169**

Journalist Thomas H. Moore details the present state of knowledge about the deleterious effects of acid rain and the improvements that will result if the 1990 Clean Air amendments are fully implemented. Economics professor William Anderson cites the testimony of one soil scientist, whose arguments that the proven effects of acid rain do not warrant new stringent regulations were ignored by the EPA and Congress.

ISSUE 10. Is the Widespread Use of Pesticides Required to Feed the World's People?   178

YES: William R. Furtick, from "Uncontrolled Pests or Adequate Food," in D. L. Gunn and J. G. R. Stevens, eds., *Pesticides and Human Welfare*   180

NO: Shirley A. Briggs, from "Silent Spring: The View from 1990," *The Ecologist*   188

Crop protection specialist William R. Furtick warns that pesticides are essential for the intensive agriculture required to prevent mass starvation. Environmentalist Shirley A. Briggs counters that pesticides have failed to decrease crop loss while causing the widespread ecological harm predicted in Rachel Carson's book *Silent Spring*.

ISSUE 11. Hazardous Waste: Are Cleanup and Control Efforts Succeeding?   202

YES: Jack Lewis, from "Superfund, RCRA, and UST: The Clean-up Threesome," *EPA Journal*   204

NO: Thomas P. Grumbly, from "Superfund: Candidly Speaking," *EPA Journal*   214

EPA Journal assistant editor Jack Lewis describes the progress that the regulatory agency is making in aggressively implementing U.S. federal hazardous waste legislation. Thomas P. Grumbly, president of Clean Sites, Inc., characterizes the EPA's hazardous waste strategy as poorly defined, not based on objective criteria, and inconsistently administered.

ISSUE 12. Municipal Waste: Should Recycling Be Promoted as the Key to Refuse Management?   222

YES: Daniel Lazare, from "Recycled But Not Used," *The Amicus Journal*   224

NO: Virginia I. Postrel and Lynn Scarlett, from "Talking Trash," *Reason*   231

Journalist Daniel Lazare examines the serious problems that must be overcome to realize the potential of recycling for bringing the municipal waste glut and natural resource depletion under control. Virginia I. Postrel, editor of the libertarian journal *Reason*, and solid waste researcher Lynn Scarlett argue that mandatory recycling programs and efforts to promote the use of recycled materials are failing because they are ill-conceived and not cost-effective.

ISSUE 13. Nuclear Waste: Is Yucca Mountain an Appropriate Site for Permanent Waste Disposal? 242

YES: Luther J. Carter, from "Siting the Nuclear Waste Repository: Last Stand at Yucca Mountain," *Environment* 244

NO: William Poole, from "Gambling With Tomorrow," *Sierra* 254

Science journalist Luther J. Carter describes a variety of technical and political considerations that support the choice of Yucca Mountain for the nuclear waste dump. Free-lance writer William Poole describes the opposition to the Nevada site and the unresolved safety issues, and he concludes that the choice was based more on politics than on science.

ISSUE 14. Can Incentives Devised by Industrial Nations Combat Tropical Deforestation? 264

YES: Martin T. Katzman and William G. Cale, Jr., from "Tropical Forest Preservation Using Economic Incentives," *BioScience* 266

NO: Hannah Finan Roditi and James B. Goodno, from "Rainforest Crunch: Combating Tropical Deforestation," *Dollars and Sense* 275

Economist Martin T. Katzman and science and mathematics dean William G. Cale, Jr., propose a scheme whereby a consortium of industrialized nations would develop, fund, and help administer an economic incentive program they claim could preserve tropical forests at a reasonable cost. *Dollars and Sense* editorial associate Hannah Finan Roditi and staff editor James B. Goodno emphasize the importance of grass-roots tactics and the involvement of representatives of indigenous populations in creating equitable plans to combat tropical deforestation.

ISSUE 15.   Should the Phaseout of Chlorofluorocarbons Be
Accelerated to Protect the Ozone Layer from Further
Depletion?   282

YES: Francesca Lyman, from "As the Ozone Thins, the Plot
Thickens," *The Amicus Journal*   284

NO: Ronald Bailey, from "The Hole Story: The Science Behind
the Scare," *Reason*   293

Environmental journal editor Francesca Lyman details the history of the
struggle to protect the ozone layer, including new data that have caused
environmentalists to demand an accelerated pace for the chlorofluorocarbon
phaseout. Environmental policy critic Ronald Bailey claims that the National
Aeronautic and Space Administration's recent warning that ozone depletion
zones were expanding was simply a political scare tactic designed to promote
its own case for increased funding.

ISSUE 16.   Are Aggressive International Efforts Needed to Slow
Global Warming?   304

YES: Richard Elliot Benedick, from "Equity and Ethics in a
Global Climate Convention," *America*   306

NO: S. Fred Singer, from "Warming Theories Need Warning
Label," *The Bulletin of the Atomic Scientists*   315

U.S. environmental diplomat Richard Elliot Benedick presents the case for
a global climate convention modeled on the ozone protection treaties and
warns that waiting for scientific certainty about global warming could be
disastrous. Environmental science professor S. Fred Singer claims that most
experts do not think that greenhouse gases will lead to catastrophic warming
and that the world should not invest huge sums of money in response to a
"phantom threat."

ISSUE 17.   Are Abundant Resources and an Improved
Environment Likely Future Prospects for the World's
People?   324

YES: Julian L. Simon, from "Life on Earth Is Getting Better, Not
Worse," *The Futurist*   326

NO: Lindsey Grant, from "The Cornucopian Fallacies: The Myth
of Perpetual Growth," *The Futurist*   332

Economist Julian L. Simon is optimistic about the likelihood that human minds and muscle will overcome resource and environmental problems. Environmental consultant Lindsey Grant fears that unless a "sustainable relationship between people and earth" is developed, the future may bring famine and ecological disaster.

ISSUE 18. Will Environmental Degradation Be a Feature of International Conflicts in the Future?   342

YES: Peter H. Gleick, from "Environment and Security: The Clear Connections," *The Bulletin of the Atomic Scientists*   344

NO: Daniel Deudney, from "Environment and Security: Muddled Thinking," *The Bulletin of the Atomic Scientists*   350

Research institute director Peter H. Gleick cites the use of the environment as a military target in the Persian Gulf War and argues that we may be entering an era of environmental conflict. Science and technology researcher Daniel Deudney argues that the transboundary nature of environmental controversies is more likely to undermine the nationalism that leads to war than to result in military conflict.

FAMILY AND PERSONAL RELATIONSHIPS,
First Edition

ISSUE 1.   Are Gender Differences Present at Birth?   2

YES: Steven Goldberg, from "Reaffirming the Obvious," *Society*   4

NO: Cynthia Fuchs Epstein, from "Inevitabilities of Prejudice,"
Society   9

Sociologist Steven Goldberg argues that there are basic physiological differences between women and men that lead men to do whatever is necessary to attain dominance in society. Sociologist Cynthia Fuchs Epstein counters that Goldberg's thesis ignores the pervasive societal constraints on women's lives as well as evidence of historical changes in women's status and roles despite such constraints.

ISSUE 2.   Are Women Only Victims in Their Roles as Social
            Support Providers?   16

YES: Deborah Belle, from "Gender Differences in the Social
Moderators of Stress," in Rosalind Barnett et al., eds., *Gender and
Stress*   18

NO: Micaela di Leonardo, from "The Female World of Cards and
Holidays: Women, Families, and the Work of Kinship," *Signs:
Journal of Women in Culture and Society*   28

Assistant professor of psychology Deborah Belle maintains that, in comparison to men, women are more highly involved as support providers. She claims that women often suffer from "support gap" stress. Micaela di Leonardo, an associate professor of anthropology and women's studies, asserts that women's involvement with kin and friends, despite its drawbacks, provides them with satisfaction as well as power within the family.

ISSUE 3. Have Men's Family Roles Changed? 36

YES: Joseph H. Pleck, from "The Contemporary Man," in Murry Scher et al., eds., *Handbook of Counseling and Psychotherapy with Men* 38

NO: Steven L. Nock and Paul William Kingston, from "Time With Children: The Impact of Couples' Work-Time Commitments," *Social Forces* 42

Professor of sociology Joseph H. Pleck argues that men married to employed women have substantially increased their involvement in housework and child care. Professors of sociology Steven L. Nock and Paul William Kingston contend that the emergence of the dual-earner family has not influenced men to increase their participation in family life.

ISSUE 4. Is Marriage Good for You? 52

YES: Bryce J. Christensen, from "The Costly Retreat from Marriage," *The Public Interest* 54

NO: Liz Hodgkinson, from *Unholy Matrimony: The Case for Abolishing Marriage* 60

Bryce J. Christensen, director of The Rockford Institute Center on the Family in America, argues that being married has positive mental and physical health benefits for individuals and society. Free-lance writer Liz Hodgkinson asserts that modern marriage should be abolished because it is dysfunctional for individuals and society as a whole.

ISSUE 5. Should Gays and Lesbians Fight for the Right to Marry? 74

YES: Andrew Sullivan, from "Here Comes the Groom," *The New Republic* 76

NO: Paula L. Ettelbrick, from "Since When Is Marriage a Path to Liberation?" *OUT/LOOK* 80

Andrew Sullivan, a former editor of *The New Republic*, proposes that allowing gay couples to marry would have social and legal advantages. Gay rights activist Paula L. Ettelbrick argues that marriage would further constrain lesbians and gay men, making it easier for society to refuse to validate relationships that do not include marriage.

ISSUE 6.   Is It Possible to Be Pro-Life and Pro-Choice?   88

YES: Carl Sagan and Ann Druyan, from "Is It Possible to Be
Pro-Life and Pro-Choice?" *Parade Magazine*   90

NO: Orrin G. Hatch, from *The Value of Life*   99

Astronomer Carl Sagan and writer Ann Druyan argue that the abortion issue
is not a simple dichotomy, pro-life *or* pro-choice, but one that has many
facets worth considering. They explore the reasons to uphold the view that
it is possible to value life and support abortion. Senator Orrin G. Hatch, a
supporter of a constitutional amendment to overturn the Supreme Court *Roe
v. Wade* decision on abortion, argues that the pro-choice position is morally
and legally without foundation and goes against biblical injunctions.

ISSUE 7.   Is Parenthood Necessary for a Good Marriage?   110

YES: Irving Sarnoff and Suzanne Sarnoff, from *Love-Centered
Marriage in a Self-Centered World*   112

NO: J. E. Veevers, from *Childless by Choice*   126

Psychologists Irving Sarnoff and Suzanne Sarnoff discuss their holistic
model of love-centered marriage and argue that the satisfaction of love needs
through marriage and parenthood is essential to self-realization and fulfillment. Sociologist J. E. Veevers describes the stages that lead to childlessness
and concludes that having children is not a solution for an unhappy marriage
nor a necessity for a happy marriage.

**ISSUE 8.   Should Surrogate Parenting Be Permitted for Infertile
            Couples?**   136

YES: John A. Robertson, from "Surrogate Mothers: Not So Novel
After All," *Hastings Center Report*   138

NO: Herbert T. Krimmel, from "The Case Against Surrogate
Parenting," *Hastings Center Report*   145

Professor of law John A. Robertson argues that the legal and ethical problems
associated with surrogate motherhood are not significantly different from
those that already exist with artificial insemination by a donor and adop-
tion. Professor of law Herbert T. Krimmel questions the morality of bearing
children for the purpose of giving them up, especially for payment.

ISSUE 9. Should Pregnant Teens Marry the Fathers of Their
Babies?   154

YES: P. Lindsay Chase-Lansdale and Maris A. Vinovskis, from
"Should We Discourage Teenage Marriage?" *The Public Interest*   156

NO: Naomi Farber, from "The Significance of Race and Class in
Marital Decisions Among Unmarried Adolescent Mothers," *Social
Problems*   164

Family researcher P. Lindsay Chase-Lansdale and professor of history Maris
A. Vinovskis call for a reexamination of research findings and current policies
that cast doubt on the benefits of having adolescent mothers and fathers rear
their own children. Human services educator Naomi Farber replies that, although adolescent mothers value marriage, they express legitimate concerns
about rushing into marriage simply because they are pregnant or have given
birth.

ISSUE 10. Does Arrest Reduce Domestic Violence?   178

YES: Joan Meier, from "Battered Justice," *The Washington Monthly*   180

NO: Franklyn W. Dunford, David Huizinga, and Delbert S.
Elliott, from "The Role of Arrest in Domestic Assault: The Omaha
Police Experiment," *Criminology*   186

Attorney Joan Meier, after reviewing several reports on domestic violence,
maintains that arrest is the most effective deterrent to continued assault.
Criminologists Franklyn W. Dunford, David Huizinga, and Delbert S. Elliott
argue that there is no clear-cut best approach to minimizing the continuation
of wife abuse.

ISSUE 11. Would a "Mommy Track" Benefit Employed Women?   192

YES: Felice N. Schwartz, from "Management Women and the
New Facts of Life," *Harvard Business Review*   194

NO: Barbara Ehrenreich and Deirdre English, from "Blowing the
Whistle on the 'Mommy Track,'" *Ms.*   202

Felice N. Schwartz, president and founder of an organization that consults
with corporations on the leadership development of women, argues that it is
in the best interests of corporations to retain valued managerial women by
creating two career paths within the organization, one for "career-primary"
women and the other for "career-and-family" women. Journalists Barbara
Ehrenreich and Deirdre English maintain that the "mommy track" notion is
based on stereotypical assumptions about women and ignores the real issue

of why corporations continue to promote work policies that are incompatible with family life.

ISSUE 12. Should the Government Establish Special Programs and Policies for Black Youths and Their Families?   208

YES: Ronald L. Taylor, from "Black Youth: The Endangered Generation," *Youth and Society*   210

NO: Jean M. Granger, from "African American Family Policy or National Family Policy: Are They Different?" *Urban League Review*   215

Sociologist Ronald L. Taylor argues that black youths and their families are disproportionately affected by poverty, crime, and unemployment and should therefore be targeted for federal and state support. Jean M. Granger, a professor of social work, asserts that the needs of black families should not be separated and distinguished from the needs of all American families. Singling out black families would only perpetuate negative myths concerning the black family.

ISSUE 13. Husband Battering: Is It a Social Problem?   224

YES: Suzanne K. Steinmetz and Joseph A. Lucca, from "Husband Battering," in Vincent B. Van Hasselt et al., eds., *Handbook of Family Violence*   226

NO: R. Emerson Dobash and Russell P. Dobash, from "Research as Social Action: The Struggle for Battered Women," in Kersti Yllö and Michele Bograd, eds., *Feminist Perspectives on Wife Abuse*   233

Professor of sociology Suzanne K. Steinmetz and professor of physical therapy Joseph A. Lucca contend that the detrimental consequences of husband battering are real but are being ignored because wives' violence against husbands is not considered a serious social problem. R. Emerson Dobash and Russell P. Dobash, professors at the University of Stirling in Scotland, argue that husband battering is not a real social problem because women do not typically evidence patterns of severe, persistent, and intimidating violence against their husbands.

**ISSUE 14. Are Extramarital Relationships Becoming More
Frequent?**   242

YES: Lynn Atwater, from *The Extramarital Connection: Sex,
Intimacy, and Identity*   244

NO: Andrew M. Greeley, Robert T. Michael, and Tom W. Smith,
from "Americans and Their Sexual Partners," *Society*   254

Associate professor of sociology Lynn Atwater argues that the incidence
of extramarital involvement has been increasing over the past half-century
in the United States. Sociologist Andrew M. Greeley, economist Robert T.
Michael, and survey researcher Tom W. Smith critique research purporting
an increased frequency of extramarital affairs and provide data indicating
that extramarital liaisons are at a relatively low level.

ISSUE 15. Children of Divorce: Are They at Greater Risk?   266

YES: Judith S. Wallerstein, from "Children of Divorce: The
Dilemma of a Decade," in Elam W. Nunnally, Catherine S.
Chilman, and Fred M. Cox, eds., *Troubled Relationships*   268

NO: David H. Demo and Alan C. Acock, from "The Impact of
Divorce on Children," *Journal of Marriage and the Family*   276

Clinician and researcher Judith S. Wallerstein contends that children whose
parents divorce are at greater risk of mental and physical health problems
than are children whose families are intact. Sociologists David H. Demo
and Alan C. Acock argue that much of the research on children of divorce
is theoretically or methodologically flawed and, consequently, the findings
cannot always be trusted.

**ISSUE 16. Do Stepchildren Need Special Policies and Programs
on Their Behalf?**   292

YES: Margaret Crosbie-Burnett and Ada Skyles, from
"Stepchildren in Schools and Colleges: Recommendations for
Educational Policy Changes," *Family Relations*   294

NO: Lawrence H. Ganong and Marilyn Coleman, from "A
Comparison of Clinical and Empirical Literature on Children in
Stepfamilies," *Journal of Marriage and the Family*   301

Margaret Crosbie-Burnett, associate professor of education and psychology,
and Ada Skyles, a J.D. candidate, maintain that stepchildren face uniquely
stressful problems related to their family situations that require special educational policies and programs. Professors of family studies Lawrence H.
Ganong and Marilyn Coleman argue that the information currently avail-

able on stepchildren and their families is theoretically and methodologically flawed. As a consequence, inaccurate images of stepchildren and their families as deviant and dysfunctional are perpetuated.

ISSUE 17. Is the Success of Remarriage Doomed?   310

YES: Andrew Cherlin, from "Remarriage as an Incomplete Institution," *American Journal of Sociology*   312

NO: Ann Goetting, from "The Six Stations of Remarriage: Developmental Tasks of Remarriage After Divorce," *Family Relations*   326

Sociologist Andrew Cherlin discusses why remarriage is less successful than marriage and proposes that this is primarily because remarriage in its present form has not been accepted by society. Professor of sociology Ann Goetting argues that remarriage is a process and that for it to be successful it must progress through a series of developmental stages.

HEALTH AND SOCIETY,
First Edition

ISSUE 1. Should the United States Adopt a National Health Insurance Program? 2

YES: Vicente Navarro, from "A National Health Program Is Necessary," *Challenge* 4

NO: John K. Iglehart, from "Canada's Health Care System Faces Its Problems," *The New England Journal of Medicine* 10

Professor Vicente Navarro maintains that health care is a basic human right and must be made available to all through a government-provided national health insurance program similar to the Canadian system. Correspondent and editor John K. Iglehart argues that although the Canadian system is admired by much of the Western world, it faces escalating problems, such as financial constraints and inadequate consumer access to high-technology medicine.

ISSUE 2. Should Doctors Ever Help Terminally Ill Patients Commit Suicide? 24

YES: Timothy E. Quill, from "Death and Dignity: A Case of Individualized Decision Making," *The New England Journal of Medicine* 26

NO: Leon R. Kass, from "Suicide Made Easy: The Evil of 'Rational' Humaneness," *Commentary* 29

Physician Timothy E. Quill, who describes a physician-assisted suicide, believes that doctors have roles other than healing and fighting against death. Physician Leon R. Kass argues that the weakening of the taboos against physician-assisted suicide is a bad idea whose time must never come.

ISSUE 3. Should Health Care for the Elderly Be Limited? 40

YES: Daniel Callahan, from "Aging and the Ends of Medicine," *Annals of the New York Academy of Sciences* 42

NO: Nat Hentoff, from "The Pied Piper Returns for the Old Folks," *The Village Voice* 51

Hastings Center director Daniel Callahan believes that medical care for elderly people at the end of their natural life expectancy should consist only of pain relief rather than expensive health care services, which serve only to forestall death. Author Nat Hentoff argues that it is immoral to limit health care services to any one segment of the population.

ISSUE 4. Is AIDS Getting More Than Its Share of Resources and Media Attention? 56

YES: **Michael Fumento,** from "Are We Spending Too Much on AIDS?" *Commentary* 58

NO: **Timothy F. Murphy,** from "No Time for an AIDS Backlash," *Hastings Center Report* 62

Writer and attorney Michael Fumento points out that Congress continues to allocate substantial amounts of money for research and the treatment of AIDS, which he feels is disproportionate to the number of people who die annually from the disease. Professor of philosophy Timothy F. Murphy argues that the AIDS epidemic is still fairly new and that AIDS is a lethal, contagious disease affecting thousands of Americans; thus, current funding is justified.

ISSUE 5. Will Practicing Positive Health Behaviors and Emphasizing Prevention Improve Health? 74

YES: **Albert L. Huebner,** from "The No-Win War on Cancer," *East West: The Journal of Natural Health and Living* 76

NO: **Lenn E. Goodman and Madeleine J. Goodman,** from "Prevention—How Misuse of a Concept Undercuts Its Worth," *Hastings Center Report* 83

Professor of physics Albert L. Huebner believes that practicing healthy behaviors could both prevent and decrease the incidence of cancer. Professors Lenn E. Goodman and Madeleine J. Goodman argue that the ability to prevent disease, especially cancer, is exaggerated and limited.

ISSUE 6. Can a Positive Mental Attitude Overcome Disease? 94

YES: **Bernard Dixon,** from "Dangerous Thoughts," *Science86 Magazine,* a publication of the American Association for the Advancement of Science 96

NO: **Marcia Angell,** from "Disease as a Reflection of the Psyche," *The New England Journal of Medicine* 101

Writer and editor Bernard Dixon discusses studies indicating that stress negatively impacts the immune system and, conversely, that a positive mental attitude can prevent illness. Physician Marcia Angell argues that there is no proof that a positive mental attitude can slow or prevent disease.

ISSUE 7. Do Smokers Have a Right to Smoke in Public Places? 108

YES: B. Bruce-Briggs, from "The Health Police Are Blowing Smoke," *Fortune* 110

NO: Robert E. Goodin, from "The Ethics of Smoking," *Ethics* 114

Policy analyst B. Bruce-Briggs believes that the war on passive smoking, which he argues is based on inaccurate data relating passive smoking with a myriad of health problems, is both a campaign against smokers and a trial run for a larger program of social manipulation. Professor of political and moral philosophy Robert E. Goodin argues that the health of nonsmokers suffers when they are forced to breathe tobacco smoke and that nonsmokers should have the right to a smoke-free environment.

ISSUE 8. Should Alcoholism Be Treated as a Disease? 124

YES: George E. Vaillant, from "We Should Retain the Disease Concept of Alcoholism," *Harvard Medical School Mental Health Letter* 126

NO: Herbert Fingarette, from "We Should Reject the Disease Concept of Alcoholism," *Harvard Medical School Mental Health Letter* 130

Physician George E. Vaillant maintains that since alcoholism is genetically transmitted, it should be treated as a disease and not as a character flaw. Philosophy professor Herbert Fingarette argues that alcohol consumption is voluntary behavior, within the drinker's control, and that the role of heredity and genes in alcoholism is limited.

ISSUE 9. Should Drugs Be Legalized? 136

YES: Richard J. Dennis, from "The Economics of Legalizing Drugs," *The Atlantic Monthly* 138

NO: James A. Inciardi and Duane C. McBride, from "The Case *Against* Legalization," in James A. Inciardi, ed., *The Drug Legalization Debate* 144

Richard J. Dennis, chairman of the Advisory Board of the Drug Policy Foundation, believes that the war on drugs has failed to reduce substance abuse or crime and argues that legalizing marijuana and cocaine would reduce the social and economic costs of drug abuse. Professors James A. Inciardi and Duane C. McBride maintain that the legalization of drugs would cause an increase in crime and produce an even greater number of addicts.

ISSUE 10. Does Sex Education Prevent Teen Pregnancy?   **156**

YES: Michael A. Carrera and Patricia Dempsey, from "Restructuring Public Policy Priorities on Teen Pregnancy: A Holistic Approach to Teen Development and Teen Services," *SIECUS Report*   **158**

NO: Sarah Glazer, from "Sex Education: How Well Does It Work?" *Editorial Research Reports*   **165**

Professors Michael A. Carrera and Patricia Dempsey discuss the success of sex education programs characterized by multiple intervention strategies, which they feel have decreased teenage pregnancy rates. Author Sarah Glazer argues that, in the United States, sex education does not prevent teenage pregnancy or reduce teenage sexual activity.

ISSUE 11. Can Abortion Be a Morally Acceptable Choice?   **178**

YES: Mary Gordon, from "A Moral Choice," *The Atlantic Monthly*   **180**

NO: Jason DeParle, from "Beyond the Legal Right: Why Liberals and Feminists Don't Like to Talk About the Morality of Abortion," *The Washington Monthly*   **187**

Author Mary Gordon believes that abortion is an acceptable means for ending an unwanted pregnancy and that women who have abortions are neither selfish nor immoral. Editor Jason DeParle argues that liberals and feminists refuse to acknowledge that the 3 out of 10 pregnancies that currently end in abortion raise many moral questions.

ISSUE 12. Is Cholesterol Reduction an Important Health Priority?   **200**

YES: Timothy Johnson, from "The Cholesterol Controversy," *Harvard Medical School Health Letter*   **202**

NO: Thomas J. Moore, from "The Cholesterol Myth," *The Atlantic Monthly*   **205**

Physician Timothy Johnson discusses evidence indicating that the higher one's serum cholesterol is, the greater the statistical risk of having a heart attack. Journalist Thomas J. Moore argues that there is no legitimate evidence proving that lowering serum cholesterol will prevent a heart attack.

ISSUE 13. Can Large Doses of Vitamins Improve Health?   **216**

YES: Linus Pauling, from *How to Live Longer and Feel Better*   **218**

NO: Editors of *Harvard Medical School Health Letter*, from "Vitamin C—When Is Enough Enough?" *Harvard Medical School Health Letter*   **226**

Biochemist Linus Pauling argues that taking megadoses of vitamins, particularly vitamin C, can help people achieve superior health. The editors of the *Harvard Medical School Health Letter* acknowledge that humans have a need for vitamin C; however, they argue that claims that megadoses will prevent colds, prevent cancer, and will prolong life are unsubstantiated.

ISSUE 14. Does Exercise Increase Longevity?   **232**

YES: Joel Gurin, from "Linking Exercise With Longevity," *Runner's World*   **234**

NO: Henry A. Solomon, from *The Exercise Myth*   **240**

American Health editor Joel Gurin claims that there is conclusive evidence that regular exercise will increase longevity. Cardiologist Henry A. Solomon argues that longevity is based on a complex interaction of genetics and lifestyle and that claims that exercise is a major variable in increasing longevity are exaggerated, unsubstantiated, and based on conflicting data.

ISSUE 15. Are Pesticides in Foods Harmful to Human Health?   **246**

YES: Lawrie Mott and Karen Snyder, from "Pesticide Alert," *Amicus Journal*   **248**

NO: Bruce Ames, from "Too Much Fuss About Pesticides," *Consumers' Research*   **256**

Pesticide researchers Lawrie Mott and Karen Snyder maintain that the very foods consumers are trying to eat more of—fresh fruits and vegetables— are those most contaminated with harmful pesticide residues. Professor of biochemistry and molecular biology Bruce Ames argues that risks, if any, from pesticides in foods are minimal and such fears are greatly exaggerated.

ISSUE 16. Is Acid Rain a Serious Environmental Problem? 262

YES: Jon R. Luoma, from "Acid Murder No Longer a Mystery,"
Audubon 264

NO: William M. Brown, from "Hysteria About Acid Rain,"
Fortune 271

Science writer Jon R. Luoma believes that there is convincing evidence implicating acid rain as a long-term threat to some aquatic ecosystems, forests, and public health. William M. Brown, director emeritus of energy and technological studies at the Hudson Institute in Indianapolis, argues that the dangers of acid rain have been greatly exaggerated and that scientists do not know what has caused the decline of some forests and waterways.

**ISSUE 17. Should All Children Be Immunized Against
Childhood Diseases?** 278

YES: Royce Flippin, from "The Vaccine Debate: Kids at Risk?"
American Health: Fitness of Body and Mind 280

NO: Richard Leviton, from "Who Calls the Shots?" *East West: The
Journal of Natural Health and Living* 285

Health writer Royce Flippin argues that since measles and some other potentially dangerous childhood diseases are making a comeback, all children should be immunized against them. Health journalist Richard Leviton maintains that many vaccines are neither safe nor effective and that parents should have a say in whether or not their children receive them.

ISSUE 18. Are Chiropractors Legitimate Health Providers? 298

YES: Ellen Ruppel Shell, from "The Getting of Respect," *The
Atlantic Monthly* 300

NO: Editors of *Harvard Medical School Health Letter*, from
"Low Back Pain: What About Chiropractors?" *Harvard Medical
School Health Letter* 305

Associate professor of journalism Ellen Ruppel Shell maintains that it is in the public's best interest that chiropractors continue to provide care for the millions who have back pain. The editors of the *Harvard Medical School Health Letter* argue that although some people may be helped by chiropractic treatment, many chiropractors adhere to a philosophy that is unproven at best, and harmful at worst.

HUMAN SEXUALITY,
Fourth Edition

ISSUE 1. Are Gender Differences Rooted in the Brain?   2

YES: Doreen Kimura, from "Sex Differences in the Brain,"
Scientific American   4

NO: Carol Tavris, from *The Mismeasure of Woman*   14

Doreen Kimura, a professor of psychology, describes a wide range of cognitive variations between the genders that reflect differing hormonal influences on fetal brain development. She maintains that differences between the female and the male brains help explain differences in occupational interests and capabilities between the sexes. Carol Tavris, a social psychologist, finds that scientific efforts conducted over the past century to prove gender differences originate in the brain have yielded enough conflicting views and distorted findings to invalidate such a hypothesis. She maintains that although biology is not irrelevant to human behavior, this research has consistently been used to define women as fundamentally different from and inferior to men in body, psyche, and brain.

ISSUE 2. Can Sex Be an Addiction?   24

YES: Patrick Carnes, from "Progress in Sex Addiction: An
Addiction Perspective," *SIECUS Report*   26

NO: Marty Klein, from "Why There's No Such Thing as Sexual
Addiction—And Why It Really Matters," *Annual Meeting of the
Society for the Scientific Study of Sex*   32

Patrick Carnes, a therapist who has established an inpatient program for sexual dependency, argues that a significant number of people have identified themselves as sexual addicts—persons with "unstoppable" repetitive behavior patterns that are destructive to the addict and to his or her family. Sexual addiction can best be treated, he claims, by using systems theory and techniques developed by Alcoholics Anonymous, obesity clinics, and substance-abuse rehabilitation programs. Marty Klein, a sex therapist and marriage and family counselor, challenges sexual addiction as being vaguely defined and often diagnosed by nonsexologists. He claims that the symptoms of sexual addiction are arbitrary and that its promulgation promotes unhealthy, negative, and immature attitudes toward natural human sexuality.

ISSUE 3.   Is Rape Motivated by Aggression Instead of Sex?   42

YES: A. Nicholas Groth and H. Jean Birnbaum, from *Men Who Rape: The Psychology of the Offender*   44

NO: Craig T. Palmer, from "Twelve Reasons Why Rape Is Not Sexually Motivated: A Skeptical Examination," *Journal of Sex Research*   52

Clinical psychologists A. Nicholas Groth and H. Jean Birnbaum argue that rape is not primarily a sexual act but one of hostility, degradation, and anger, often not resulting in sexual arousal at all. Professor Craig T. Palmer claims that the arguments that present rape as being motivated primarily by anger, rage, the need for power, or sadism are illogical, based on inaccurate definitions, untestable, or inconsistent with the actual behavior of rapists.

ISSUE 4.   Does Sexual Infidelity Destroy a Relationship?   62

YES: Frank Pittman, from "What Price Camelot?" *The Family Therapy Networker*   64

NO: Sandra C. Finzi, from "Così Fan Tutte: 'So Does Everyone,'" *The Family Therapy Networker*   71

Frank Pittman, a family therapist and the author of *Private Lies: Infidelity and the Betrayal of Intimacy,* maintains that infidelity is the primary disrupter of families, the most dreaded and devastating experience in marriage. He identifies and refutes seven myths about adultery that are true some of the time but that are not as universal as most people think. Sandra C. Finzi, a family therapist, argues that the European approach to extramarital "arrangements" is much more realistic than the American tradition of viewing every extramarital sexual encounter as an indication of a deep flaw in the character of the "wandering" spouse or a fatal flaw in the marriage. Finzi claims that marriages in which couples learn to distinguish between the long-term solidarity of the relationship and the passing infatuation may not collapse in the wake of an extramarital affair.

ISSUE 5.   Is Pornography Harmful?   78

YES: James C. Dobson, from *Final Report of the Attorney General's Commission on Pornography*   80

NO: Philip Nobile and Eric Nadler, from *United States of America vs. Sex: How the Meese Commission Lied About Pornography*   87

Psychologist James C. Dobson, the founder and president of Focus on the Family, a publishing and broadcasting organization dedicated to the maintenance of "traditional values," feels that the U.S. Attorney General's Commission on Pornography saw and heard enough evidence to be convinced that pornography causes untold harm to adolescents and women. Philip Nobile and Eric Nadler, two journalists who followed the U.S. Attorney General's Commission on Pornography around the nation to report on its theory and practice, solicited the opinions of 11 citizens—feminists, journalists, sex therapists, and civil libertarians—who considered the attorney general's report. This Shadow Commission, as Nobile and Nadler called the group, contends that the report has many biases and does not demonstrate a causal connection between pornography and possible harms, such as rape.

ISSUE 6. Should RU 486 Be Legalized? 100

YES: Janet Callum and Rebecca Chalker, from "RU 486: Yes," *Ms.* 102

NO: Janice Raymond, Renate Klein, and Lynette Dumble, from "RU 486: No," *Ms.* 105

Janet Callum, former director of administrative services for the Feminist Women's Health Center, and Rebecca Chalker, an author and women's health advocate, claim that the risks of using RU 486 for abortion are exceedingly low. They argue that the ban against RU 486 should be lifted in the United States because it is less intrusive than surgical abortion, it leaves women in control, and it appears to be a safe and effective abortion alternative, which they feel women need. Janice Raymond, a professor of women's studies, Renate Klein, a lecturer in the humanities, and Lynette Dumble, a research fellow in the surgery department at the University of Melbourne, believe that feminists should not advocate a dubious and dangerous technology such as RU 486, but instead should fight to take conventional abortion methods out of the hands of physicians and promote the licensing of trained laywomen to handle most abortions.

ISSUE 7. Should Schools Distribute Condoms? 110

YES: Center for Population Options, from *Condom Availability in Schools: A Guide for Programs* 112

NO: Edwin J. Delattre, from "Condoms and Coercion: The Maturity of Self Determination," *Vital Speeches of the Day* 119

The Center for Population Options outlines what is known about the sexual behavior and risks of teens today and then examines strategies for reducing these risks, specifically encouraging abstinence and condom use. Considering all the options and all the risks, the center concludes that making condoms available to students through the schools with counseling and education is the best course of action. Professor of education Edwin J. Delattre, in opposing condom distribution in schools, notes several flaws in the argument that we have a moral obligation to distribute condoms to save lives. He dismisses the claim that this is purely a health issue, and he discusses various moral issues involved in promoting casual sexual involvement, which he believes condom distribution does.

ISSUE 8. Should Surrogate Motherhood Be Outlawed?   126

YES: Richard John Neuhaus, from "Renting Women, Buying Babies and Class Struggles," *Society*   128

NO: Monica B. Morris, from "Reproductive Technology and Restraints," *Society*   133

Richard John Neuhaus, director of the Rockford Institute Center on Religion and Society, argues that the renting of wombs and buying of babies associated with surrogate motherhood exploits the lower class and raises hostilities in America and therefore should be outlawed. Professor of sociology Monica B. Morris supports the practice of surrogate mothering and maintains that it should be regulated by law to avoid widespread misuse.

ISSUE 9. Abortion and the "Pro-Life" v. "Pro-Choice" Debate: Should the Human Fetus Be Considered a Person?   142

YES: Knights of Columbus, from *Amicus Curiae, William L. Webster, Attorney General of Missouri, et al. v. Reproductive Health Services,* U.S. Supreme Court   144

NO: Janet Benshoof, from "Fetal 'Personhood' and the Law," in Edd Doerr and James W. Prescott, eds., *Abortion Rights and Fetal "Personhood"*   150

The Knights of Columbus, a national organization of lay Catholics, argue that the concept of "viability" on which the case of *Roe v. Wade* was based has changed and that, in terms of the Fourteenth Amendment, ability to survive outside the mother's womb is not a proper basis for defining the word *person.* Hence, the unborn child should be protected as a person from conception on. Janet Benshoof argues that, historically, the law has never regarded the fetus as a person. She warns that recent attempts to force legal recognition of fetal personhood have already created a frightening array of restrictions on women

and their right to privacy, from court-ordered obstetrical interventions to lawsuits and legislation for feticide, fetal abuse, and fetal neglect.

ISSUE 10. Is There a Date Rape Crisis on College Campuses?   158

YES: Robin Warshaw, from *I Never Called It Rape: The* Ms. *Report on Recognizing, Fighting, and Surviving Date and Acquaintance Rape*   160

NO: Katie Roiphe, from "Date Rape's Other Victim," *The New York Times Magazine*   167

Robin Warshaw, a journalist specializing in social issues, examines the data from a nationwide survey conducted by *Ms.* magazine and psychologist Mary P. Koss and concludes that date rape is "happening all around us." Katie Roiphe, author of *The Morning After: Sex, Fear and Feminism on Campus*, claims that feminist prophets of a rape crisis wrongfully redefine sexual harassment and rape to include almost any encounter between women and men. She argues that shifting the criteria for harassment and rape from force and coercion to male political power promotes a destructive and sexist image of women as delicate, naive, unable to express their true feelings, and incapable of resisting men.

ISSUE 11. Does Government Have a Constitutional Right to Prohibit Certain Kinds of Sexual Conduct?   176

YES: Byron R. White, from Majority Opinion, *Michael J. Bowers, Attorney General of Georgia, v. Michael Hardwick, and John and Mary Doe,* U. S. Supreme Court   178

NO: Harry A. Blackmun, from Dissenting Opinion, *Michael J. Bowers, Attorney General of Georgia, v. Michael Hardwick, and John and Mary Doe,* U. S. Supreme Court   182

Supreme Court justice Byron R. White, arguing the majority opinion, claims that, unlike heterosexuals, homosexuals do not have a constitutional right to privacy when it comes to engaging in oral or anal sex, even in the privacy of their homes, because of the traditional social and legal condemnation of sodomy. Supreme Court justice Harry A. Blackmun, dissenting from the majority opinion, argues that since the right to be left alone is the most comprehensive of human rights and the one most valued by civilized people, the state has no right or compelling reason to prohibit any sexual acts engaged in privately by consenting adults.

**ISSUE 12. Do Parental Notification Laws Benefit Minors
Seeking Abortions?**   188

YES: Focus on the Family and Family Research Council, from
*Amicus Curiae, State of Ohio, Appellant, v. Akron Center for
Reproductive Health et al.,* U.S. Supreme Court   190

NO: Fran Avallone, from *Parental Consent and Notification Laws*   197

Focus on the Family, an organization dedicated to the preservation of traditional values, and the Family Research Council argue that the state has many legitimate and compelling reasons to require parental notification and consent for teenagers seeking abortions. Such laws permit parents to deal with issues underlying adolescent pregnancy and to provide emotional and psychological support for whatever decision the pregnant minor makes. Fran Avallone, state coordinator for Right to Choose of New Jersey, favors parental involvement in a minor's abortion decision but opposes laws requiring parental notification or consent. She argues that the only real effect of such laws is to delay abortions and further traumatize pregnant minors, especially among the poor.

**ISSUE 13. Should the Policy Banning Gays from the Military Be
Lifted?**   208

YES: Randy Shilts, from "What's Fair in Love and War,"
Newsweek   210

NO: Eugene T. Gomulka, from "Why No Gays?" *Proceedings*   214

Randy Shilts, national correspondent for the *San Francisco Chronicle,* argues that the military handling of the homosexual issue in World War II, the Korean War, the Vietnam War, and the Gulf War documents the hypocrisy of the policy that embraces gay men and lesbians in times of war and discharges them in times of peace. Eugene T. Gomulka, a commander in the U.S. Navy Chaplain Corps, argues that the ban must be maintained because of "widespread sexual compulsion," a high rate of suicide, and high rates of alcoholism, STDs, and HIV infection among gays, as well as "behavioral problems" and tensions that come with housing gay and heterosexual personnel together in tight quarters.

ISSUE 14. Should Prostitution Be Decriminalized?   220

YES: Norma Jean Almodovar, from "Prostitution and the
Criminal Justice System," *The Truth Seeker*   222

NO: Charles Winick, from "Debate on Legalization of
Prostitution," *Medical Aspects of Human Sexuality*   229

Norma Jean Almodovar, a prostitutes' rights activist and the author of *Cop to Call Girl*, argues that the real problem with prostitution lies not with some women's choice to exchange sexual favors for money but with the consequences of laws that make this exchange illegal. Charles Winick, coauthor of *The Lively Commerce—Prostitution in the United States*, argues that prostitution serves no function except to exploit women and to encourage other illegal activities and that it should therefore be eliminated entirely.

ISSUE 15. Should Society Recognize Gay Marriages?   234

YES: Brent Hartinger, from "A Case for Gay Marriage: In Support
of Loving and Monogamous Relationships," *Commonweal*   236

NO: Dennis O'Brien, from "Against Gay Marriage: What
Heterosexuality Means," *Commonweal*   242

Brent Hartinger, a free-lance writer, argues that "domestic partnership" legislation and other legal strategies used by gay men and lesbians to protect their relationship rights are inadequate and actually weaken the traditional institution of marriage. Society, he argues, has a clear interest in committed, long-lasting relationships and strong family structures, whether these are heterosexual or same-gender. Legalizing gay marriages, Hartinger concludes, would promote social stability and enhance heterosexual marriage. Dennis O'Brien, president of the University of Rochester, defends deep and abiding homosexual relationships, but he is not convinced that legally recognizing these unions as marriages would accomplish anything that cannot be accomplished equally as well with existing legal strategies. The religious or moral meaning of marriage, he contends, poses an even more substantial argument against recognizing gay unions as marriages.

ISSUE 16. Is Sexual Harassment a Pervasive Problem?   248

YES: Catharine R. Stimpson, from "Over-Reaching: Sexual
Harassment and Education," *Initiatives*   250

NO: Gretchen Morgenson, from "May I Have the Pleasure,"
National Review   255

Catharine R. Stimpson, graduate dean at Rutgers University, claims that sexual harassment is epidemic in American society and will remain epidemic as long as males are in power and control. Although some significant progress has been made in creating resistance to sexual harassment, she believes the only way to create a harassment-free society is to redefine the historical connections between sexuality, gender, and power. Gretchen Morgenson, senior editor of *Forbes* magazine, argues that statistics on the prevalence of sexual harassment are grossly exaggerated by "consultants" who make a good

livelihood instituting corporate anti-harassment programs. She argues that, in reality, the problem of sexual harassment has and will continue to become less of a problem.

ISSUE 17. Has the Federal Government Spent Enough on AIDS Research?   262

YES: Michael Fumento, from "Are We Spending Too Much on AIDS?" *Commentary*   264

NO: Timothy F. Murphy, from "No Time for an AIDS Backlash," *Hastings Center Report*   269

Michael Fumento, a former AIDS analyst for the U.S. Commission on Civil Rights, is disturbed that the Public Health Service spent more money in 1990 for AIDS research and education than it allocated for any other fatal disease. He points out that each year many times more Americans die of heart disease and cancer than of AIDS, and he asserts that the time has come to stop spending so much money and time on the disease. Assistant professor of philosophy Timothy F. Murphy maintains that the massive funding for AIDS research and prevention is justified. He argues that a communicable, lethal disease like AIDS ought to receive priority over noncommunicable diseases like cancer and heart disease, both of which can also be medically managed to allow patients to live to old age.

LEGAL ISSUES,
Fifth Edition

ISSUE 1.   **Is the Legal System Damaging the American Economy?**   2

YES: Peter Huber, from Statement Before the Subcommittee on the Consumer, Committee on Commerce, Science, and Transportation, U.S. Senate   4

NO: Kenneth Jost, from "Tampering With Evidence: The Liability and Competitiveness Myth," *ABA Journal*   13

Attorney Peter Huber claims that litigation and liability laws deter innovation and advances in quality and discourage improvements in product safety. Journalist Kenneth Jost contests claims that the American legal system hurts economic competitiveness, and he asserts that such arguments are based on flawed evidence.

ISSUE 2.   **Should Lawyers Be Prohibited from Presenting a False Case?**   24

YES: Harry I. Subin, from "The Criminal Lawyer's 'Different Mission': Reflections on the 'Right' to Present a False Case," *Georgetown Journal of Legal Ethics*   26

NO: John B. Mitchell, from "Reasonable Doubts Are Where You Find Them: A Response to Professor Subin's Position on the Criminal Lawyer's 'Different Mission,'" *Georgetown Journal of Legal Ethics*   40

Professor of law Harry I. Subin examines the ethical responsibilities of criminal defense lawyers and argues that greater responsibility should be placed on lawyers not to pervert the truth to help their clients. Attorney John B. Mitchell disputes the contention that the goal of the criminal justice process is to seek the truth and argues that it is essential that there be independent defense attorneys to provide protection against government oppression.

ISSUE 3.   Should Plea Bargaining Be Abolished?   52

YES: Kenneth Kipnis, from "Criminal Justice and the Negotiated
Plea," *Ethics*   54

NO: Nick Schweitzer, from "Plea Bargaining: A Prosecutor's
View," *Wisconsin Bar Bulletin*   67

Professor of philosophy Kenneth Kipnis makes the case that justice cannot be traded on the open market and that plea bargaining often subverts the cause of justice. District Attorney Nick Schweitzer finds that plea bargaining is fair, useful, desirable, necessary, and practical.

**ISSUE 4.   Is Drug Use Testing Permitted Under the Fourth
             Amendment?**   76

YES: Anthony Kennedy, from Majority Opinion, *National Treasury
Employees Union v. William Von Raab,* U.S. Supreme Court   78

NO: Antonin Scalia, from Dissenting Opinion, *National Treasury
Employees Union v. William Von Raab,* U.S. Supreme Court   89

Supreme Court justice Anthony Kennedy believes that drug tests of Customs Service officials are reasonable under the Fourth Amendment of the Constitution even when there is no probable cause or individualized suspicion. Justice Antonin Scalia, in dissent, argues that the Customs Service rules were not justified, serve no reasonable purpose, and are unnecessary invasions of privacy.

ISSUE 5.   Is "Hate Speech" Fully Protected by the Constitution?   96

YES: Antonin Scalia, from Majority Opinion, *R. A. V. v. City of St.
Paul, Minnesota,* U.S. Supreme Court   98

NO: John Paul Stevens, from Concurring Opinion, *R. A. V. v. City
of St. Paul, Minnesota,* U.S. Supreme Court   105

Supreme Court justice Antonin Scalia finds that the St. Paul ordinance punishing "hate speech" cannot be constitutional because it regulates speech depending on the subject the speech addresses. Justice John Paul Stevens concurs that this particular ordinance is not constitutional, but he argues that it is perhaps simply overbroad.

ISSUE 6.   Do Prayers at Public School Graduation Ceremonies
Violate the Constitution?   116

YES: Anthony Kennedy, from Majority Opinion, *Robert E. Lee et
al. v. Daniel Weisman et al.*, U.S. Supreme Court   118

NO: Antonin Scalia, from Dissenting Opinion, *Robert E. Lee et al.
v. Daniel Weisman et al.*, U.S. Supreme Court   128

Supreme Court justice Anthony Kennedy finds that prayers offered at middle
school graduation ceremonies were coercive and violated the Constitution's
Establishment Clause. Justice Antonin Scalia finds neither coercion nor government involvement to a degree warranting invalidation of the practices in
question.

ISSUE 7.   Is Abortion Protected by the Constitution?   138

YES: Sandra Day O'Connor, from Majority Opinion, *Planned
Parenthood of Southeastern Pennsylvania et al. v. Robert P. Casey et al.*,
U.S. Supreme Court   140

NO: William H. Rehnquist, from Dissenting Opinion, *Planned
Parenthood of Southeastern Pennsylvania et al. v. Robert P. Casey et al.*,
U.S. Supreme Court   152

Supreme Court justice Sandra Day O'Connor upholds a woman's constitutional right to abortion under most circumstances and reaffirms the central
holding of *Roe v. Wade*. Chief Justice William H. Rehnquist argues that Pennsylvania regulations on abortion should be upheld and that it is appropriate
to overrule *Roe v. Wade*.

ISSUE 8.   Should Pornography Be Protected by the First
Amendment?   160

YES: Sarah Evans Barker, from *American Booksellers Association,
Inc. v. William H. Hudnut III*, U.S. Court of Appeals for the Seventh
Circuit   162

NO: Andrea Dworkin, from *Amicus Curiae, American Booksellers
Association, Inc. v. William H. Hudnut III*, U.S. Court of Appeals for
the Seventh Circuit   173

Judge Sarah Evans Barker argues that the ordinances banning pornography
as a violation of the civil rights of women are unconstitutional infringements
on freedom of speech. Author Andrea Dworkin maintains that pornography
should not be constitutionally protected because it is destructive, abusive,
and detrimental to women, and it violates their civil rights.

ISSUE 9. Is Affirmative Action Constitutional? 184

YES: Thurgood Marshall, from Dissenting Opinion, *Regents of the University of California v. Allan Bakke*, U.S. Supreme Court 186

NO: Potter Stewart, from Dissenting Opinion, *H. Earl Fullilove v. Philip M. Klutznick*, U.S. Supreme Court 195

Supreme Court justice Thurgood Marshall points to past discrimination and argues that we must find a way to compensate for the years of disadvantage. Justice Potter Stewart contends that the law and the Constitution must not discriminate on the basis of race, for whatever reason.

ISSUE 10. Can States Restrict the Right to Die? 200

YES: William H. Rehnquist, from Majority Opinion, *Nancy Beth Cruzan v. Director, Missouri Department of Health*, U.S. Supreme Court 202

NO: William J. Brennan, Jr., from Dissenting Opinion, *Nancy Beth Cruzan v. Director, Missouri Department of Health*, U.S. Supreme Court 214

Supreme Court chief justice William H. Rehnquist recognizes that a competent individual may refuse medical treatment but believes a showing of clear and convincing proof of the individual's wishes is required before allowing the termination of feeding to an incompetent person. Justice William J. Brennan, Jr., argues that the Court is erecting too high a standard for allowing an individual's wishes to be followed and that Nancy Cruzan did indeed wish to have her feeding discontinued.

ISSUE 11. Should Homosexuality Bar a Parent from Being Awarded Custody of a Child? 224

YES: Hewitt P. Tomlin, Jr., from Concurring Opinion, *Leonard Arthur Collins v. Beverly Jo Clendenan Collins*, Court of Appeals of Tennessee 226

NO: Melvin P. Antell, from Majority Opinion, *M. P. v. S. P.*, Superior Court of New Jersey, Appellate Division 235

Judge Hewitt P. Tomlin, Jr., argues that an award of child custody to a homosexual parent cannot be in the best interests of the child. Justice Melvin P. Antell refuses to allow one parent's homosexuality to be a deciding factor in the custody decision of the court.

ISSUE 12. Should the Death Penalty Be Abolished?   246

YES: Jack Greenberg, from "Against the American System of
Capital Punishment," *Harvard Law Review*   248

NO: Ernest van den Haag, from "The Ultimate Punishment: A
Defense," *Harvard Law Review*   255

Law professor Jack Greenberg argues that capital punishment should be
banned because it is applied erratically and in a racially and regionally biased
manner. Distinguished scholar Ernest van den Haag responds that the death
penalty is moral and just and should be employed against those who commit
murder.

ISSUE 13. Should the Exclusionary Rule Be Abolished?   262

YES: Malcolm Richard Wilkey, from "The Exclusionary Rule:
Why Suppress Valid Evidence?" *Judicature*   264

NO: Yale Kamisar, from "The Exclusionary Rule in Historical
Perspective: The Struggle to Make the Fourth Amendment More
Than 'an Empty Blessing,'" *Judicature*   276

Former U.S. Court of Appeals judge Malcolm Richard Wilkey raises objections to the exclusionary rule on the grounds that it may suppress evidence
and allow the guilty to go free. Professor of law Yale Kamisar argues that
the exclusionary rule is necessary to prevent abuses by police and to protect
citizens' rights.

**ISSUE 14. Should "Battered Wife Syndrome" Be Barred as a
            Defense in a Murder Case?**   288

YES: Burley B. Mitchell, Jr., from Majority Opinion, *State of North
Carolina v. Judy Ann Laws Norman,* Supreme Court of North
Carolina   290

NO: Harry C. Martin, from Dissenting Opinion, *State of North
Carolina v. Judy Ann Laws Norman,* Supreme Court of North
Carolina   299

Justice Burley B. Mitchell, Jr., is unwilling to recognize "battered wife syndrome" as meeting the standards of immediacy and necessity needed for
a self-defense claim in a homicide case. Justice Harry C. Martin, dissenting
in the same case, believes that, given the actions of the husband, the wife's
behavior can be viewed in such a way as to meet the standards of self-defense.

ISSUE 15.   Should a National Gun Control Policy Be Established?   308

YES: Mark Udulutch, from "The Constitutional Implications of Gun Control and Several Realistic Gun Control Proposals," *American Journal of Criminal Law*   310

NO: James D. Wright, from "Second Thoughts About Gun Control," *The Public Interest*   320

Law student Mark Udulutch examines the gun control problem and asserts that gun control is necessary and that effective and enforceable federal regulations are feasible. Professor of sociology James D. Wright concludes, after examining how guns are used, that banning guns would not be beneficial.

ISSUE 16.   Does Caller ID Invade Privacy?   332

YES: Janlori Goldman, from Statement Before the Subcommittee on Technology and the Law, Committee on the Judiciary, U.S. Senate   334

NO: Arthur R. Miller, from Statement Before the Subcommittee on Technology and the Law, Committee on the Judiciary, U.S. Senate   342

Attorney Janlori Goldman believes that regulation of Caller ID is needed to protect privacy and to prevent misuse of the technology that reveals the telephone number of callers. Professor Arthur R. Miller evaluates the rights of callers and those being called and concludes that the privacy rights of the latter are deserving of more protection, which Caller ID provides.

ISSUE 17.   Should the Insanity Defense Be Abolished?   346

YES: Jonathan Rowe, from "Why Liberals Should Hate the Insanity Defense," *The Washington Monthly*   348

NO: Richard Bonnie, from Statement Before the Committee on the Judiciary, U.S. Senate   358

Editor Jonathan Rowe examines the insanity defense as it is now administered and finds that it is most likely to be used by white middle- or upper-class defendants and that its application is unfair and leads to unjust results. Professor of law Richard Bonnie argues that the abolition of the insanity defense would be immoral and leaves no alternative for those who are not responsible for their actions.

MASS MEDIA,
Second Edition

ISSUE 1.   Are American Values Shaped by the Mass Media?   **2**

YES: Neil Postman, from *Amusing Ourselves to Death*   **4**

NO: Edwin Diamond, from *Good News, Bad News*   **9**

Professor of media studies Neil Postman argues that television promotes triviality by speaking in only one voice—the voice of entertainment. Thus, television is transforming American culture into show business, to the detriment of rational public discourse. Professor of journalism Edwin Diamond resists the dominant view of television as a reshaper of politics, manners, and society. Television is play and is treated as such by audiences.

**ISSUE 2.   Are Positive Images of African Americans Increasing
in the Media?**   **16**

YES: J. Fred MacDonald, from *Blacks and White TV: African Americans in Television Since 1948*, 2d ed.   **18**

NO: Ash Corea, from "Racism and the American Way of Media," in John Downing et al., eds., *Questioning the Media: A Critical Introduction*   **24**

According to professor J. Fred MacDonald, advertisers now realize that African Americans make up a significant target audience. As a result, images of African Americans in the media have improved. Professor Ash Corea argues that African Americans have been and still are underrepresented in the media, and she argues that news stories and the public's reactions to the way minorities are framed in the media perpetuate negative stereotypes.

ISSUE 3.   Is Television Harmful for Children?   **32**

YES: Marie Winn, from *Unplugging the Plug-In Drug*   **34**

NO: Daniel R. Anderson, from "How TV Influences Your Kids," *TV Guide*   **41**

Author and children's advocate Marie Winn argues that television has a negative influence on children and their families and worries that time spent with television displaces other activities, such as family time, reading, and play. Daniel R. Anderson, a professor of psychology, does not find evidence that television turns children into "zombies." He believes that television, used properly, can be a source of positive education and entertainment.

ISSUE 4.   Are Media Messages About Women Improving?   46

YES: Diana M. Meehan, from "The Strong-Soft Woman: Manifestations of the Androgyne in Popular Media," in Stuart Oskamp, ed., *Television as a Social Issue*   48

NO: Susan Faludi, from *Backlash: The Undeclared War Against American Women*   55

Diana M. Meehan, an author and communications professor, notes that there have been some changes in the portrayal of female characters in the popular media. The image of a strong, autonomous female that combines aspects of "masculine" strength with "feminine" caring and warmth has emerged and is an encouraging sign for those who advocate more varied gender portrayals. Susan Faludi, a Pulitzer Prize–winning journalist, writes about a "backlash" that is under way in American society against equality for women and women's rights. The media is contributing to this backlash by putting out the disturbing and insidious message that women who have attempted to pursue goals of social equality and respect, economic sufficiency, or political participation have been sold a bill of goods.

ISSUE 5.   Should the Content of Records Be Censored?   68

YES: Parents Music Resource Center, from Statement Before the Committee on Commerce, Science, and Transportation, U.S. Senate   70

NO: Frank Zappa, from Statement Before the Committee on Commerce, Science, and Transportation, U.S. Senate   75

The Parents Music Resource Center (PMRC) requests that Congress encourage the manufacturers of record albums, casette tapes, and compact discs to place warning labels on their products that contain explicit or violent lyrics. Musician Frank Zappa advocates protecting musicians' First Amendment right to free speech and endorses the use of printed texts of music lyrics rather than a labeling system.

ISSUE 6.   Should the Names of Rape Victims Be Published?   84

YES: Michael Gartner, from "Naming the Victim," *Columbia Journalism Review*   86

NO: Katha Pollitt, from "Naming and Blaming: Media Goes Wilding in Palm Beach," *The Nation*   89

President of NBC news Michael Gartner justifies his decision to name the accuser in the William Kennedy Smith rape case, claiming that names add credibility to a story. He further argues that a policy of identifying accusers in rape cases will destroy many of society's wrongly held impressions and stereotypes about the crime of rape. Katha Pollitt, journalist and social critic, looks at six reasons commonly cited by proponents of naming alleged rape victims and argues that not one of them justifies the decision to reveal victims' identities without their consent.

ISSUE 7.   Is Objectivity Still a Criterion for Journalism?   100

YES: William E. Rowley and William V. Grimes, from "Three-Dimensional Objectivity," *The Quill*   102

NO: Theodore L. Glasser, from "Objectivity Precludes Responsibility," *The Quill*   110

William E. Rowley, who spent 17 years as a newspaper reporter and was a professor of journalism, and philosopher William V. Grimes argue that objectivity is an enduring and central value of journalism, and one that has been too simplistically portrayed. Theodore L. Glasser, the director of Stanford University's Graduate Program in Journalism, contends that objectivity has unfortunate consequences for reporters—it strips them of their creativity, engagement, and intellectual challenge.

ISSUE 8.   Is the Public Best Served by a Marketplace Approach to Regulation?   120

YES: Mark S. Fowler and Daniel L. Brenner, from "A Marketplace Approach to Broadcast Regulation," *Texas Law Review*   122

NO: Robert M. Entman and Steven S. Wildman, from "Reconciling Economic and Noneconomic Perspectives on Media Policy: Transcending the 'Marketplace of Ideas,'" *Journal of Communication*   131

Mark S. Fowler, former chairman of the Federal Communications Commission, and his legal assistant Daniel L. Brenner articulate a rationale for deregulating the communication industries and argue that the public interest would best be served by a "marketplace" approach to regulation. Professors of communication studies Robert M. Entman and Steven S. Wildman argue that most of the controversy over media regulation comes from proponents of either the "market economics" or "social values" schools of thought. They support a combination of these two approaches as the most effective form of media regulation today.

ISSUE 9.   Should Pornography Be Protected as Free Speech?   140

YES: Frank Easterbrook, from *American Booksellers Association, Inc. v. William H. Hudnut III*, U.S. Court of Appeals for the Seventh Circuit   142

NO: James C. Dobson, from *Final Report of the U.S. Attorney General's Commission on Pornography*   150

Judge Frank Easterbrook holds that an ordinance regulating pornography is an unconstitutional infringement on freedom of speech and press. Psychologist James C. Dobson is convinced of the devastation inflicted on victims of pornography. He lists nine ways in which pornography does harm and calls for new and heavily enforced legislation to control it.

ISSUE 10. Do Presidential TV Ads Manipulate Voters?   160

YES: Joe McGinniss, from *The Selling of the President, 1968*   162

NO: Thomas E. Patterson and Robert D. McClure, from *The Unseeing Eye: The Myth of Television Power in National Elections*   168

Author and reporter Joe McGinniss is convinced that political campaigning is merely a matter of projecting the right image on the television screen to sell the politician to the public. Political scientists Thomas E. Patterson and Robert D. McClure explore the effects of political ads on television and conclude that the public is better informed and better able to make decisions as a result of exposure to televised political commercials.

ISSUE 11. Do Speech Codes Suppress Freedom of Expression?   176

YES: Nat Hentoff, from "'Speech Codes' on the Campus: And Problems of Free Speech," *Dissent*   178

NO: Stanley Fish, from "There's No Such Thing as Free Speech and It's a Good Thing Too," *Boston Review*   184

Columnist Nat Hentoff is concerned that speech codes on American college campuses will inhibit the discussion of important issues, and he argues that they impede the free exchange of ideas and violate First Amendment principles. Professor of English and law Stanley Fish argues that free speech in and of itself "is not an independent value but a political prize." When the aim of a form of speech is to cause harm or to perpetuate lies, it does not deserve protection under a claim of freedom of expression.

ISSUE 12. Are the Results of Polls Misleading?   194

YES: Christopher Hitchens, from "Voting in the Passive Voice: What Polling Has Done to American Democracy," *Harper's Magazine*   196

NO: Philip Meyer, from "Stop Pulling Punches With Polls," *Columbia Journalism Review*   207

Editor and author Christopher Hitchens traces the origins and describes the methods of polling, and he warns of the dangers that arise from relying on this type of public opinion measurement. Professor of journalism Philip Meyer argues that polling reinforces the democratic process and warns that opponents to political polls are exercising a form of censorship.

ISSUE 13. Do Ratings Serve the Viewing Public's Interest?   216

YES: Hugh Malcolm Beville, Jr., from *Audience Ratings: Radio, Television, and Cable*   218

NO: Erik Larson, from "Watching Americans Watch TV," *The Atlantic Monthly*   227

Hugh Malcolm Beville, Jr., a ratings pioneer, defends the credibility and utility of ratings and argues that ratings provide networks with the information necessary to make decisions about what the public wants. Writer and journalist Erik Larson finds that ratings are inherently imperfect and criticizes the power they have in the industry.

ISSUE 14. Is Advertising Ethical?   240

YES: Theodore Levitt, from "The Morality(?) of Advertising," *Harvard Business Review*   242

NO: Douglas Kellner, from "Advertising and Consumer Culture," in John Downing et al., eds., *Questioning the Media: A Critical Introduction*   249

Professor of business administration Theodore Levitt presents a philosophical treatment of the human values of advertising as compared with the values of other "imaginative" disciplines and argues that embellishment is expected by consumers. Professor of philosophy Douglas Kellner calls advertising a "parasitic industry," and he urges the public to become more aware of the strategies advertisers use to manipulate habits and behaviors.

ISSUE 15. Media Monopolies: Does Concentration of Ownership Jeopardize Media Content? 258

YES: Ben H. Bagdikian, from *The Media Monopoly*, 3rd ed. 260

NO: Benjamin M. Compaine, from "The Expanding Base of Media Competition," *Journal of Communication* 269

Ben H. Bagdikian, Pulitzer Prize–winning journalist and professor, contends that only 23 corporations control America's mass media and that this has sobering consequences. Information systems consultant Benjamin M. Compaine argues that new technologies provide ample options for accessing and distributing a diversity of ideas, mitigating concerns about the influence of concentration on the marketplace of ideas.

ISSUE 16. Can Network News Survive? 280

YES: Edwin Diamond, from *The Media Show: The Changing Face of the News, 1985–1990* 282

NO: Jon Katz, from "Say Good Night, Dan," *Rolling Stone* 288

Edwin Diamond, professor of journalism and media critic, examines the influence of budget cuts on network news operations and predicts that even as network news takes on a new look, it will nonetheless survive. Journalist Jon Katz examines the impact of cable television and the effects of new network ownership on network news, specifically looking at what happened to network news coverage during the 1991 Persian Gulf War, and concludes that we may have seen the beginning of the end for network television news.

ISSUE 17. Does Technology Transfer by Multinational Firms Benefit the Development of Third World Nations? 300

YES: Eun Young Kim, from "Multinationals: Preparation for International Technology Transfer," in Frederick Williams and David V. Gibson, eds., *Technology Transfer: A Communication Perspective* 302

NO: Gerald J. Kruijer, from *Development Through Liberation* 308

Eun Young Kim, president of a communication consulting firm in Korea, argues that a major part of international business has to do with technology transfer and that multinationals can forge strategic alliances between the industrialized world and the developing countries. Professor of sociology Gerald J. Kruijer cites evidence to show how multinational firms exert power over developing countries by creating systems of inequality in trade, and he argues that many developing countries inherit positions of powerlessness through ties to multinationals.

ISSUE 18. Can Modern Mass Communication Promote a Better World?   318

YES: Ithiel de Sola Pool, from *Technologies of Freedom*   320

NO: Jacques Ellul, from "Preconceived Ideas About Mediated Information," in Everett Rogers and Francis Balle, eds., *The Media Revolution in America and in Western Europe*   330

Professor of political science Ithiel de Sola Pool argues that the abundance of new technologies allows greater interaction among individuals and nations. Professor of communication Jacques Ellul warns that real communication may be lost by too great a reliance on these new technologies to do what only human beings can do.

MORAL ISSUES,
Fourth Edition

ISSUE 1. Must Contemporary Moral Disagreements End in Deadlock?   2

YES: Alasdair MacIntyre, from *After Virtue: A Study in Moral Theory,* 2d ed.   4

NO: James Rachels, from "Can Ethics Provide Answers?" *Hastings Center Report*   8

Philosopher Alasdair MacIntyre argues that although it is possible for each side in a moral disagreement to produce a valid argument for its position, no overarching point of view exists that can decide between them. Philosopher James Rachels argues that there *is* a way out of seemingly deadlocked moral disagreements but that solutions involve careful attention to facts, logic, and argument.

ISSUE 2. Is Morality Relative to Culture?   20

YES: Melville J. Herskovits, from "Cultural Relativism and Cultural Values," in Frances Herskovits, ed., *Cultural Relativism: Perspectives in Cultural Pluralism*   22

NO: James Rachels, from *The Elements of Moral Philosophy*   31

American anthropologist Melville J. Herskovits (1895–1963) takes the position that morality has no absolute identity but is a social and cultural phenomenon that varies according to the customs and beliefs of different cultural groups. In his view, the great enemy of relativism is ethnocentrism, especially as expressed by European colonialism. Philosopher James Rachels argues that a general relativism about moral matters is false and that certain particular values must be maintained by every society.

ISSUE 3. Is Morality Subjective?   40

YES: Bertrand Russell, from *Religion and Science*   42

NO: Brand Blanshard, from "The New Subjectivism in Ethics," *Philosophy and Phenomenological Research*   48

British philosopher Bertrand Russell (1872–1970) holds that morality is subjective, moral judgments express personal emotions, and differences in value judgments are due to differences in taste. American philosopher Brand Blanshard (1892–1987) rejects all of these views and maintains that subjectivism in ethics is untenable. He argues that when one makes a moral judgment about something, one is making a judgment about that object (an objective judgment), not simply expressing one's (subjective) feelings.

ISSUE 4.   Is Morality Grounded in Religion?   56

YES: Jack Bemporad, from "Morality and Religion," in H.
Tristram Engelhardt, Jr., and Daniel Callahan, eds., *Knowledge,
Value, and Belief*   58

NO: John Arthur, from "Morality Without God," in Garry
Brodsky et al., eds., *Contemporary Readings in Social and Political
Ethics*   65

Professor of philosophy Jack Bemporad argues that only in religion is there a true foundation for ethics. He claims that if ethical questions are pushed far enough, they must eventually go beyond themselves into the religious realm; and here, the Judeo-Christian monotheistic tradition is particularly relevant. Philosopher John Arthur, in arguing that morality is independent of religion, does not claim that religious doctrines are false but rather that both the believer and the nonbeliever have to approach moral questions in the same way: by considering the merits of each case.

ISSUE 5.   Is Capitalism Viable for the Future?   76

YES: Russell Kirk, from "Is Capitalism Still Viable?" *Journal of
Business Ethics*   78

NO: Michael Harrington, from "Is Capitalism Still Viable?"
Journal of Business Ethics   83

Author and scholar Russell Kirk argues that capitalism has contributed to the enormous success of the United States and will continue to do so. Michael Harrington, social critic and political theorist, argues that capitalism, as well as it has worked in the past and continues to work in the present, is on its way out.

ISSUE 6.   Should Animals Be Liberated?   90

YES: Peter Singer, from *Animal Liberation*, rev. ed.   92

NO: Michael P. T. Leahy, from *Against Liberation: Putting Animals in Perspective*   99

Australian philosopher Peter Singer argues that since animals can suffer pain, and since pain is a bad experience for whatever being has that experience, human beings need to take the suffering of animals into consideration. He denounces speciesism because, like racism and sexism, it takes the view that the suffering of one group does not count as much as the suffering of another. British philosopher Michael P. T. Leahy argues that although it may be necessary to be more humane to animals, drastic changes in human behavior toward animals are not called for. He maintains that abolishing meat-eating, a practice that is indulged in by millions of people, would be severely disruptive to people's lives and cannot be justified by concerns for so-called animals' rights.

ISSUE 7.   Is Feminism a Positive Value for Society?   108

YES: Ruth Sidel, from *On Her Own: Growing Up in the Shadow of the American Dream*   110

NO: Nicholas Davidson, from *The Failure of Feminism*   117

Author and social scientist Ruth Sidel argues that feminism has made some progress but that it holds the promise of even greater progress in the future toward a more caring society. Author and historian Nicholas Davidson argues that although it has made some positive contributions, ultimately feminism has simply substituted one oppressive ideal for another.

ISSUE 8.   Should Drugs Be Legalized?   126

YES: Ethan A. Nadelmann, from "America's Drug Problem: A Case for Decriminalization," *Dissent*   128

NO: James Q. Wilson, from "Against the Legalization of Drugs," *Commentary*   135

Ethan A. Nadelmann, professor of political science and public affairs, considers the costs and benefits of current drug policies in the United States and argues that, from a moral point of view, society should legalize drugs and change the drug problem from a criminal justice problem to a public health problem. James Q. Wilson, professor of management and public policy, argues that the war on drugs has successfully reduced drug use and that laws against drugs are necessary to keep people away from highly addictive and damaging drugs such as heroin and cocaine.

ISSUE 9.   Does Society Have an Obligation to Care for the Less
Well Off?   146

YES: Trudy Govier, from "The Right to Eat and the Duty to
Work," *Philosophy of the Social Sciences*   148

NO: Irving Kristol, from *Two Cheers for Capitalism*   157

Canadian philosopher Trudy Govier argues that society does have an obligation to care for the less well off and that welfare should be provided without
being made contingent upon something (a willingness to work, for example).
Author and social critic Irving Kristol argues that society should not redis-
tribute wealth to the less well off but should promote economic growth in
general.

ISSUE 10. Should "Hate Speech" Be Tolerated?   164

YES: Nat Hentoff, from "'Speech Codes' on the Campus: And
Problems of Free Speech," *Dissent*   166

NO: Stanley Fish, from "There's No Such Thing as Free Speech
and It's a Good Thing Too," *Boston Review*   172

Author and social critic Nat Hentoff, in defending the value of free speech,
argues that as much as we may take exception to "hate speech," it must be
tolerated in a free society. In his view, speech codes on college campuses that
prohibit offensive speech are wrong. Legal theorist Stanley Fish argues that
appeals to the empty and abstract idea of freedom of speech in defense of
"hate speech" are useless because such a freedom of speech does not exist.
He supports the invocation of codes that restrict certain kinds of speech.

ISSUE 11. Should Homosexuality Be Accepted by Society?   184

YES: Richard D. Mohr, from "Gay Basics: Some Questions, Facts,
and Values," in James Rachels, ed., *The Right Thing to Do*   186

NO: Paul Cameron, from "A Case Against Homosexuality," *The
Human Life Review*   195

Professor of philosophy Richard D. Mohr argues that homosexuals suffer
from unjust discrimination, and he defends homosexuality against charges
that it is immoral and unnatural. Psychologist Paul Cameron claims that homosexuality is associated with many negative personal traits, and he argues
that society would be making a mistake if it allows homosexuality equal
status with heterosexuality.

ISSUE 12. Is Pornography Immoral?   204

YES: Ann Garry, from "Pornography and Respect for Women,"
Social Theory and Practice   206

NO: James A. Gould, from "Why Pornography Is Valuable," *The International Journal of Applied Philosophy*   215

Professor of philosophy Ann Garry argues that pornography—as it exists today—degrades women and therefore is immoral. Pornographic materials violate principles of respect, and they send a message that calls for the violation of respect for women. Professor of philosophy James A. Gould argues that although pornography has been under attack by both political conservatives and feminists, neither side has made a convincing case. He maintains that pornography has many positive values and that many materials that are called "pornographic" are really contributions to the advancement of the arts.

ISSUE 13. Is Abortion Immoral?   220

YES: Don Marquis, from "Why Abortion Is Immoral," *The Journal of Philosophy*   222

NO: Jane English, from "Abortion and the Concept of a Person," *Canadian Journal of Philosophy*   230

Professor of philosophy Don Marquis argues that abortion is generally wrong for the same reason that killing an innocent adult human being is generally wrong: it deprives the individual of a future that he or she would otherwise have. Philosopher Jane English (1947–1978) argues that there is no well-defined line dividing persons from nonpersons. She claims that both the conservative and the liberal positions are too extreme and that some abortions are morally justifiable and some are not.

ISSUE 14. Should Capital Punishment Be Abolished?   242

YES: Hugo Adam Bedau, from "Capital Punishment," in Tom Regan, ed., *Matters of Life and Death*, 2d ed.   244

NO: Ernest van den Haag, from "The Ultimate Punishment: A Defense," *Harvard Law Review*   250

Professor of philosophy Hugo Adam Bedau argues that the idea of "an eye for an eye" (retribution in kind) has not historically supported capital punishment; in actuality, very different kinds of offenses have been punished by death. Today, he asserts, the death penalty claims the lives of the least well defended (including some innocent people) rather than the most serious criminals. Ernest van den Haag, legal professor and social critic, argues

that capital punishment is a fitting punishment for murder and that there are some crimes that are so terrible that the most appropriate response is the death penalty.

ISSUE 15. Is Euthanasia Immoral?   258

YES: J. Gay-Williams, from "The Wrongfulness of Euthanasia," in Ronald Munson, ed., *Intervention and Reflection: Basic Issues in Medical Ethics*   260

NO: Richard Brandt, from "A Moral Principle About Killing," in Marvin Kohl, ed., *Beneficent Euthanasia*   264

J. Gay-Williams believes that euthanasia is immoral because it violates one's natural personal will to survive. He argues that a public policy allowing euthanasia would have severe negative practical effects. Moral philosopher Richard Brandt argues that killing human beings ordinarily injures them and violates their preferences. But in cases of euthanasia, when both of these conditions are lacking, the killing could be allowable.

ISSUE 16. Is Affirmative Action Morally Justifiable?   272

YES: Richard Wasserstrom, from "A Defense of Programs of Preferential Treatment," *National Forum: The Phi Kappa Phi Journal*   274

NO: Barry R. Gross, from "Is Turn About Fair Play?" in Barry R. Gross, ed., *Reverse Discrimination*   280

Professor of philosophy Richard Wasserstrom, in defense of affirmative action programs, refutes criticisms designed to persuade that however well intentioned affirmative action programs might be, they are fundamentally flawed. Philosopher Barry R. Gross argues that programs of affirmative action fail to fit any reasonable model of reparation or compensation and that they introduce undesirable consequences of their own. He maintains that affirmative action programs are all cases of reverse discrimination and are all fundamentally unjust.

ISSUE 17. Is Terrorism Ever Justified?   290

YES: Virginia Held, from "Terrorism, Rights, and Political Goals," in R. G. Frey and Christopher W. Morris, eds., *Violence, Terrorism, and Justice*   292

NO: Paul Wilkinson, from *Terrorism and the Liberal State*, 2d ed.   301

Philosopher Virginia Held argues that terrorism is not inherently wrong, and, although she does not wish to encourage terrorism, she believes that it is justifiable in cases in which human rights are grossly violated. Political scientist Paul Wilkinson argues that terrorism is criminal and that it is contrary to the values of civilized society.

ISSUE 18. Are Human Rights Basic to Justice?   310

YES: Rhoda E. Howard, from "Human Rights and the Necessity for Cultural Change," *Focus on Law Studies*   312

NO: Vinay Lal, from "The Imperialism of Human Rights," *Focus on Law Studies*   316

Rhoda E. Howard, a Canadian sociologist, argues that universal human rights are so basic and so important that sometimes cultures have to change in order to accommodate them. Vinay Lal, a professor of humanities, argues that the idea of human rights is fundamentally a Western concept that is alien to most cultural traditions in the Third World. To impose human rights policies on these cultures is a form of Western imperialism.

ISSUE 19. Is Patriotism a Virtue?   322

YES: Stephen Nathanson, from "In Defense of 'Moderate Patriotism,'" *Ethics*   324

NO: Paul Gomberg, from "Patriotism Is Like Racism," *Ethics*   332

Philosopher Stephen Nathanson argues that "moderate patriotism" is virtuous because it recognizes the demands of a universal morality but still allows one to favor one's country over those of other people. Philosopher Paul Gomberg argues that any form of patriotism must violate the demands of a universal morality founded on respect for all individuals and is therefore akin to racism.

ISSUE 20. Do Rich Nations Have an Obligation to Help Poor Nations?   340

YES: Peter Singer, from *Practical Ethics*   342

NO: Garrett Hardin, from "Lifeboat Ethics: The Case Against Helping the Poor," *Psychology Today*   350

Professor of philosophy Peter Singer argues that citizens of rich nations can help those in poor nations without great harm to themselves and that, therefore, they *should* help. Biologist Garrett Hardin argues that since birthrates in poorer nations are high and the Earth can provide only finite resources, future generations of all nations will be hurt if wealthy nations help poor nations.

POLITICAL ISSUES,
Eighth Edition

ISSUE 1. Is American Government Dominated by Big Business?   2

YES: Thomas Byrne Edsall, from *The New Politics of Inequality: How Political Power Shapes Economic Policy*   4

NO: David Vogel, from *Fluctuating Fortunes: The Political Power of Business in America*   15

Political reporter Thomas Byrne Edsall argues that the power of big business is stronger than ever because of the increasing political sophistication of big business coupled with the breakdown of political parties. Professor of business administration David Vogel contends that the power of business fluctuates with the times and is currently being kept in check by other forces in U.S. society.

ISSUE 2. Has Party Reform Succeeded?   28

YES: William J. Crotty, from *Decision for the Democrats: Reforming the Party Structure*   30

NO: Tom Wicker, from "Let Some Smoke In," *The New York Times Magazine*   39

Political scientist William J. Crotty contends that modern reform has opened up the political process and has given unprecedented influence to each party's rank and file. Political columnist Tom Wicker concludes that the presidential nominating process too often fails to produce the candidate who is most able or most likely to win the greatest popular support.

ISSUE 3. Do Political Action Committees Undermine Democracy?   46

YES: Fred Wertheimer, from "Campaign Finance Reform: The Unfinished Agenda," *THE ANNALS of the American Academy of Political and Social Science*   48

NO: Herbert E. Alexander, from "The Case for PACs," A Public Affairs Council Monograph   52

Common Cause president Fred Wertheimer argues that PACs exert too much influence over the electoral process, allowing special interests to get the ear of elected officials at the expense of the national interest. Political analyst Herbert E. Alexander insists that PACs have made significant contributions to the American political system.

ISSUE 4. Do the News Media Have a Liberal Bias?   58

YES: William A. Rusher, from *The Coming Battle for the Media: Curbing the Power of the Media Elite*   60

NO: Edward S. Herman and Noam Chomsky, from "Propaganda Mill," *The Progressive*   66

Media analyst William A. Rusher argues that the media are biased against conservatives and that news coverage promotes liberal opinions. Professors Edward S. Herman and Noam Chomsky critique the mass media from the perspective of the left and find the media to be a "propaganda mill" in the service of the wealthy and powerful.

ISSUE 5. Does Congress Need to Be Radically Reformed?   76

YES: Paula Dwyer and Douglas Harbrecht, from "Congress: It Doesn't Work. Let's Fix It," *Business Week*   78

NO: Nelson W. Polsby, from "Congress-Bashing for Beginners," *The Public Interest*   87

Journalists Paula Dwyer and Douglas Harbrecht conclude that the legislative performance of Congress is dismal, and they identify several areas in which radical reforms would lead to vast improvement. Political scientist Nelson W. Polsby believes that "Congress-bashing" is a misguided attack upon the legislative power and undermines the constitutional separation of powers.

ISSUE 6. The Presidency Versus Congress: Should Divided Government Be Ended?   96

YES: James L. Sundquist, from *Constitutional Reform and Effective Government*   98

NO: Richard P. Nathan, from "The Presidency After Reagan: Don't Change It—Make It Work," in Larry Berman, ed., *Looking Back on the Reagan Presidency*   104

Political scientist James L. Sundquist suggests that a president and Congress from the same party might put an end to governmental deadlocks. Richard P. Nathan, director of the Rockefeller Institute of Government at the State University of New York at Albany, argues that major structural changes in the relationship between the president and Congress are neither necessary nor desirable.

ISSUE 7.   Does the Government Regulate Too Much?   112

YES: Thomas Gale Moore, from "Regulation, Reregulation, or Deregulation," in Annelise Anderson and Dennis L. Bark, eds., *Thinking About America: The United States in the 1990s*   114

NO: David Bollier and Joan Claybrook, from "Regulations That Work," *The Washington Monthly*   121

Economist Thomas Gale Moore argues that deregulating economic markets lowers costs, benefits consumers, and makes the American economy more competitive in the world. Journalist David Bollier and political activist Joan Claybrook provide evidence that existing government regulations have prevented serious human and environmental harm in the past, and they argue that the purpose of regulations should not be obscured by economic considerations.

ISSUE 8.   Should the Federal Courts Be Bound by the "Original Intent" of the Framers?   132

YES: Robert H. Bork, from "The Case Against Political Judging," *National Review*   134

NO: Leonard W. Levy, from *Original Intent and the Framers' Constitution*   142

Educator and former judge Robert H. Bork argues that the "original intent" of the framers of the Constitution can and should be upheld by the federal courts, because not to do so is to have judges perform a political role they were not given. Professor of history Leonard W. Levy believes that the "original intent" of the framers cannot be found, and, even if it could, given these changing times, it could not be applied in dealing with contemporary constitutional issues.

ISSUE 9. Will Tougher Sentencing Reduce Crime?   152

YES: Stanley C. Brubaker, from "In Praise of Punishment," *The Public Interest*   154

NO: Linda Rocawich, from "Lock 'Em Up: America's All-Purpose Cure for Crime," *The Progressive*   163

Political scientist Stanley C. Brubaker argues that punishment for crime, whether or not it deters crime or rehabilitates criminals, is important because it helps to underscore the community's sense of right and wrong. Editor Linda Rocawich contends that locking people up is inhumane, is often applied in a racially discriminatory manner, and does not deter crime.

ISSUE 10. Is Capital Punishment Justified?   172

YES: Walter Berns, from *For Capital Punishment: Crime and the Morality of the Death Penalty*   174

NO: Mary Meehan, from "The Death Penalty in the United States: Ten Reasons to Oppose It," *America*   181

Professor of government Walter Berns is convinced that the death penalty has a place in modern society and that it serves a need now, as it did when the Constitution was framed. Social writer Mary Meehan gives a variety of reasons, from the danger of killing the innocent to the immorality of killing even the guilty, why she thinks the death penalty is wrong.

ISSUE 11. Is Affirmative Action Reverse Discrimination?   188

YES: Stephen L. Carter, from *Reflections of an Affirmative Action Baby*   190

NO: Herbert Hill, from "Race, Affirmative Action, and the Constitution," Rosenberg/Humphrey Lecture at City College of New York   194

Law professor Stephen L. Carter expresses his concern that affirmative action programs may lower standards and deprive African Americans of the incentive necessary to achieve excellence. Professor of African American studies Herbert Hill argues that affirmative action is necessary to reverse America's long history of racist practices.

ISSUE 12. Should "Hate Speech" Be Protected?   202

YES: Nat Hentoff, from "'Speech Codes' on the Campus: And Problems of Free Speech," *Dissent*   204

NO: Stanley Fish, from "There's No Such Thing as Free Speech and It's a Good Thing Too," *Boston Review*   210

Columnist Nat Hentoff is worried that political orthodoxy and "politically correct" speech codes on American college campuses will inhibit discussion of important issues. Professor of law Stanley Fish argues that speech in and of itself has no value, and when its only aim is to humiliate people, it does not deserve protection.

ISSUE 13. Should Drugs Be Legalized?   220

YES: Ethan A. Nadelmann, from "The Case for Legalization," *The Public Interest*   222

NO: James Q. Wilson, from "Against the Legalization of Drugs," *Commentary*   233

Assistant professor of politics and public affairs Ethan A. Nadelmann contends that drug legalization would help put the criminal drug dealers out of business while protecting the rights of adults to make their own choices, free of criminal sanctions. Political scientist James Q. Wilson argues that drug legalization would vastly increase dangerous drug use and the social ills created by such usage.

ISSUE 14. Are the Poor Being Harmed by Welfare?   244

YES: Robert Rector, from "Requiem for the War on Poverty: Rethinking Welfare After the L.A. Riots," *Policy Review*   246

NO: Barbara Ehrenreich, from "The New Right Attack on Social Welfare," in Fred Block et al., eds., *The Mean Season: The Attack on the Welfare State*   255

Social policy analyst Robert Rector argues that the welfare system undermines the work ethic and discourages the formation of two-parent families. He feels that true welfare reform would encourage personal responsibility and effort. Journalist Barbara Ehrenreich believes that social welfare should not be blamed for the ills of the poor, and she argues that unfettered free enterprise and the consumer culture are responsible for the permissiveness and perceived moral decline of modern America.

ISSUE 15. Is the National Debt a National Liability? 264

YES: **Benjamin M. Friedman,** from *Day of Reckoning: The Consequences of American Economic Policy Under Reagan and After* 266

NO: **Robert L. Bartley,** from *Seven Fat Years and How to Do It Again* 273

Professor of political economics Benjamin M. Friedman believes that the steeply rising national debt of the 1980s led to a sharp decline in the economy, the reversal of which requires radical economic remedies. *Wall Street Journal* editor Robert L. Bartley holds that the significance of the deficit is exaggerated and that it takes attention away from fiscal policies that will enhance our economic growth.

ISSUE 16. Does the United States Need Socialized Medicine? 280

YES: **Nancy Watzman,** from "Socialized Medicine Now—Without the Wait," *The Washington Monthly* 282

NO: **John C. Goodman,** from "An Expensive Way to Die," *National Review* 290

Policy analyst Nancy Watzman argues that the Canadian model of universal medical insurance can be adapted and improved in order to provide superior and less expensive care for all Americans. John C. Goodman, president of the National Center for Policy Analysis, maintains that Americans get more and better health care more promptly than do individuals in countries with compulsory schemes of national health insurance.

ISSUE 17. Was *Roe v. Wade* a Mistake? 296

YES: **William H. Rehnquist,** from Dissenting Opinion, *Planned Parenthood of Southeastern Pennsylvania v. Robert P. Casey,* U.S. Supreme Court 298

NO: **Harry A. Blackmun,** from Concurring Opinion, *Planned Parenthood of Southeastern Pennsylvania v. Robert P. Casey,* U.S. Supreme Court 304

Supreme Court chief justice William H. Rehnquist believes that the Court wrongly decided *Roe v. Wade* and that states should have the right to establish their own abortion laws. Supreme Court justice Harry A. Blackmun believes that *Roe* was correctly decided, and he opposes any law that would limit a woman's access to an abortion beyond the limits set in that case.

ISSUE 18. Should There Be a "Wall of Separation" Between Church and State? 312

YES: Edd Doerr, from "Does Religion Belong in Our Public Schools?" *USA Today Magazine* (a publication of the Society for the Advancement of Education) 314

NO: George Goldberg, from *Reconstructing America* 321

Edd Doerr, executive director of Americans for Religious Liberty, believes that public schools should promote and reflect shared values, leaving religious instruction and celebration to the home and place of worship. George Goldberg, a writer and lawyer, holds that school prayer and the teaching of religion are permissible as long as all religions are accorded equal treatment.

ISSUE 19. Should National Self-Interest Be the Basis of American Foreign Policy? 330

YES: Alan Tonelson, from "What Is the National Interest?" *The Atlantic Monthly* 332

NO: Joshua Muravchik, from *Exporting Democracy: Fulfilling America's Destiny* 340

Alan Tonelson, research director of the Economic Strategy Institute in Washington, D.C., advocates "interest-based" pragmatism in the formulation of American foreign policy and warns against utopian internationalism. Joshua Muravchik, a writer and scholar, warns against "the folly of realism" and argues that *interest* should be understood in the broadest sense, which includes an interest in democracy and human rights.

ISSUE 20. Is America Declining? 348

YES: Edward N. Luttwak, from "Is America on the Way Down? Yes," *Commentary* 350

NO: Robert L. Bartley, from "Is America on the Way Down? No," *Commentary* 359

Foreign policy strategist Edward N. Luttwak believes that Japan and Europe will soon be richer than the United States because of the failure of America's economic policies and social programs. *Wall Street Journal* editor Robert L. Bartley asserts that America is, and will remain, the wealthiest country and that it will continue to play the role of world leader.

PSYCHOLOGICAL ISSUES,
Seventh Edition

ISSUE 1.   Can Deception in Research Be Justified?   2

YES: Stanley Milgram, from "Subject Reaction: The Neglected
Factor in the Ethics of Experimentation," *Hastings Center Report*   4

NO: Thomas H. Murray, from "Learning to Deceive," *Hastings
Center Report*   13

Professor of psychology Stanley Milgram makes his case for the suspension
of normal ethical standards when a social scientist is seeking to benefit society. Research associate Thomas H. Murray holds that social scientists must
consider the costs of deception to the individual scientist, the subject, and the
society at large, and determine if the information produced is worth those
costs.

**ISSUE 2.   Should Psychologists Study Memory Through
             Controlled Laboratory Experiments?**   22

YES: Mahzarin R. Banaji and Robert G. Crowder, from "The
Bankruptcy of Everyday Memory," *American Psychologist*   24

NO: Ulric Neisser, from "A Case of Misplaced Nostalgia,"
American Psychologist   32

Cognitive psychologists Mahzarin R. Banaji and Robert G. Crowder argue
that laboratory studies under controlled conditions are the best means of
understanding the general principles of memory. Cognitive psychologist Ulric Neisser contends that memory researchers need to study the practical
problems of memory in the natural settings in which these problems occur.

ISSUE 3.   Can Experiments Using Animals Be Justified?   38

YES: John R. Cole, from "Animal Rights and Wrongs," *The
Humanist*   40

NO: Steven Zak, from "Ethics and Animals," *The Atlantic Monthly*   46

Anthropologist John R. Cole argues that although animal research has declined in recent years, some animal research is still necessary and beneficial
to society. Attorney Steven Zak asserts that animals have the right to not
be treated like instruments for the betterment of humankind and that legal
barriers should be erected to prevent animal exploitation.

ISSUE 4.   Is Our Behavior Primarily Determined by Biological Processes?   58

YES: Richard Restak, from "Is Free Will a Fraud?" *Science Digest*   60

NO: Joseph F. Rychlak, from "Free Will: 'Doing Otherwise, All Circumstances Remaining the Same,'" *An Original Essay Written for This Volume*   65

Forensic neurologist Richard Restak interprets physiological research as suggesting that free will is a delusion; therefore, biological processes control behaviors. Noted humanistic psychologist Joseph F. Rychlak contends that when the concepts of free will and determinism are fully understood, physiological research generally supports the existence of free will.

ISSUE 5.   Is the "Disease" of Alcoholism a Myth?   74

YES: Herbert Fingarette, from "Alcoholism: The Mythical Disease," *The Public Interest*   76

NO: William Madsen, from "Thin Thinking About Heavy Drinking," *The Public Interest*   87

Professor of philosophy Herbert Fingarette proposes that the concept of alcoholism as a disease is a myth that has been generated and is currently sustained by those whose own economic interests are served by the myth. Professor of anthropology William Madsen alleges that Fingarette's assertions are based on unscientific research and misunderstanding and are harmful in the long run to alcoholics and to society.

ISSUE 6.   Is Our State of Mind Responsible for Our State of Health?   94

YES: Bernard Dixon, from "Dangerous Thoughts," *Science86 Magazine*, a publication of the American Association for the Advancement of Science   96

NO: Ellen Switzer, from "Blaming the Victim," *Vogue*   101

Bernard Dixon, an editor and writer who specializes in science and health issues, presents a series of studies that show the relationship between our state of mind and the workings of our immune system. Free-lance writer Ellen Switzer, who specializes in medicine, psychology, and law, asserts that there is no credible evidence for the claims that the course of a serious illness can be altered by the state of mind of an individual afflicted with a disease.

ISSUE 7.   Has Science Discredited ESP?   110

YES: C. E. M. Hansel, from *ESP and Parapsychology: A Critical
Reevaluation*   112

NO: David Loye, from *The Sphinx and the Rainbow*   121

Psychologist C. E. M. Hansel examines the available research that is used to support the existence of ESP and concludes that all of the studies fail to meet the criteria he establishes for scientific research. Psychologist David Loye contends that no research of any kind could meet the criteria that Hansel establishes, and he finds that parapsychologists are far ahead of their critics in reliability and objectivity.

ISSUE 8.   Can Computers Help Us Understand the Human
            Mind?   128

YES: Herbert A. Simon, from "Using Cognitive Science to Solve
Human Problems," *Science and Public Policy Seminar*   130

NO: Ulric Neisser, from "Computers Can't Think," *Creative
Computing*   135

Professor of computer science and psychology Herbert A. Simon contends that computers, like humans, have problem-solving and decision-making abilities. Professor of psychology Ulric Neisser argues that the computer's ability to answer questions and store information does not constitute thought in the way it is performed by humans.

ISSUE 9.   Can Intelligence Be Increased?   144

YES: Robert J. Sternberg, from "How Can We Teach
Intelligence?" *Educational Leadership*   146

NO: Arthur R. Jensen, from "Compensatory Education and the
Theory of Intelligence," *Phi Delta Kappan*   157

Psychologist Robert J. Sternberg presents his view that intelligence is a changeable and multifaceted characteristic, and he suggests that intelligence can be taught through training programs, three of which he summarizes. Psychologist Arthur R. Jensen contends that efforts to increase intelligence have not resulted in any appreciable gains and that programs designed for this purpose had a faulty understanding of the nature of intelligence.

ISSUE 10. Do Gender Differences Originate from Biological Factors?   **168**

YES: Steven Goldberg, from "Reaffirming the Obvious," *Society*   **170**

NO: Cynthia Fuchs Epstein, from "Inevitabilities of Prejudice," *Society*   **175**

Sociologist Steven Goldberg contends that the biological differences between men and women explain any psychological differences observed in behavior, emotion, or attitude. Sociologist Cynthia Fuchs Epstein counters Goldberg's claim by citing empirical evidence and recent social developments that she feels indicate the cultural origins of gender differences.

ISSUE 11. Is Day Care Harmful?   **182**

YES: Burton L. White, from "Should You Stay Home With Your Baby?" *Young Children*   **184**

NO: Joanne Curry O'Connell, from "Children of Working Mothers: What the Research Tells Us," *Young Children*   **191**

Burton L. White, educator and researcher, contends that the absence of a primary caretaker during a child's first few years produces serious emotional and psychological debilitation. Joanne Curry O'Connell, a professor of educational psychology, asserts that child development investigators have found no consistent adverse effects of out-of-home child day care.

ISSUE 12. Are Children of Divorced Parents at Greater Risk?   **200**

YES: Judith S. Wallerstein, from "Children of Divorce: The Dilemma of a Decade," in Elam W. Nunnally, Catherine S. Chilman, and Fred M. Cox, eds., *Troubled Relationships*   **202**

NO: David H. Demo and Alan C. Acock, from "The Impact of Divorce on Children," *Journal of Marriage and the Family*   **210**

Clinician and researcher Judith S. Wallerstein contends that children of divorced parents are at greater risk than children of intact families for mental and physical problems. Sociologists David H. Demo and Alan C. Acock question the idea that intact, two-parent families are always best for children, and they argue that divorce often includes many positive changes.

ISSUE 13. Should Adolescents Be Allowed to Make Decisions About Abortion Without Parental Involvement?   220

YES: APA Interdivisional Committee on Adolescent Abortion, from "Adolescent Abortion: Psychological and Legal Issues," *American Psychologist*   222

NO: Everett L. Worthington, Jr., David B. Larson, Malvin W. Brubaker, Cheryl Colecchi, James T. Berry, and David Morrow, from "The Benefits of Legislation Requiring Parental Involvement Prior to Adolescent Abortion," *American Psychologist*   229

A committee of psychologists affiliated with the American Psychological Association (APA) argues that empirical research shows that adolescents are competent enough to make their own decisions concerning abortion. Psychologist Everett L. Worthington, Jr., et al. summarize research that they feel evidences the benefits of adolescents involving the family in decisions such as abortion.

ISSUE 14. Should Psychotherapists Allow Suicide?   238

YES: Thomas Szasz, from "The Case Against Suicide Prevention," *American Psychologist*   240

NO: George A. Clum, from "Abandon the Suicidal? A Reply to Szasz," *American Psychologist*   248

Psychiatrist and psychoanalyst Thomas Szasz considers the patients of psychotherapists to be moral agents who are able to decide for themselves whether or not suicide is a viable option. Psychologist and suicide researcher George A. Clum views suicidal behavior as temporary and impulsive, and he argues that suicidal patients need external restraint to reduce the danger.

ISSUE 15. Do Diagnostic Labels Hinder the Effective Treatment of Persons With Mental Disorders?   254

YES: D. L. Rosenhan, from "On Being Sane in Insane Places," *Science*   256

NO: Robert L. Spitzer, from "On Pseudoscience in Science, Logic in Remission and Psychiatric Diagnosis: A Critique of 'On Being Sane in Insane Places,'" *Journal of Abnormal Psychology*   271

Psychologist D. L. Rosenhan describes an experiment that, he contends, demonstrates that once a patient is labeled as schizophrenic, his behavior is seen as such by mental health workers regardless of the true state of the patient's mental health. Psychiatrist Robert L. Spitzer argues that diagnostic

labels are necessary and valuable and that Rosenhan's experiment has many flaws.

ISSUE 16. Should Psychotherapy Include Religious Values?   286

YES: **Allen E. Bergin,** from "Psychotherapy and Religious Values," *Journal of Consulting and Clinical Psychology*   288

NO: **Albert Ellis,** from "Psychotherapy and Atheistic Values: A Response to A. E. Bergin's 'Psychotherapy and Religious Values,'" *Journal of Consulting and Clinical Psychology*   297

Clinical psychologist and researcher Allen E. Bergin advocates injecting theistic religious values into the psychotherapeutic context. Albert Ellis, president of the Institute for Rational-Emotive Therapy, feels that extreme religiosity leads to emotional disturbance, and he advances values that are based upon a humanistic-atheistic system of beliefs.

ISSUE 17. Is Electroconvulsive Therapy Safe?   302

YES: **Raymond R. Crowe,** from "Electroconvulsive Therapy: A Current Perspective," *The New England Journal of Medicine*   304

NO: **Leonard Roy Frank,** from "Electroshock: Death, Brain Damage, Memory Loss, and Brainwashing," *The Journal of Mind and Behavior*   310

Psychiatrist Raymond R. Crowe argues that ECT is not only safe and effective, but it also acts quickly after many other treatments have failed. Former ECT patient Leonard Roy Frank asserts that ECT only seems effective and that many practitioners of ECT underestimate its risks.

ISSUE 18. Should Psychologists Be Allowed to Prescribe Drugs?   324

YES: **Ronald E. Fox,** from "Prescription Privileges: Their Implications for the Practice of Psychology," *Psychotherapy*   326

NO: **Garland Y. DeNelsky,** from "Prescription Privileges for Psychologists: The Case Against," *Professional Psychology: Research and Practice*   332

Clinical psychologist Ronald E. Fox argues that prescription privileges for psychologists is a logical extension of psychological practice. Clinical psychologist Garland Y. DeNelsky argues that such privileges would make psychology a medical specialty and remove psychology's uniqueness as a discipline.

**ISSUE 19. Would Legalizing Drugs Have Beneficial Effects on
        Society?**   338

YES: Richard J. Dennis, from "The Economics of Legalizing
Drugs," *The Atlantic Monthly*   340

NO: James Q. Wilson, from "Against the Legalization of Drugs,"
Commentary   346

Richard J. Dennis, chairman of the Advisory Board of the Drug Policy Foundation, argues that legalizing most drugs would reduce crime, save money, and not increase the number of addicts. Professor of management and public policy James Q. Wilson feels that legalizing drugs would lead to an increase in use, accidents, and drug-related violence.

RACE AND ETHNICITY,
First Edition

ISSUE 1. Are Nonethnic Scholars Able to Successfully Research Minorities?　2

YES: Robert K. Merton, from "Insiders and Outsiders: A Chapter in the Sociology of Knowledge," *American Journal of Sociology*　4

NO: Patricia Hill Collins, from "Learning from the Outsider Within: The Sociological Significance of Black Feminist Thought," *Social Problems*　15

Columbia University professor emeritus Robert K. Merton politely but pointedly challenges claims that superior insights automatically result from membership in a specific group. In so doing, he generates several useful hypotheses for researching and understanding ethnic and racial minorities. Sociologist Patricia Hill Collins, while acknowledging the value of Merton and others, discusses the merits of the insider's claim to better understanding. She combines criticism of traditional methods for researching and theorizing about racial minorities, especially Black females, with suggestions for how sociology can be enriched by the insights of Black feminist scholars.

ISSUE 2. Is the Concept of the Underclass Useful for Studying Race and Ethnic Relations?　26

YES: William Julius Wilson, from *The Truly Disadvantaged: The Inner City, the Underclass, and Public Policy*　28

NO: José Hernández, from "Latino Alternatives to the Underclass Concept," *Latino Studies Journal*　32

University of Chicago sociologist and president of the American Sociological Association William Julius Wilson insists that factors such as the shift of heavy manufacturing industries out of cities, the movement of the middle classes out of the cities, and the segregation and isolation of many of the people who remain have all contributed to the decay of poorer urban areas. This has created a permanent underclass or urban poor, who are often neglected by policymakers and researchers. Hunter College Black and Puerto Rican studies professor José Hernández rejects the term *underclass* as just another example of dominant group efforts to denigrate and humiliate the poor. He feels that when the term is applied to any category of people, and especially to Latinos, it is inaccurate and charged with negative connotations.

ISSUE 3.   Are Asian Americans a "Model Minority"?   42

YES: David A. Bell, from "America's Greatest Success Story: The Triumph of Asian-Americans," *The New Republic*   44

NO: Ronald Takaki, from *Strangers from a Different Shore: A History of Asian Americans*   55

Journalist and historian David Bell reflects on the current, frequently expressed enthusiasm for the successes of Asian Americans that appears in the mass media. Although he acknowledges some difficulties and hurdles faced by Asian Americans, Bell nevertheless portrays the road taken by Asian Americans as "America's greatest success story." University of California-Berkeley historian Ronald Takaki faults the mass media and some ethnic studies scholars for misunderstanding the statistics and examples used as "proof" that Asians are a model minority. Takaki argues that within Asian groups there are vast differences in success, and he reviews the prejudice and exploitation experienced by Asian Americans.

ISSUE 4.   Do Italian Americans Reject Assimilation?   64

YES: Kathleen Neils Conzen, David A. Gerber, Ewa Morawska, George E. Pozzetta, and Rudolph J. Vecoli, from "The Invention of Ethnicity: A Perspective from the U.S.A.," *Journal of American Ethnic History*   66

NO: Herbert J. Gans, from "Comment: Ethnic Invention and Acculturation, A Bumpy-Line Approach," *Journal of American Ethnic History*   73

Historians and sociologists Kathleen Conzen, David Gerber, Ewa Morawska, George Pozzetta, and Rudolph Vecoli reject many standard theories of ethnic acculturation and assimilation. Instead, they attempt to prove, with several cases, including the Italian one presented here, that many ethnic groups elect to remain separate in important ways from the dominant culture. Columbia University sociologist Herbert J. Gans insists that even recent ethnic groups, as well as the Italians, while sometimes following an indirect or uneven path to assimilation, are still far more American than not, and prefer it that way.

ISSUE 5.   Should We Call Ourselves African Americans?   84

YES: John Sibley Butler, from "Multiple Identities," *Society*   86

NO: Walter E. Williams, from "Myth Making and Reality Testing," *Society*   95

Professor of sociology John Sibley Butler briefly traces the history of the terms that Black Americans have applied to themselves, and he contrasts their ethnic-racial identities with those of other Americans. He argues that it makes sense to be African Americans. Walter E. Williams, professor of economics, acknowledges the baggage contained in the labels that people select for themselves. He dismisses those who opt for African American (or related terms) in order to achieve cultural integrity among Blacks. He says that there are serious problems in the Black community that need to be addressed, none of which will be solved by a new name.

ISSUE 6.   Do Cultural Differences Between Home and School Explain the High Dropout Rates for American Indian Students?   102

YES: Jon Reyhner, from "American Indians Out of School: A Review of School-Based Causes and Solutions," *Journal of American Indian Education*   104

NO: Susan Ledlow, from "Is Cultural Discontinuity an Adequate Explanation for Dropping Out?" *Journal of American Indian Education*   113

Professor of curriculum and instruction John Reyhner argues that the school dropout rate for Native Americans is almost double that of other groups. He blames this on schools, teachers, and curricula that ignore the needs and potentials of North American Indian students. Educator Susan Ledlow argues that data on dropout rates for North American Indians is sparse. She questions the meaning and measurement of "cultural discontinuity," and she faults this perspective for ignoring important structural factors, such as employment, in accounting for why Native American students drop out of school.

ISSUE 7.   Should Bilingual Education Programs Be Stopped?   124

YES: Diane Ravitch, from "Politicization and the Schools: The Case of Bilingual Education," *Proceedings of the American Philosophical Society*   126

NO: Donaldo Macedo, from "English Only: The Tongue-Tying of America," *Journal of Education*   135

History of education professor Diane Ravitch analyzes the ways in which politics has commingled with education in the United States, particularly in regards to bilingual education programs. She argues that certain cultural, ideological, and political interest groups are usurping students' educational needs in order to impose their own agendas. Associate professor of linguis-

tics Donaldo Macedo dismisses Ravitch and other education traditionalists who attack bilingual education as misguided at best, dishonest at worse. He insists that learning in public schools is not simply a matter of acquiring a neutral body of information. Instead, for non-English-speaking minorities, it frequently entails dehumanization through forced repetition of dominant group values.

ISSUE 8.   Should Black Women Join the Feminist Movement?   146

YES: bell hooks, from *Talking Back: Thinking Feminist, Thinking Black*   148

NO: Vivian V. Gordon, from *Black Women, Feminism and Black Liberation: Which Way?*   154

Scholar and writer bell hooks argues that Black and white women have worked together for generations to solve mutual problems. They have shown that they are able to transcend racism. Hooks feels that Black activists should not avoid the feminist movement or maintain separate memberships in Black movement groups only. The extent of sexism among Blacks and whites necessitates women working together. Activist-scholar Vivan V. Gordon maintains that she is not a racist but has good reasons to urge Blacks to separate themselves from a white-dominated feminist movement. She contends that, historically, white women as a group, no matter how benign some individuals may have been, benefited from and encouraged the exploitation of Blacks. In spite of the sexism of some Black males, Gordon feels that Black women would be better off to maintain their own agenda for liberation.

ISSUE 9.   Are Positive Images of African Americans Increasing in the Media?   160

YES: J. Fred MacDonald, from *Blacks and White TV: African Americans in Television Since 1948,* 2d ed.   162

NO: Ash Corea, from "Racism and the American Way of Media," in John Downing et al., eds., *Questioning the Media: A Critical Introduction*   168

Professor J. Fred MacDonald sees the need for improvements in images of African Americans presented on television, yet he feels that TV producers, because of their desire to reach Black consumers, have significantly altered, for the better, images of Blacks in the media. Professor Ash Corea insists that Blacks remain underrepresented as actors, directors, and executives in the television media. Some roles for Blacks are demeaning, and Blacks, like other minorities, are disproportionately linked on television with crime.

ISSUE 10. Should Minorities Continue to Demand More Rights? 178

YES: David Hatchett, from "The Future of Civil Rights in the
Twenty-first Century," *Crisis: The Journal of Lay Catholic Opinion* 180

NO: Glenn Loury, from "The Struggle to Return to Self-Help,"
Issues and Views 186

Writer and social commentator David Hatchett sees greater internationaliza-
tion in the future of the civil rights movement. And he completely concurs
with several prominent Black leaders that the desperation of many Black
communities alone justifies continued demands for more rights. Boston University professor of economics Glenn Loury traces the debate between Black
leaders W. E. B. Du Bois and Booker T. Washington that rocked the Black
intellectual community 80 years ago. Loury sides with Washington in recom-
mending self-help over government favors, which he says casts Blacks into
playing the role of the victim.

**ISSUE 11. Does "Lower-Class" Culture Perpetuate Poverty
Among Urban Minorities?** 192

YES: Edward Banfield, from *The Unheavenly City* 194

NO: William Ryan, from *Blaming the Victim* 199

Political scientist Edward Banfield, in a classic debate, argues that it is the
life-styles of the poor that keep them impoverished. This so-called culture
of poverty thesis examines the values and behaviors of the poor and finds
in them the causes of poverty. Social critic and psychologist William Ryan
counters that Banfield's thesis is a corruption of science and only functions
to blame the victim for society's ills. Economic discrimination, racism, and a
history of maltreatment explains poverty among urban minorities, not life-
styles that are often rational efforts to survive in an irrational situation.

ISSUE 12. Is Affirmative Action Reverse Discrimination? 208

YES: Shelby Steele, from *The Content of Our Character* 210

NO: Herman Schwartz, from "In Defense of Affirmative Action,"
Dissent 215

Associate professor of English Shelby Steele contends that instead of solving
racial inequality problems, affirmative action mandates have generated racial
discrimination in reverse. Professor of law Herman Schwartz argues that we
must somehow undo the cruel consequences of racism that still plague our
society and its victims.

ISSUE 13. Are Hispanics Making Significant Progress?   222

YES: Linda Chavez, from *Out of the Barrio: Toward a New Politics of Hispanic Assimilation*   224

NO: Robert Aponte, from "Urban Hispanic Poverty: Disaggregations and Explanations," *Social Problems*   233

Scholar and former political candidate Linda Chavez takes great pride in documenting the accomplishments of Hispanics. They are making it in America, she says. Michigan State University social scientist Robert Aponte suggests that social scientists, following an agenda driven by government policy, have concentrated on Black poverty, which has resulted in a lack of accurate data and information on the economic status of Hispanics. Researchers have also tended to treat Hispanics as a whole. Aponte argues that disaggregation of demographic data shows that Hispanics are increasingly poor.

ISSUE 14. Is Systemic Racism in Criminal Justice a Myth?   242

YES: William Wilbanks, from "The Myth of a Racist Criminal Justice System," *Criminal Justice Research Bulletin*   244

NO: Coramae Richey Mann, from "The Reality of a Racist Criminal Justice System," *Criminal Justice Research Bulletin*   249

Florida International University criminology professor William Wilbanks advances the thesis that the criminal justice system is not now racist, and he says that claims that it is are myths. Indiana University criminologist Coramae Richey Mann generously welcomes Wilbanks's ideas as part of a healthy debate. However, after careful research and thought, she dismisses them as analytically and empirically flawed, and permeated with elitism.

ISSUE 15. Is Italy Solving Its Immigration Problem?   258

YES: Marco Martiniello, from "Italy: Two Perspectives—Racism in Paradise?" *Race and Class*   260

NO: Paul Kazim, from "Italy: Two Perspectives—Racism Is No Paradise!" *Race and Class*   265

Marco Martiniello, a professor at the European Institute of Florence University in Italy, admits that the suddenness of Italy's immigration problem caught Italians off-guard, yet he feels that rational steps are being taken to resolve the problem. Film researcher Paul Kazim argues that Italy is far more racist than it cares to admit. To him, the government's responses to the problem of immigration as well as the growing hostility toward immigrants demonstrates this. The government's amnesty program, he feels, sometimes results in little more than "authorized starving."

ISSUE 16. Is There an Ethnic Revolt Against the Melting Pot?   272

YES: Editors of *Social Justice,* from "Five Hundred Years of Genocide, Repression, and Resistance," *Social Justice*   274

NO: Arthur M. Schlesinger, Jr., from *The Disuniting of America: Reflections on a Multicultural Society*   278

The editors of *Social Justice* reject almost all previous formulation of ethnicity and assimilation in the United States. Their aim is to "reclaim the true history" of the continent, which, they say, is one of enslavement, torture, and repression of people of color, who are now in revolt against lies and exploitation. Harvard University historian, and advisor to President Kennedy, Arthur M. Schlesinger, Jr., argues that the genius of the United States lies in its unity—the ability of its citizens to embrace basic, common values while accepting cultural diversity. He bitterly attacks "ethnic ideologues" who are bent on disuniting America, not bringing about positive changes.

SOCIAL ISSUES,
Seventh Edition

ISSUE 1.   Does "Multiculturalism" Debase the Curriculum?   2

YES: Dinesh D'Souza, from "The Visigoths in Tweed," *Forbes*   **4**

NO: Troy Duster, from "They're Taking Over! and Other Myths About Race on Campus," *Mother Jones*   **12**

Dinesh D'Souza, a research fellow at the American Enterprise Institute, argues that poorly conceived attempts by many colleges to change their curriculums by including minority and Third World studies have distorted and politicized higher education in the United States. Professor of sociology Troy Duster applauds the changes made by colleges and universities to accommodate today's diverse student body.

ISSUE 2.   Are Liberal Values Propagated by the News Media?   20

YES: William A. Rusher, from *The Coming Battle for the Media*   **22**

NO: Edward S. Herman and Noam Chomsky, from "Propaganda Mill," *The Progressive*   **28**

William A. Rusher, a media analyst and former publisher of the *National Review*, argues that the media are biased against conservatives and that news coverage promotes liberal opinions. Professors Edward S. Herman and Noam Chomsky critique the mass media from the perspective of the left and find the media to be a "propaganda mill" in the service of the wealthy and powerful.

ISSUE 3.   Has Individualism Become Excessive?   36

YES: Robert N. Bellah et al., from *Habits of the Heart: Individualism and Commitment in American Life*   **38**

NO: Henry Fairlie, from *The Spoiled Child of the Western World: The Miscarriage of the American Idea in Our Time*   **47**

Sociologist Robert N. Bellah and his associates argue that the tendency of Americans has been to become absorbed in the self at the expense of transcendent values and the good of the community. British commentator Henry Fairlie suggests that the critics of "consumerism" fail to appreciate the extraordinary degree of freedom enjoyed by modern "mass man."

ISSUE 4. Is Feminism a Harmful Ideology?   58

YES: Michael Levin, from *Feminism and Freedom*   60

NO: Marilyn French, from *Beyond Power*   68

Professor of philosophy Michael Levin faults feminism for trying to impose an inappropriate equality on men and women that conflicts with basic biological differences between the sexes. Novelist and literary scholar Marilyn French advocates both equality between the sexes and the transformation of existing patriarchal structures to elevate feminine values to the same level as masculine values.

ISSUE 5. Would a "Mommy Track" Benefit Employed Women?   76

YES: Felice N. Schwartz, from "Management Women and the New Facts of Life," *Harvard Business Review*   78

NO: Barbara Ehrenreich and Deirdre English, from "Blowing the Whistle on the 'Mommy Track,'" *Ms.*   85

Felice N. Schwartz, president and founder of Catalyst, an organization that advises corporations on the development of women leaders, argues that some women are truly career minded and should be treated just as men are in terms of both demands and opportunities. However, for other women who are not so inclined, corporations should give them a less demanding path with fewer opportunities in order to facilitate their family lives. Journalists Barbara Ehrenreich and Deirdre English attack Schwartz's suggestion for a less demanding and less rewarding second path as unwarranted not only because Schwartz has no empirical evidence for her premises but also because her suggestion seems to be a justification for not treating women equally.

ISSUE 6. Is Sexual Harassment a Pervasive Problem in America?   90

YES: Catharine R. Stimpson, from "Over-Reaching: Sexual Harassment and Education," *Initiatives*   92

NO: Gretchen Morgenson, from "May I Have the Pleasure," *National Review*   97

Catharine R. Stimpson, graduate dean at Rutgers University, argues that sexual harassment is a form of male domination in America and that the real problem is not wrongful accusations of harassment but the refusal of the wronged to file complaints. Gretchen Morgenson, senior editor of *Forbes* magazine, argues that the notion of pervasive sexual harassment in the workplace is largely the product of hype by an "anti-harassment industry" and its supporters.

ISSUE 7. Should Traditional Families Be Preserved?   104

YES: David Popenoe, from "Breakup of the Family: Can We Reverse the Trend?" *USA Today Magazine* (a publication of the Society for the Advancement of Education)   106

NO: Judith Stacey, from *Brave New Families: Stories of Domestic Upheaval in Late Twentieth Century America*   112

Sociologist David Popenoe decries the demise of the traditional nuclear family, explains its causes, and recommends corrective actions. Sociologist Judith Stacey argues that the falsely labeled traditional family with the wife confined to the home is not an option for many women and is not the preferred family practice for a majority of women.

ISSUE 8. Is Economic Inequality Beneficial to Society?   122

YES: George Gilder, from *Wealth and Poverty*   124

NO: William Ryan, from *Equality*   136

Social critic George Gilder praises the American political economy that provides so many incentives for people to get ahead and make money. He maintains that the economy is dynamic and that all classes of people benefit. Professor of psychology William Ryan contends that income inequalities in America are excessive and immoral because they vastly exceed differences of merit and result in tremendous hardships for the poor.

ISSUE 9. Does "Lower-Class" Culture Perpetuate Poverty?   148

YES: Edward Banfield, from *The Unheavenly City*   150

NO: William Ryan, from *Blaming the Victim*   155

Sociologist Edward Banfield suggests that it is the cultural outlook of the poor that tends to keep them in poverty. Professor of psychology William Ryan responds that attacking the culture of the poor is a form of "blaming the victims" for the conditions that surround them.

ISSUE 10. Is Black Self-Help the Solution to Racial Inequality?   164

YES: Glenn C. Loury, from "A Prescription for Black Progress," *The Christian Century*   166

NO: John E. Jacob, from "The Future of Black America," *Vital Speeches of the Day*   173

Professor of political economy Glenn C. Loury contends that government programs aimed at relieving black poverty often become job programs for middle-class professionals, and he argues that, historically, self-help has been the key to black progress. National Urban League president John E. Jacob argues that the notion of blacks pulling themselves out of poverty by their own bootstraps is a myth without basis in fact or in history.

ISSUE 11. Is Affirmative Action Reverse Discrimination? 182

YES: Shelby Steele, from *The Content of Our Character* 184

NO: Herman Schwartz, from "In Defense of Affirmative Action," *Dissent* 189

Associate professor of English Shelby Steele contends that instead of solving racial inequality problems, affirmative action mandates have generated racial discrimination in reverse. Professor of law Herman Schwartz argues that we must somehow undo the cruel consequences of racism that still plague our society and its victims.

ISSUE 12. Helping the Homeless: Do We Need More Government Regulation? 196

YES: Peter Dreier and Richard Appelbaum, from "American Nightmare: Homelessness," *Challenge* 198

NO: William Tucker, from "How Housing Regulations Cause Homelessness," *The Public Interest* 207

Peter Dreier, a housing authority administrator, and sociologist Richard Appelbaum explain homelessness as largely due to skyrocketing housing prices and federal housing cuts. The solution to the housing crisis lies not in freeing up the market but in implementing government programs, including subsidies. Journalist William Tucker blames the housing crisis and homelessness in large part on government policies, particularly rent control.

ISSUE 13. Is Government Dominated by Big Business? 220

YES: Thomas Byrne Edsall, from *The New Politics of Inequality: How Political Power Shapes Economic Policy* 222

NO: David Vogel, from *Fluctuating Fortunes: The Political Power of Business in America* 233

Political reporter Thomas Byrne Edsall argues that the power of big business is stronger than ever because of the increasing political sophistication of big business coupled with the breakdown of political parties. Professor of business administration David Vogel contends that the power of business fluctuates with the times and is currently being kept in check by other forces in U.S. society.

ISSUE 14. Does Welfare Do More Harm Than Good?   246

YES: Murray Weidenbaum, from "Beyond Handouts," *Across the Board*   248

NO: Theodore R. Marmor, Jerry L. Mashaw, and Philip L. Harvey, from *America's Misunderstood Welfare State: Persistent Myths, Enduring Realities*   253

Economist Murray Weidenbaum argues that the extensive system of welfare set up during the 1960s and early 1970s has mired the poor in dependency, making their condition worse, not better. Social analysts Theodore R. Marmor, Jerry L. Mashaw, and Philip L. Harvey contend that the American welfare state has been widely misunderstood by its critics and that conservative "reforms" will only increase the misery of the poor.

ISSUE 15. Does the Breakup of Communism Show the Success of Capitalism?   262

YES: Milton Friedman, from "Four Steps to Freedom," *National Review*   264

NO: Robert Pollin and Alexander Cockburn, from "The World, the Free Market and the Left," *The Nation*   268

Economist Milton Friedman contends that the countries newly liberated from communist dictatorships can emerge from economic ruin by adopting laissez-faire capitalism. Economist Robert Pollin and Alexander Cockburn, columnist for *The Nation*, argue that the collapse of Soviet communism does not invalidate the role of socialist planning as an essential tool for broadening democracy and making the economy serve human needs.

ISSUE 16. Is Street Crime More Harmful Than White-Collar Crime?   280

YES: John J. DiIulio, Jr., from "The Impact of Inner-City Crime," *The Public Interest*   282

NO: Jeffrey H. Reiman, from *The Rich Get Richer and the Poor Get Prison*   288

Associate professor of politics and public affairs John J. DiIulio, Jr., analyzes the enormous harm done—especially to the urban poor and, by extension, to all of society—by street criminals and their activities. Professor of criminal justice Jeffrey H. Reiman suggests that the dangers visited on society by corporations and white-collar criminals are a great menace, and he reviews how some of those dangers threaten society.

ISSUE 17. Should Drugs Be Legalized?   298

YES: Claudia Mills, from "The War on Drugs: Is It Time to Surrender?" *QQ: Report from the Institute for Philosophy and Public Policy*   300

NO: James Q. Wilson and John J. DiIulio, Jr., from "Crackdown," *The New Republic*   307

Claudia Mills, a writer and student of philosophy, concludes that the cost of fighting drugs—in financial and human terms—outweighs any benefits obtained from waging the battle against drugs, and she argues that they should therefore be legalized. Political scientists James Q. Wilson and John J. DiIulio, Jr., argue that drug legalization would vastly increase dangerous drug use and the social ills that are created by such usage.

ISSUE 18. Is Incapacitation the Answer to the Crime Problem?   316

YES: James Q. Wilson, from *Thinking About Crime*   318

NO: David L. Bazelon, from "Solving the Nightmare of Street Crime," *USA Today Magazine* (a publication of the Society for the Advancement of Education)   325

Criminologist and sociologist James Q. Wilson argues that imprisoning everyone convicted of a serious offense for several years would greatly reduce these crimes. He contends that incapacitation is the one policy that works. Judge David L. Bazelon discusses the moral and financial costs of the incapacitation approach and argues that society must attack the brutal social and economic conditions that are the root causes of street crime.

ISSUE 19.   Does Population Growth Threaten Humanity?   336

YES: Lester R. Brown, from "The New World Order," in Lester R.
Brown et al., *State of the World 1991*   338

NO: Julian L. Simon, from "Population Growth Is Not Bad for
Humanity," *National Forum: The Phi Kappa Phi Journal*   347

Lester R. Brown, president of the Worldwatch Institute, describes the major
ways in which the environment is deteriorating due to economic and population growth. Professor of economics and business administration Julian L.
Simon challenges the factual correctness of the negative effects of population
growth that are cited by environmentalists.

ISSUE 20.   Is America's Socioeconomic System Breaking Down?   354

YES: Werner Meyer-Larsen, from "America's Century Will End
with a Whimper," *World Press Review*   356

NO: Herbert Stein, from "The U.S. Economy: A Visitors' Guide,"
The American Enterprise   363

Journalist Werner Meyer-Larsen describes the many problems of the American economy and society and concludes that the United States has declined
considerably from its economic preeminence of three decades ago. Economist
Herbert Stein puts America's economic problems in comparative perspective
and concludes that the United States is still the richest country in the world
and problems like the national debt are relatively small and quite manageable.

WORLD POLITICS,
Fifth Edition

ISSUE 1. Is a "New World Order" a Realistic Possibility for
International Politics?   2

YES: Richard Falk, from "In Search of a New World Model,"
Current History   4

NO: Robert W. Tucker, from "Realism and the New Consensus,"
The National Interest   11

Falk contends that it is necessary and feasible to work toward a new world order, one based on cooperation and the development of a global community. Tucker argues that the standard of *national* interest remains the most reasonable one for the formulation of foreign policy.

ISSUE 2. Will Democracy Survive in Russia?   18

YES: Nina Belyaeva, from "Russian Democracy: Crisis as
Progress," *The Washington Quarterly*   20

NO: Walter Laqueur, from "Russian Nationalism," *Foreign Affairs*   28

Belyaeva maintains that although Russia will face crises in its governance, democracy will prevail. Laqueur maintains that the democratic tradition in Russia is weak and that, amid turmoil, an authoritarian system based on nationalist populism is likely to occur.

ISSUE 3. Should the United States Abandon Its Superpower
Role?   36

YES: Alan Tonelson, from "Clinton's World," *The Atlantic Monthly*   38

NO: Elliott Abrams, from "Why America Must Lead," *The
National Interest*   44

Tonelson argues that the level of strong internationalism exhibited by the United States during the cold war period is no longer politically required, nor is it economically viable. Abrams contends that the United States can best serve its own interests and contribute to world stability by maintaining a high level of international involvement.

ISSUE 4.   Will the European Community Increase Its Level of Integration?   52

YES: Walter Goldstein, from "Europe After Maastricht," *Foreign Affairs*   54

NO: Angelo M. Codevilla, from "The Euromess," *Commentary*   64

Goldstein contends that the European Community's setbacks can be overcome if it follows a more gradual, realistic path toward integration. Codevilla argues that disapproval of the EC has been building and that its framework and the future of integration are doubtful.

ISSUE 5.   Will the North American Free Trade Agreement Benefit All Its Member Countries?   74

YES: Jaime Jose Serra Puche, from "The North American Free Trade Agreement: A Source of Competitiveness," *Vital Speeches of the Day*   76

NO: Sheldon Friedman, from "NAFTA as Social Dumping," *Challenge*   83

Serra Puche maintains that NAFTA will be mutually beneficial to Americans, Canadians, and Mexicans. Friedman charges that NAFTA will work to the disadvantage of all workers, particularly those at the lowest end of the wage scale.

ISSUE 6.   Is Islamic Fundamentalism a Threat to Political Stability?   90

YES: Judith Miller, from "The Challenge of Radical Islam," *Foreign Affairs*   92

NO: Leon T. Hadar, from "What Green Peril?" *Foreign Affairs*   100

Miller argues that the radical Islamic movement in the greater Middle East region has created a combustible mixture that threatens domestic and international political stability. Hadar maintains that Islam is neither unified nor a threat to political stability.

ISSUE 7.   Will China Become an Asian Superpower?   110

YES: Zhao Xiaowei, from "The Threat of a New Arms Race Dominates Asian Geopolitics," *Global Affairs*   112

NO: Samuel S. Kim, from "China as a Regional Power," *Current History*   119

Zhao Xiaowei predicts that as China modernizes and becomes more stable domestically, it is likely to engage in an arms race designed to build itself up to a regional, even global, superpower. Kim maintains that China is a weak state that will be hard pressed to survive the multiple threats from within.

ISSUE 8. Was Intervention in Somalia Strictly for Humanitarian Purposes?   126

YES: Herman J. Cohen, from Statement Before the Committee on Foreign Affairs, U.S. House of Representatives   128

NO: John Pilger, from "The US Fraud in Africa: Operation Restore Hope Is Part of New Age Imperialism," *New Statesman*   132

Cohen characterizes the U.S. decision to join the UN military force sent to Somalia as based on humanitarian concerns. Pilger argues that intervention in Somalia was based on political motivations and is a symptom of a new age of imperialism.

ISSUE 9. Does Japan Represent a Worldwide Economic Threat?   142

YES: Diane D. Pikcunas, from "Japan's Economic 'Pearl Harbor' Threatens the United States," *Conservative Review*   144

NO: Koji Taira, from "Japan, an Imminent Hegemon?" *The Annals of the American Academy of Political and Social Science*   151

Pikcunas argues that Japan has emerged as a determined and serious adversary to the United States in the economic field. Taira says that although Japan has been thrust into a leading world role it is not likely to economically dominate the world.

ISSUE 10. Should the Developed North Increase Aid to the Less Developed South?   162

YES: Ivan L. Head, from "South-North Dangers," *Foreign Affairs*   164

NO: Peter Bauer, from "Creating the Third World: Foreign Aid and Its Offspring," *Encounter*   175

Head contends that the South's continued poverty constitutes a threat to developed countries. It is, therefore, in their interests to increase their efforts to help the South. Bauer maintains that foreign aid goes to the wrong recipients and that it usually does not help, and may in fact be detrimental to, economic development.

ISSUE 11. Should the Global Arms Trade Be Severely
    Restricted?   188

YES: William D. Hartung, from "Why Sell Arms? Lessons from
the Carter Years," *World Policy Journal*   190

NO: John F. McDonnell, from "Pax Pacifica: Defense Exports,"
Vital Speeches of the Day   197

Hartung contends that controlling the proliferation of weapons throughout the world by restricting arms sales should be a top foreign policy priority. McDonnell argues that selling weapons to allies enhances the security of both the seller and the buyer and promotes economic prosperity in the seller country.

ISSUE 12. Does the Global Environmental Movement Threaten
    Economic Prosperity?   204

YES: James M. Sheehan, from "The UN's Environmental Power
Grab," *The World & I*   206

NO: Thea Browder, from "Good Environmentalism Is Good
Business," *The World & I*   212

Sheehan charges that many ecological zealots want to use central planning to create strict environmental restrictions, which will negatively affect economic activity, causing national prosperity and individual standards of living to be diminished. Browder contends that concerns about the economic costs of protecting the environment are overdrawn and that creative planning can drastically reduce the adverse effects of environmental protection.

ISSUE 13. Is It Possible to Drastically Reduce Defense
    Expenditures and Remain Secure?   220

YES: Jerome B. Wiesner, Philip Morrison, and Kosta Tsipis, from
"Ending Overkill," *The Bulletin of the Atomic Scientists*   222

NO: Colin L. Powell, from "U.S. Forces: Challenges Ahead,"
Foreign Affairs   234

Wiesner et al. maintain that U.S. defense expenditures can be reduced dramatically, while still ensuring the physical safety of the United States and protecting its vital interests. Powell argues that drastic cuts will harm national security and are unacceptable.

ISSUE 14. Should the United Nations Take on Greater Military Capabilities and Roles? 242

YES: Boutros Boutros-Ghali, from *An Agenda for Peace: Preventive Diplomacy, Peacemaking and Peacekeeping* 244

NO: Jeffrey R. Gerlach, from "A U.N. Army for the New World Order?" *Orbis: A Journal of World Affairs* 255

Boutros-Ghali contends that both the scope of the United Nation's security mission and the extent of the UN's military capabilities should be expanded significantly in the interest of world peace. Gerlach criticizes the recommendations of Boutros-Ghali. He is concerned that such expansion would lead to the United Nations imposing its "international collectivist" will on others, especially small, Third World countries.

ISSUE 15. Would Women in Combat Weaken National Security? 268

YES: David Horowitz, from "The Feminist Assault on the Military," *National Review* 270

NO: Sue Tunnicliffe, from "War, Peace and Feminist Theory," *Paper presented to the International Studies Association 33rd Annual Convention* 275

Horowitz maintains that there are many purposes behind the feminists' efforts to restructure the military, but national security is not one of them. Tunnicliffe contends that opposition to women in combat positions is *not* based on concerns about national security; rather, it is primarily an attempt to perpetuate male political domination.

ISSUE 16. Is the Kidnapping of Criminal Suspects from Foreign Countries Justifiable? 282

YES: Robert Bork, from "The Reach of American Law," *The National Interest* 284

NO: Jack R. Binns, from "Reflections on Mr. Bumble: Extraterritorial Kidnapping," *Foreign Service Journal* 292

Bork contends that trying criminal suspects kidnapped from other countries does not violate the law. Binns argues that bringing suspects to the United States for trial by kidnapping them, rather than through the legal process of extradition, is bad law and worse foreign policy.

**ISSUE 17. Should Morality and Human Rights Strongly
Influence Foreign Policy-Making?**   302

YES: Cyrus R. Vance, from "The Human Rights Imperative,"
Foreign Policy   304

NO: George Shultz, from "Morality and Realism in American
Foreign Policy," *Department of State Bulletin*   312

Vance contends that a commitment to human rights must be a central principle of foreign policy. Shultz asserts that foreign policy must avoid idealism if it conflicts with the national interest.

ISSUE 18. Are Global Standards of Human Rights Desirable?   318

YES: Rhoda E. Howard, from "Human Rights and the Necessity
for Cultural Change," *Focus on Law Studies*   320

NO: Vinay Lal, from "The Imperialism of Human Rights," *Focus
on Law Studies*   324

Howard contends that some human rights are so fundamental to justice that they are universal. Lal argues that, to a significant degree, human rights are based on the cultural traditions of the West; therefore, pressuring countries to abide by global standards of human rights is mostly a tactic used by Western nations to maintain their power over weaker ones.

ISSUE 19. Is There a World Population Crisis?   330

YES: Nafis Sadik, from "World Population Continues to Rise,"
The Futurist   332

NO: Julian L. Simon, from "Population Growth Is Not Bad for
Humanity," *National Forum: The Phi Kappa Phi Journal*   338

Sadik argues that the world's 5 billion people are already straining resources and that population continues to grow too fast in regions least able to support increases. Simon contends that claims of the many alleged harms from population growth have proved to be incorrect and that population growth should be viewed as beneficial.

ISSUE 20. Can Modern War Be Just?   346

YES: Robert L. Phillips, from *War and Justice*   348

NO: Robert L. Holmes, from *On War and Morality*   355

Phillips contends that the concept of a just war, and the rules for waging a just war, continue to apply in the modern era. Holmes argues that modern means of conducting war have made the concept of just war obsolete.

ISSUE LIST

Sample Entry

<Do Political Action Committees
Undermine Democracy?>[1] <Pol,>[2]
<Issue 3>[3]

---

1. Issue
2. Taking Sides volume in which issue appears
   (abbreviation)
3. Issue number within the Taking Sides volume

— A —

Abortion and the "Pro-Life" v.
"Pro-Choice" Debate: Should the Human
Fetus Be Considered a Person? *HS,*
Issue 9

Are Abundant Resources and an Improved
Environment Likely Future Prospects for
the World's People? *Env,* Issue 17

Are Aggressive International Efforts
Needed to Slow Global Warming? *Env,*
Issue 16

Are American Values Shaped by the Mass
Media? *MM,* Issue 1

Are Asian Americans a "Model Minority"?
RER, Issue 3

Are Children of Divorced Parents at
Greater Risk? *Psy,* Issue 12

Are Chiropractors Legitimate Health
Providers? *Hea,* Issue 18

Are Current Sex Education Programs
Lacking in Moral Guidance? *Edu,*
Issue 19

Are Drug Addicts Always in Control of
Their Addiction? *Dru,* Issue 15

Are Extramarital Relationships Becoming
More Frequent? *Fam,* Issue 14

Are Federal "Marketing Orders" Unfair?
BE, Issue 13

Are Gender Differences Present at Birth?
Fam, Issue 1

Are Gender Differences Rooted in the
Brain? *HS,* Issue 1

Are General Theories of Crime Possible?
CR, Issue 2

Are Global Standards of Human Rights
Desirable? *WP,* Issue 18

Are Hispanics Making Significant Progress?
RER, Issue 13

Are Human Rights Basic to Justice? *CR,*
Issue 18; *Mor,* Issue 18

Are Liberal Values Propagated by the
News Media? *Soc,* Issue 2

Are Media Messages About Women
Improving? *MM,* Issue 4

Are Nonethnic Scholars Able to
Successfully Research Minorities? *RER,*
Issue 1

Are Pesticides in Foods Harmful to Human
Health? *Hea,* Issue 15

Are Positive Images of African Americans
Increasing in the Media? *MM,* Issue 2;
RER, Issue 9

Are Private Prisons a Good Idea? *CR,*
Issue 15

Are Profits the Only Business of Business?
Eco, Issue 1

Are Programs of Preferential Treatment
Unjustifiable? *BE,* Issue 5

Are Rent Controls the Cause of America's
Homelessness? *Eco,* Issue 5

Are the Dangers of Steroids Exaggerated?
Dru, Issue 17

Are the Effects of Acid Rain Serious
Enough to Justify Strict Enforcement of
Clean Air Legislation? *Env,* Issue 9

Are the Poor Being Harmed by Welfare?
Pol, Issue 14

Are There Limits to Confidentiality? *Bio,*
Issue 8

Are the Results of Polls Misleading? *MM,*
Issue 12

Are Women Only Victims in Their Roles as
Social Support Providers? *Fam,* Issue 2

Are Women Paid Less Than Men Because
Their Working Conditions Are More
Favorable? *Eco,* Issue 4

—C—

Can Abortion Be a Morally Acceptable Choice? *Hea*, Issue 11

Can a Positive Mental Attitude Overcome Disease? *Hea*, Issue 6

Can Caffeine Be Bad for Your Health? *Dru*, Issue 9

Can "Choice" Lead the Way to Educational Reform? *Edu*, Issue 9

Can Computers Help Us Understand the Human Mind? *Psy*, Issue 8

Can Corporate Codes of Ethics Promote Ethical Behavior? *BE*, Issue 2

Can Current Pollution Strategies Improve Air Quality? *BE*, Issue 17; *Env*, Issue 8

Can Deception in Research Be Justified? *Psy*, Issue 1

Can Experiments Using Animals Be Justified? *Psy*, Issue 3

Can Hostile Takeovers Be Justified? *BE*, Issue 14

Can Incentives Devised by Industrial Nations Combat Tropical Deforestation? *Env*, Issue 14

Can Intelligence Be Increased? *Psy*, Issue 9

Can Large Doses of Vitamins Improve Health? *Hea*, Issue 13

Can Modern Mass Communication Promote a Better World? *MM*, Issue 18

Can Modern War Be Just? *WP*, Issue 20

Can Network News Survive? *MM*, Issue 16

Can Schools Prevent Urban Dropouts? *Edu*, Issue 12

Can Sex Be an Addiction? *HS*, Issue 2

Can States Restrict the Right to Die? *Leg*, Issue 10

Can Traditional Criminology Make Sense Out of Domestic Violence? *CR*, Issue 11

Can Whistle-Blowing Be Clearly Justified? *BE*, Issue 7

Children of Divorce: Are They at Greater Risk? *Fam*, Issue 15

Could the United States Have Prevented the Fall of South Vietnam? *AH2*, Issue 15

—D—

Did American Slaves Develop a Distinct African American Culture in the Eighteenth Century? *AH1*, Issue 5

Did Capitalist Values Motivate the American Colonists? *AH1*, Issue 4

Did Nestlé Act Irresponsibly in Marketing Infant Formula to the Third World? *BE*, Issue 19

Did President Jefferson Outfederalize the Federalists? *AH1*, Issue 9

Did President Reagan Win the Cold War? *AH2*, Issue 17

Did Reaganomics Fail? *Eco*, Issue 9

Did Slaves Exercise Religious Autonomy? *AH1*, Issue 12

Did the Election of 1828 Represent a Democratic Revolt of the People? *AH1*, Issue 10

Did the Great Society Fail? *AH2*, Issue 14

Did the Progressives Fail? *AH2*, Issue 7

Did the United Nations Earth Summit Produce Useful Results? *Env*, Issue 1

Did the Westward Movement Transform the Traditional Roles of Women in the Late Nineteenth Century? *AH2*, Issue 5

Did World War II Liberate American Women? *AH2*, Issue 11

Do Alcoholics Have to Maintain a Lifetime of Abstinence? *Dru*, Issue 16

Do Black Students Need an Afrocentric Curriculum? *Edu*, Issue 14

Do Cultural Differences Between Home and School Explain the High Dropout Rates for American Indian Students? *RER*, Issue 6

Do Diagnostic Labels Hinder the Effective Treatment of Persons With Mental Disorders? *Psy*, Issue 15

Do "Discipline Programs" Promote Ethical Behavior? *Edu*, Issue 18

Do Drug Education Programs Prevent Drug Abuse? *Dru*, Issue 11

Do Employees Have a Moral Right to Meaningful Work? *BE*, Issue 4

Do Employers Have an Obligation to Provide Parental Leave Policies for Their Employees? *BE*, Issue 6

Does a Common Curriculum Promote Equality? *Edu*, Issue 6

Does Arrest Reduce Domestic Violence? *Fam*, Issue 10

Does Caller ID Invade Privacy? *Leg*, Issue 16

Does Congress Need to Be Radically Reformed? *Pol*, Issue 5

Does Drug Testing Violate Civil Rights? *Dru*, Issue 3

Does Exercise Increase Longevity? *Hea*, Issue 14

Does Global Warming Require Immediate Government Action? *Eco*, Issue 17

Does Government Have a Constitutional Right to Prohibit Certain Kinds of Sexual Conduct? *HS*, Issue 11

Does Insider Trading Serve a Useful Purpose? *BE*, Issue 15

Does Japan Represent a Worldwide Economic Threat? *WP*, Issue 9

Does "Lower-Class" Culture Perpetuate Poverty? *Soc*, Issue 9

Does "Lower-Class" Culture Perpetuate Poverty Among Urban Minorities? *RER*, Issue 11

Does "Multiculturalism" Debase the Curriculum? *Soc*, Issue 1

Does Population Growth Threaten Humanity? *Soc*, Issue 19

Does Sex Education Prevent Teen Pregnancy? *Hea*, Issue 10

Does Sexual Infidelity Destroy a Relationship? *HS*, Issue 4

Does Society Have an Obligation to Care for the Less Well Off? *Mor*, Issue 9

Does Technology Transfer by Multinational Firms Benefit the Development of Third World Nations? *MM*, Issue 17

Does the Breakup of Communism Show the Success of Capitalism? *Soc*, Issue 15

Does the Global Environmental Movement Threaten Economic Prosperity? *WP*, Issue 12

Does the Government Regulate Too Much? *Pol*, Issue 7

Does the United States Need Socialized Medicine? *Pol*, Issue 16

Does the United States Save Enough? *Eco*, Issue 12

Does Tracking Create Educational Inequality? *Edu*, Issue 16

Does Welfare Do More Harm Than Good? *Soc*, Issue 14

Does Wilderness Have Intrinsic Value? *Env*, Issue 2

Do Federal Budget Deficits Matter? *Eco*, Issue 10

Do Gender Differences Originate from Biological Factors? *Psy*, Issue 10

Do Hostile Takeovers Harm Society? *Eco*, Issue 6

Do Ignition Interlocks Reduce Drunk Driving Arrests? *CR*, Issue 12

Do Italian Americans Reject Assimilation? *RER*, Issue 4

Do Parental Notification Laws Benefit Minors Seeking Abortions? *HS*, Issue 12

Do Physicians Have an Ethical Duty to Treat AIDS Patients? *Bio*, Issue 9

Do Political Action Committees Undermine Democracy? *Pol*, Issue 3

Do Prayers at Public School Graduation Ceremonies Violate the Constitution? *Leg*, Issue 6

Do Presidential TV Ads Manipulate Voters? *MM*, Issue 10

Do Ratings Serve the Viewing Public's Interest? *MM*, Issue 13

Do Rich Nations Have an Obligation to Help Poor Nations? *Mor*, Issue 20

Do Smokers Have a Right to Smoke in Public Places? *Hea*, Issue 7

Do Speech Codes Suppress Freedom of Expression? *MM*, Issue 11

Do Stepchildren Need Special Policies and Programs on Their Behalf? *Fam*, Issue 16

Do the News Media Have a Liberal Bias? *Pol*, Issue 4

—H—

Has Individualism Become Excessive? *Soc*, Issue 3

Has Party Reform Succeeded? *Pol,* Issue 2

Has Science Discredited ESP? *Psy,* Issue 7

Has the Federal Government Spent Enough on AIDS Research? *HS,* Issue 17

Have Men's Family Roles Changed? *Fam,* Issue 3

Hazardous Waste: Are Cleanup and Control Efforts Succeeding? *Env,* Issue 11

Helping the Homeless: Do We Need More Government Regulation? *Soc,* Issue 12

Husband Battering: Is It a Social Problem? *Fam,* Issue 13

—I—

Is Abortion Immoral? *Mor,* Issue 13

Is Abortion Protected by the Constitution? *Leg,* Issue 7

Is Acid Rain a Serious Environmental Problem? *Hea,* Issue 16

Is Advertising Ethical? *MM,* Issue 14

Is Advertising Fundamentally Deceptive? *BE,* Issue 10

Is Affirmative Action Constitutional? *Leg,* Issue 9

Is Affirmative Action Morally Justifiable? *Mor,* Issue 16

Is Affirmative Action Reverse Discrimination? *Pol,* Issue 11; *RER,* Issue 12; *Soc,* Issue 11

Is AIDS Getting More Than Its Share of Resources and Media Attention? *Hea,* Issue 4

Is Alcoholism Hereditary? *Dru,* Issue 10

Is America Declining? *Pol,* Issue 20

Is American Government Dominated by Big Business? *Pol,* Issue 1

Is America's Socioeconomic System Breaking Down? *Soc,* Issue 20

Is a "New World Order" a Realistic Possibility for International Politics? *WP,* Issue 1

Is Black Self-Help the Solution to Racial Inequality? *Soc,* Issue 10

Is Bribery Ever Justified? *BE,* Issue 20

Is Capitalism Viable for the Future? *BE,* Issue 1; *Mor,* Issue 5

Is Capital Punishment Justified? *Pol,* Issue 10

Is Choice a Panacea for the Ills of Public Education? *Eco,* Issue 8

Is Cholesterol Reduction an Important Health Priority? *Hea,* Issue 12

Is Church-State Separation Being Threatened? *Edu,* Issue 5

Is Crime Functional? *CR,* Issue 1

Is Criminal Behavior Biologically Determined? *CR,* Issue 3

Is Criminal Justice Free of Systemic Racism? *CR,* Issue 6

Is Day Care Harmful? *Psy,* Issue 11

Is Drug Testing an Unwarranted Invasion of Employee Privacy? *BE,* Issue 8

Is Drug Use Testing Permitted Under the Fourth Amendment? *Leg,* Issue 4

Is Economic Inequality Beneficial to Society? *Soc,* Issue 8

Is Electroconvulsive Therapy Safe? *Psy,* Issue 17

Is Euthanasia Immoral? *Mor,* Issue 15

Is Feminism a Harmful Ideology? *Soc,* Issue 4

Is Feminism a Positive Value for Society? *Mor,* Issue 7

Is Government Dominated by Big Business? *Soc,* Issue 13

Is "Hate Speech" Fully Protected by the Constitution? *Leg,* Issue 5

Is Home Schooling a Viable Alternative? *Edu,* Issue 11

Is Incapacitation the Answer to the Crime Problem? *Soc,* Issue 18

Is Islamic Fundamentalism a Threat to Political Stability? *WP,* Issue 6

Is Italy Solving Its Immigration Problem? *RER,* Issue 15

Is It Ethical for Scientists to Use Data from the Nazi Experiments? *Bio,* Issue 14

Is It Ethical to Withhold the Truth from Dying Patients? *Bio,* Issue 5

Is It Ever Morally Right to Withhold Food and Water from Dying Patients? *Bio,* Issue 7

Is It Possible to Be Pro-Life and Pro-Choice? *Fam,* Issue 6

Is It Possible to Drastically Reduce Defense Expenditures and Remain Secure? *WP,* Issue 13

Is It Unethical to Implant Animal Parts in Humans? *Bio,* Issue 13

Is Japan a Threat to America's Economic and National Security? *Eco,* Issue 16

Is Litigation the Best Way to Compensate Asbestos Workers for Disease and Risk? *BE,* Issue 9

Is Mainstreaming Beneficial to All? *Edu,* Issue 17

Is Marriage Good for You? *Fam,* Issue 4

Is Mass Transit the Answer to Improving U.S. Energy Efficiency? *Eco,* Issue 7

Is Morality Grounded in Religion? *Mor,* Issue 4

Is Morality Relative to Culture? *Mor,* Issue 2

Is Morality Subjective? *Mor,* Issue 3

Is National Service at Odds With American National Interest? *Eco,* Issue 3

Is Objectivity Still a Criterion for Journalism? *MM,* Issue 7

Is Our Behavior Primarily Determined by Biological Processes? *Psy,* Issue 4

Is Our State of Mind Responsible for Our State of Health? *Psy,* Issue 6

Is Parenthood Necessary for a Good Marriage? *Fam,* Issue 7

Is Passive Smoking Harmful to Nonsmokers? *Dru,* Issue 8

Is Patriotism a Virtue? *Mor,* Issue 19

Is Physician-Assisted Suicide Ethical? *Bio,* Issue 6

Is Population Control the Key to Preventing Environmental Deterioration? *Env,* Issue 4

Is Pornography Harmful? *HS,* Issue 5

Is Pornography Immoral? *Mor,* Issue 12

Is Punishment Good Crime Control? *CR,* Issue 5

Is Rape Motivated by Aggression Instead of Sex? *HS,* Issue 3

Is Research on Criminal Careers Helpful? *CR,* Issue 10

Is Sexual Harassment a Pervasive Problem? *HS,* Issue 16

Is Sexual Harassment a Pervasive Problem in America? *Soc,* Issue 6

Is Street Crime More Harmful Than White-Collar Crime? *Soc,* Issue 16

Is Street Crime More Serious Than White-Collar Crime? *CR,* Issue 4

Is Systemic Racism in Criminal Justice a Myth? *RER,* Issue 14

Is Television Harmful for Children? *MM,* Issue 3

Is Terrorism Ever Justified? *Mor,* Issue 17

Is the Concept of the Underclass Useful for Studying Race and Ethnic Relations? *RER,* Issue 2

Is the "Disease" of Alcoholism a Myth? *Dru,* Issue 13; *Psy,* Issue 5

Is the Kidnapping of Criminal Suspects from Foreign Countries Justifiable? *WP,* Issue 16

Is the Legal System Damaging the American Economy? *Leg,* Issue 1

Is the National Debt a National Liability? *Pol,* Issue 15

Is the Public Best Served by a Marketplace Approach to Regulation? *MM,* Issue 8

Is There a Date Rape Crisis on College Campuses? *HS,* Issue 10

Is There a Moral Right to Abortion? *Bio,* Issue 2

Is There an Ethnic Revolt Against the Melting Pot? *RER,* Issue 16

Is There a World Population Crisis? *WP,* Issue 19

Is the Success of Remarriage Doomed? *Fam,* Issue 17

Is the Victims' Rights Movement Succeeding? *CR,* Issue 16

Is the War on Drugs Misdirected? *Dru,* Issue 5

Is the Widespread Use of Pesticides Required to Feed the World's People? *Env,* Issue 10

Is Workfare a Good Substitute for Welfare? *Eco,* Issue 14

—J—

Juvenile Justice: Are Kids "Getting Away With Murder"? *CR*, Issue 7

—M—

Media Monopolies: Does Concentration of Ownership Jeopardize Media Content? *MM*, Issue 15

Municipal Waste: Should Recycling Be Promoted as the Key to Refuse Management? *Env*, Issue 12

Must Contemporary Moral Disagreements End in Deadlock? *Mor*, Issue 1

—N—

Nuclear Waste: Is Yucca Mountain an Appropriate Site for Permanent Waste Disposal? *Env*, Issue 13

—P—

Product Liability: Was Ford to Blame in the Pinto Case? *BE*, Issue 11

—S—

Should Adolescents Be Allowed to Make Decisions About Abortion Without Parental Involvement? *Psy*, Issue 13

Should Alcohol Advertising Be Limited? *Dru*, Issue 14

Should Alcoholism Be Treated as a Disease? *Hea*, Issue 8

Should All Children Be Immunized Against Childhood Diseases? *Hea*, Issue 17

Should American Farmers Be Forced to Face Market Competition? *Eco*, Issue 2

Should a National Gun Control Policy Be Established? *Leg*, Issue 15

Should a New Military-Industrial Complex Be Developed? *Eco*, Issue 18

Should Animal Experimentation Be Permitted? *Bio*, Issue 12

Should Animals Be Liberated? *Mor*, Issue 6

Should "Battered Wife Syndrome" Be Barred as a Defense in a Murder Case? *Leg*, Issue 14

Should Behaviorism Shape Educational Practices? *Edu*, Issue 3

Should Bilingual Education Programs Be Abandoned? *Edu*, Issue 15

Should Bilingual Education Programs Be Stopped? *RER*, Issue 7

Should Black Women Join the Feminist Movement? *RER*, Issue 8

Should Capital Punishment Be Abolished? *CR*, Issue 9; *Mor*, Issue 14

Should Commercial Surrogate Motherhood Be Banned? *Bio*, Issue 4

Should Courts Be Permitted to Order Women to Use Long-Acting Contraceptives? *Bio*, Issue 1

Should Doctors Be Able to Refuse Demands for "Futile" Treatment? *Bio*, Issue 11

Should Doctors Ever Help Terminally Ill Patients Commit Suicide? *Hea*, Issue 2

Should Drugs Be Legalized? *Dru*, Issue 1; *Hea*, Issue 9; *Mor*, Issue 8; *Pol*, Issue 13; *Soc*, Issue 17

Should Drug Use by Pregnant Women Be Considered Child Abuse? *Dru*, Issue 7

Should Eastern European Nations Be Encouraged to Develop Free Market Institutions? *BE*, Issue 18

Should Elderly Offenders Get Lighter Sentences? *CR*, Issue 13

Should Energy Policy Focus on Reducing the Use of Fossil Fuels? *Env*, Issue 7

Should Gays and Lesbians Fight for the Right to Marry? *Fam*, Issue 5

Should "Hate Speech" Be Protected? *Pol*, Issue 12

Should "Hate Speech" Be Tolerated? *Mor*, Issue 10

Should Health Care for the Elderly Be Limited? *Bio*, Issue 18; *Hea*, Issue 3

Should HIV-Infected Health Care Workers Be Restricted from Performing Some Procedures? *Bio*, Issue 10

Should Homosexuality Bar a Parent from Being Awarded Custody of a Child? *Leg*, Issue 11

Should Homosexuality Be Accepted by Society? *Mor*, Issue 11

Should Industry Be Held Accountable for Acid Rain? *BE*, Issue 16

Should Lawyers Be Prohibited from Presenting a False Case? *Leg*, Issue 2

Should Literacy Be Based on Traditional Culture? *Edu*, Issue 13

Should Medical Patients Be Permitted to Use Marijuana? *Dru*, Issue 2

Should Minorities Continue to Demand More Rights? *RER*, Issue 10

Should Morality and Human Rights Strongly Influence Foreign Policy-Making? *WP*, Issue 17

Should National Goals Guide School Performance? *Edu*, Issue 8

Should National Self-Interest Be the Basis of American Foreign Policy? *Pol*, Issue 19

Should Needle Exchange Programs Be Promoted? *Dru*, Issue 6

Should Newborns Without Brains Be Used as Organ Donors? *Bio*, Issue 16

Should Plea Bargaining Be Abolished? *Leg*, Issue 3

Should Plea Bargaining Continue to Be an Accepted Practice? *CR*, Issue 8

Should Pornography Be Protected as Free Speech? *MM*, Issue 9

Should Pornography Be Protected by the First Amendment? *Leg*, Issue 8

Should Pregnant Teens Marry the Fathers of Their Babies? *Fam*, Issue 9

Should Prostitution Be Decriminalized? *HS*, Issue 14

Should Psychologists Be Allowed to Prescribe Drugs? *Psy*, Issue 18

Should Psychologists Study Memory Through Controlled Laboratory Experiments? *Psy*, Issue 2

Should Psychotherapists Allow Suicide? *Psy*, Issue 14

Should Psychotherapy Include Religious Values? *Psy*, Issue 16

Should Research With Aborted Fetal Tissue Be Banned? *Bio*, Issue 15

Should Risk Assessment Methods Be Used to Set Environmental Priorities? *Env*, Issue 5

Should RU 486 Be Legalized? *HS*, Issue 6

Should Schooling Be Based on Social Experiences? *Edu*, Issue 1

Should Schools Determine What Is Learned? *Edu*, Issue 2

Should Schools Distribute Condoms? *HS*, Issue 7

Should Schools of Education Be Abolished? *Edu*, Issue 20

Should Society Recognize Gay Marriages? *HS*, Issue 15

Should Surrogate Motherhood Be Outlawed? *HS*, Issue 8

Should Surrogate Parenting Be Permitted for Infertile Couples? *Fam*, Issue 8

Should Thawing Unused Frozen Embryos Be Permitted? *Bio*, Issue 3

Should the Capital Gains Tax Be Lowered? *Eco*, Issue 13

Should the Content of Records Be Censored? *MM*, Issue 5

Should the Death Penalty Be Abolished? *Leg*, Issue 12

Should the Developed North Increase Aid to the Less Developed South? *WP*, Issue 10

Should the Drinking Age Remain at 21? *Dru*, Issue 4

Should the Endangered Species Act Be Reauthorized? *Env*, Issue 3

Should the Exclusionary Rule Be Abolished? *Leg*, Issue 13

Should the Federal Courts Be Bound by the "Original Intent" of the Framers? *Pol*, Issue 8

Should the Federal Reserve Target Zero Inflation? *Eco*, Issue 11

Should the Global Arms Trade Be Severely Restricted? *WP*, Issue 11

Should the Government Establish Special Programs and Policies for Black Youths and Their Families? *Fam*, Issue 12

Should the Insanity Defense Be Abolished? *Leg*, Issue 17

Should the Names of Rape Victims Be Published? *MM*, Issue 6

Should the "Pay-for-Performance" System Be Overhauled? *BE*, Issue 3

Should the Phaseout of Chlorofluorocarbons Be Accelerated to Protect the Ozone Layer from Further Depletion? *Env*, Issue 15

Should the Policy Banning Gays from the Military Be Lifted? *HS*, Issue 13

Should There Be a Market in Body Parts? *Bio*, Issue 17

Should There Be a "Wall of Separation" Between Church and State? *Pol*, Issue 18

Should the United Nations Take on Greater Military Capabilities and Roles? *WP*, Issue 14

Should the United States Abandon Its Superpower Role? *WP*, Issue 3

Should the United States Adopt a National Health Insurance Program? *Hea*, Issue 1

Should the United States Follow the Canadian Model of a National Health Program? *Bio*, Issue 19

Should the United States Protect Domestic Industries from Foreign Competition? *Eco*, Issue 15

Should Tobacco Advertising Be Banned? *BE*, Issue 12

Should Tobacco Advertising Be Prohibited? *Dru*, Issue 12

Should Traditional Families Be Preserved? *Soc*, Issue 7

Should Values Be Developed Rather Than Transmitted? *Edu*, Issue 4

Should We Call Ourselves African Americans? *RER*, Issue 5

— T —

The Presidency Versus Congress: Should Divided Government Be Ended? *Pol*, Issue 6

— W —

Was Abraham Lincoln America's Greatest President? *AH1*, Issue 16

Was Antebellum Reform Motivated Primarily by Humanitarian Goals? *AH1*, Issue 11

Was City Government in Late Nineteenth-Century America a "Conspicuous Failure"? *AH2*, Issue 6

Was Colonial Culture Uniquely American? *AH1*, Issue 1

Was Dwight Eisenhower a Great President? *AH2*, Issue 13

Was Early Twentieth-Century American Foreign Policy in the Caribbean Basin Dominated by Economic Concerns? *AH2*, Issue 8

Was Intervention in Somalia Strictly for Humanitarian Purposes? *WP*, Issue 8

Was It Necessary to Drop the Atomic Bomb to End World War II? *AH2*, Issue 12

Was *Roe v. Wade* a Mistake? *Pol*, Issue 17

Was Martin Luther King, Jr.'s Leadership Essential to the Success of the Civil Rights Movement? *AH2*, Issue 16

Was Race a Central Factor in the Colonists' Attitudes Toward Native Americans? *AH1*, Issue 2

Was Reconstruction a "Splendid Failure"? *AH1*, Issue 17; *AH2*, Issue 1

Was the American Labor Movement Radical? *AH2*, Issue 3

Was the American Revolution a Conservative Movement? *AH1*, Issue 7

Was the Confederacy Defeated Because of Its "Loss of Will"? *AH1*, Issue 15

Was the Great Awakening a Key to the American Revolution? *AH1*, Issue 6

Was the Ku Klux Klan of the 1920s an Extremist Movement? *AH2*, Issue 9

Was the New Deal an Effective Answer to the Great Depression? *AH2*, Issue 10

Was the Salem Witchcraft Hysteria Caused by a Fear of Women? *AH1*, Issue 3

Was U.S. Foreign Policy in the Early Nineteenth Century Imperialistic? *AH1*, Issue 13

Were Nineteenth-Century Entrepreneurs Robber Barons? *AH2*, Issue 2

Were Southern Slaveholding Women Covert Abolitionists? *AH1*, Issue 14

Were the Founding Fathers Democratic Reformers? *AH1*, Issue 8

Were the Immigrants' Old World Cultures Destroyed as They Adjusted to American Life? *AH2*, Issue 4

Will China Become an Asian Superpower? *WP*, Issue 7

Will Democracy Survive in Russia? *WP*, Issue 2

Will Drug Legalization Help the Criminal Justice System? *CR*, Issue 17

Will Environmental Degradation Be a Feature of International Conflicts in the Future? *Env*, Issue 18

Will Gun Control Reduce Crime? *CR*, Issue 14

Will Practicing Positive Health Behaviors and Emphasizing Prevention Improve Health? *Hea*, Issue 5

Will Reforming School Funding Remove "Savage Inequalities"? *Edu*, Issue 7

Will the "Edison Project" Prompt Major Reforms? *Edu*, Issue 10

Will the European Community Increase Its Level of Integration? *WP*, Issue 4

Will the "Greening" of Multinational Corporations Lead to Environmental Improvements? *Env*, Issue 6

Will the Human Genome Project Lead to Abuses in Genetic Engineering? *Bio*, Issue 20

Will the North American Free Trade Agreement Benefit All Its Member Countries? *WP*, Issue 5

Will Tougher Sentencing Reduce Crime? *Pol*, Issue 9

Would a "Mommy Track" Benefit Employed Women? *Fam*, Issue 11; *Soc*, Issue 5

Would Legalizing Drugs Have Beneficial Effects on Society? *Psy*, Issue 19

Would Women in Combat Weaken National Security? *WP*, Issue 15

TOPIC INDEX

Sample Entry

\<Pollution\>[1]

  \<Can Current Pollution Strategies
  Improve Air Quality?\>[2] \<Env,\>[3]
  \<Issue 8\>[4]

---

1. Topic
2. Issue in which topic is covered
3. Taking Sides volume in which issue appears
  (abbreviation)
4. Issue number within the Taking Sides volume

— A —

Abortion

Abortion and the "Pro-Life" *v.*
"Pro-Choice" Debate: Should the
Human Fetus Be Considered a Person?
HS, Issue 9

Can Abortion Be a Morally Acceptable
Choice? *Hea*, Issue 11

Do Parental Notification Laws Benefit
Minors Seeking Abortions? *HS*,
Issue 12

Is Abortion Immoral? *Mor*, Issue 13

Is Abortion Protected by the
Constitution? *Leg*, Issue 7

Is It Possible to Be Pro-Life and
Pro-Choice? *Fam*, Issue 6

Is There a Moral Right to Abortion? *Bio*,
Issue 2

Should Adolescents Be Allowed to Make
Decisions About Abortion Without
Parental Involvement? *Psy*, Issue 13

Should Research With Aborted Fetal
Tissue Be Banned? *Bio*, Issue 15

Should RU 486 Be Legalized? *HS*, Issue 6

Was *Roe v. Wade* a Mistake? *Pol*, Issue 17

Acid rain. *See also* **Pollution; Toxic
chemicals**

Are the Effects of Acid Rain Serious
Enough to Justify Strict Enforcement of
Clean Air Legislation? *Env*, Issue 9

Is Acid Rain a Serious Environmental
Problem? *Hea*, Issue 16

Should Industry Be Held Accountable for
Acid Rain? *BE*, Issue 16

**Acquired Immunodeficiency Syndrome.
See AIDS**

Addiction

Are Drug Addicts Always in Control of
Their Addiction? *Dru*, Issue 15

Can Sex Be an Addiction? *HS*, Issue 2

Do Alcoholics Have to Maintain a
Lifetime of Abstinence? *Dru*, Issue 16

Do Smokers Have a Right to Smoke in
Public Places? *Hea*, Issue 7

Is Passive Smoking Harmful to
Nonsmokers? *Dru*, Issue 8

Is the "Disease" of Alcoholism a Myth?
Dru, Issue 13; *Psy*, Issue 5

Should Alcoholism Be Treated as a
Disease? *Hea*, Issue 8

Should Drugs Be Legalized? *Dru*, Issue 1;
Hea, Issue 9; *Mor*, Issue 8; *Pol*, Issue 13

Would Legalizing Drugs Have Beneficial
Effects on Society? *Psy*, Issue 19

Advertising

Do Presidential TV Ads Manipulate
Voters? *MM*, Issue 10

Do Ratings Serve the Viewing Public's
Interest? *MM*, Issue 13

Is Advertising Ethical? *MM*, Issue 14

Is Advertising Fundamentally Deceptive?
BE, Issue 10

Should Alcohol Advertising Be Limited?
Dru, Issue 14

Should Tobacco Advertising Be Banned?
BE, Issue 12

Should Tobacco Advertising Be
Prohibited? *Dru*, Issue 12

Affirmative action

Are Hispanics Making Significant
Progress? *RER*, Issue 13

Are Programs of Preferential Treatment
Unjustifiable? *BE*, Issue 5

Is Affirmative Action Constitutional? *Leg*,
Issue 9

Is Affirmative Action Morally Justifiable?
Mor, Issue 16

Is Affirmative Action Reverse Discrimination? *Pol*, Issue 11; *RER*, Issue 12; *Soc*, Issue 11

African Americans. *See also* **Racial discrimination; Slavery**

Are Positive Images of African Americans Increasing in the Media? *MM*, Issue 2; *RER*, Issue 9

Did American Slaves Develop a Distinct African American Culture in the Eighteenth Century? *AH1*, Issue 5

Did Slaves Exercise Religious Autonomy? *AH1*, Issue 12

Do Black Students Need an Afrocentric Curriculum? *Edu*, Issue 14

Is Affirmative Action Reverse Discrimination? *Pol*, Issue 11

Is Black Self-Help the Solution to Racial Inequality? *Soc*, Issue 10

Is Morality Relative to Culture? *Mor*, Issue 2

Is Systemic Racism in Criminal Justice a Myth? *RER*, Issue 14

Should Black Women Join the Feminist Movement? *RER*, Issue 8

Should Literacy Be Based on Traditional Culture? *Edu*, Issue 13

Should Minorities Continue to Demand More Rights? *RER*, Issue 10

Should the Government Establish Special Programs and Policies for Black Youths and Their Families? *Fam*, Issue 12

Should We Call Ourselves African Americans? *RER*, Issue 5

Was Abraham Lincoln America's Greatest President? *AH1*, Issue 16

Was Colonial Culture Uniquely American? *AH1*, Issue 1

Was Martin Luther King, Jr.'s Leadership Essential to the Success of the Civil Rights Movement? *AH2*, Issue 16

Was Reconstruction a "Splendid Failure"? *AH1*, Issue 17; *AH2*, Issue 1

Aggression

Is Pornography Harmful? *HS*, Issue 5

Is Rape Motivated by Aggression Instead of Sex? *HS*, Issue 3

Aging

Can Large Doses of Vitamins Improve Health? *Hea*, Issue 13

Should Elderly Offenders Get Lighter Sentences? *CR*, Issue 13

Should Health Care for the Elderly Be Limited? *Bio*, Issue 18; *Hea*, Issue 3

Agriculture

Are Federal "Marketing Orders" Unfair? *BE*, Issue 13

Are Pesticides in Foods Harmful to Human Health? *Hea*, Issue 15

Did Capitalist Values Motivate the American Colonists? *AH1*, Issue 4

Did President Jefferson Outfederalize the Federalists? *AH1*, Issue 9

Does Global Warming Require Immediate Government Action? *Eco*, Issue 17

Is the Widespread Use of Pesticides Required to Feed the World's People? *Env*, Issue 10

Should American Farmers Be Forced to Face Market Competition? *Eco*, Issue 2

AIDS

Are Current Sex Education Programs Lacking in Moral Guidance? *Edu*, Issue 19

Are There Limits to Confidentiality? *Bio*, Issue 8

Do Physicians Have an Ethical Duty to Treat AIDS Patients? *Bio*, Issue 9

Has the Federal Government Spent Enough on AIDS Research? *HS*, Issue 17

Is AIDS Getting More Than Its Share of Resources and Media Attention? *Hea*, Issue 4

Should HIV-Infected Health Care Workers Be Restricted from Performing Some Procedures? *Bio*, Issue 10

Should Needle Exchange Programs Be Promoted? *Dru*, Issue 6

Should Schools Distribute Condoms? *HS*, Issue 7

Should the Policy Banning Gays from the Military Be Lifted? *HS*, Issue 13

Air pollution. *See* **Pollution**

Alcohol. *See also* **Addiction; Drug abuse**

Are Rent Controls the Cause of America's Homelessness? *Eco*, Issue 5

Do Alcoholics Have to Maintain a Lifetime of Abstinence? *Dru*, Issue 16

Do Cultural Differences Between Home and School Explain the High Dropout Rates for American Indian Students? *RER*, Issue 6

Do Ignition Interlocks Reduce Drunk Driving Arrests? *CR*, Issue 12

Is Alcoholism Hereditary? *Dru*, Issue 10

Is the "Disease" of Alcoholism a Myth? *Dru*, Issue 13; *Psy*, Issue 5

Is the War on Drugs Misdirected? *Dru*, Issue 5

Should Alcohol Advertising Be Limited? *Dru*, Issue 14

Should Alcoholism Be Treated as a Disease? *Hea*, Issue 8

Should the Drinking Age Remain at 21? *Dru*, Issue 4

American government. *See* **Congress; Constitution, U.S.; Federal government; Judicial system; Presidency**

American history, Colonial

Did Capitalist Values Motivate the American Colonists? *AH1*, Issue 4

Was Colonial Culture Uniquely American? *AH1*, Issue 1

Was Race a Central Factor in the Colonists' Attitudes Toward Native Americans? *AH1*, Issue 2

Was the American Revolution a Conservative Movement? *AH1*, Issue 7

Was the Great Awakening a Key to the American Revolution? *AH1*, Issue 6

Was the Salem Witchcraft Hysteria Caused by a Fear of Women? *AH1*, Issue 3

American history, Post–Civil War

Did Slaves Exercise Religious Autonomy? *AH1*, Issue 12

Did the Progressives Fail? *AH2*, Issue 7

Did the Westward Movement Transform the Traditional Roles of Women in the Late Nineteenth Century? *AH2*, Issue 5

Was Antebellum Reform Motivated Primarily by Humanitarian Goals? *AH1*, Issue 11

Was City Government in Late Nineteenth-Century America a "Conspicuous Failure"? *AH2*, Issue 6

Was Reconstruction a "Splendid Failure"? *AH1*, Issue 17; *AH2*, Issue 1

Was the American Labor Movement Radical? *AH2*, Issue 3

Was the Confederacy Defeated Because of Its "Loss of Will"? *AH1*, Issue 15

Was U.S. Foreign Policy in the Early Nineteenth Century Imperialistic? *AH1*, Issue 13

Were Nineteenth-Century Entrepreneurs Robber Barons? *AH2*, Issue 2

Were the Immigrants' Old World Cultures Destroyed as They Adjusted to American Life? *AH2*, Issue 4

American history, Pre–Civil War

Did President Jefferson Outfederalize the Federalists? *AH1*, Issue 9

Did the Election of 1828 Represent a Democratic Revolt of the People? *AH1*, Issue 10

Was Abraham Lincoln America's Greatest President? *AH1*, Issue 16

Were Southern Slaveholding Women Covert Abolitionists? *AH1*, Issue 14

Were the Founding Fathers Democratic Reformers? *AH1*, Issue 8

American history, Twentieth century

Could the United States Have Prevented the Fall of South Vietnam? *AH2*, Issue 15

Did President Reagan Win the Cold War? *AH2*, Issue 17

Did the Great Society Fail? *AH2*, Issue 14

Did World War II Liberate American Women? *AH2*, Issue 11

Was Dwight Eisenhower a Great President? *AH2*, Issue 13

Was It Necessary to Drop the Atomic Bomb to End World War II? *AH2,* Issue 12

Was Martin Luther King, Jr.'s Leadership Essential to the Success of the Civil Rights Movement? *AH2,* Issue 16

Was the Ku Klux Klan of the 1920s an Extremist Movement? *AH2,* Issue 9

Was the New Deal an Effective Answer to the Great Depression? *AH2,* Issue 10

American Revolution

Was the American Revolution a Conservative Movement? *AH1,* Issue 7

Was the Great Awakening a Key to the American Revolution? *AH1,* Issue 6

American-Soviet relations. *See* **United States–Soviet Union relations**

Animals. *See* **Wildlife**

Anxiety. *See* **Mental illness**

Armed forces. *See* **Military**

Arms race. *See* **Nuclear weapons**

Athletics

Are the Dangers of Steroids Exaggerated? *Dru,* Issue 17

Can Caffeine Be Bad for Your Health? *Dru,* Issue 9

Atomic bomb. *See* **Nuclear weapons**

Attorneys. *See* **Lawyers**

— B —

Banking

Does the United States Save Enough? *Eco,* Issue 12

Should the Federal Reserve Target Zero Inflation? *Eco,* Issue 11

Behavior

Are Drug Addicts Always in Control of Their Addiction? *Dru,* Issue 15

Are Extramarital Relationships Becoming More Frequent? *Fam,* Issue 14

Are Gender Differences Present at Birth? *Fam,* Issue 1

Are General Theories of Crime Possible? *CR,* Issue 2

Are the Results of Polls Misleading? *MM,* Issue 12

Can a Positive Mental Attitude Overcome Disease? *Hea,* Issue 6

Can Deception in Research Be Justified? *Psy,* Issue 1

Do Diagnostic Labels Hinder the Effective Treatment of Persons With Mental Disorders? *Psy,* Issue 15

Do "Discipline Programs" Promote Ethical Behavior? *Edu,* Issue 18

Does Government Have a Constitutional Right to Prohibit Certain Kinds of Sexual Conduct? *HS,* Issue 11

Do Gender Differences Originate from Biological Factors? *Psy,* Issue 10

Husband Battering: Is It a Social Problem? *Fam,* Issue 13

Is Bribery Ever Justified? *BE,* Issue 20

Is It Ethical to Withhold the Truth from Dying Patients? *Bio,* Issue 5

Is Morality Grounded in Religion? *Mor,* Issue 4

Is Our Behavior Primarily Determined by Biological Processes? *Psy,* Issue 4

Is Sexual Harassment a Pervasive Problem? *HS,* Issue 16

Is Sexual Harassment a Pervasive Problem in America? *Soc,* Issue 6

Is the "Disease" of Alcoholism a Myth? *Dru,* Issue 13; *Psy,* Issue 5

Should Alcoholism Be Treated as a Disease? *Hea,* Issue 8

Should Psychotherapists Allow Suicide? *Psy,* Issue 14

Behavior disorders

Are Drug Addicts Always in Control of Their Addiction? *Dru,* Issue 15

Can Sex Be an Addiction? *HS,* Issue 2

Do Diagnostic Labels Hinder the Effective Treatment of Persons With Mental Disorders? *Psy,* Issue 15

Is Criminal Behavior Biologically Determined? *CR,* Issue 3

Is Rape Motivated by Aggression Instead of Sex? *HS,* Issue 3

Should the Insanity Defense Be Abolished? *Leg,* Issue 17

Behavior modification
Do Alcoholics Have to Maintain a
Lifetime of Abstinence? *Dru,* Issue 16
Do "Discipline Programs" Promote
Ethical Behavior? *Edu,* Issue 18
Has the Federal Government Spent
Enough on AIDS Research? *HS,*
Issue 17
Is Advertising Ethical? *MM,* Issue 14
Is AIDS Getting More Than Its Share of
Resources and Media Attention? *Hea,*
Issue 4
Will Practicing Positive Health Behaviors
and Emphasizing Prevention Improve
Health? *Hea,* Issue 5

Bill of Rights. *See also* **American
Revolution; Civil rights; Constitution,
U.S.**
Does Caller ID Invade Privacy? *Leg,*
Issue 16
Does Drug Testing Violate Civil Rights?
Dru, Issue 3
Do Prayers at Public School Graduation
Ceremonies Violate the Constitution?
Leg, Issue 6
Do Speech Codes Suppress Freedom of
Expression? *MM,* Issue 11
Has Individualism Become Excessive?
Soc, Issue 3
Is Church-State Separation Being
Threatened? *Edu,* Issue 5
Is Drug Use Testing Permitted Under the
Fourth Amendment? *Leg,* Issue 4
Is "Hate Speech" Fully Protected by the
Constitution? *Leg,* Issue 5
Is Objectivity Still a Criterion for
Journalism? *MM,* Issue 7
Should "Hate Speech" Be Protected? *Pol,*
Issue 12
Should "Hate Speech" Be Tolerated? *Mor,*
Issue 10
Should Homosexuality Bar a Parent from
Being Awarded Custody of a Child?
Leg, Issue 11
Should Pornography Be Protected as Free
Speech? *MM,* Issue 9
Should Pornography Be Protected by the
First Amendment? *Leg,* Issue 8

Should the Exclusionary Rule Be
Abolished? *Leg,* Issue 13
Should the Federal Courts Be Bound by
the "Original Intent" of the Framers?
Pol, Issue 8

Biotechnology
Is It Ever Morally Right to Withhold
Food and Water from Dying Patients?
Bio, Issue 7
Is It Unethical to Implant Animal Parts
in Humans? *Bio,* Issue 13
Is Physician-Assisted Suicide Ethical? *Bio,*
Issue 6
Should Animal Experimentation Be
Permitted? *Bio,* Issue 12
Should Courts Be Permitted to Order
Women to Use Long-Acting
Contraceptives? *Bio,* Issue 1
Should Newborns Without Brains Be
Used as Organ Donors? *Bio,* Issue 16
Should Research With Aborted Fetal
Tissue Be Banned? *Bio,* Issue 15
Should Thawing Unused Frozen
Embryos Be Permitted? *Bio,* Issue 3
Should There Be a Market in Body Parts?
Bio, Issue 17
Will the Human Genome Project Lead to
Abuses in Genetic Engineering? *Bio,*
Issue 20

Blacks. *See* **African Americans**

Brain chemistry
Are Gender Differences Rooted in the
Brain? *HS,* Issue 1
Is Criminal Behavior Biologically
Determined? *CR,* Issue 3
Is Electroconvulsive Therapy Safe? *Psy,*
Issue 17
Is Our Behavior Primarily Determined by
Biological Processes? *Psy,* Issue 4

Brain research
Are Gender Differences Rooted in the
Brain? *HS,* Issue 1
Is Electroconvulsive Therapy Safe? *Psy,*
Issue 17
Is Our Behavior Primarily Determined by
Biological Processes? *Psy,* Issue 4

Should Newborns Without Brains Be Used as Organ Donors? *Bio,* Issue 16

Business. *See* **Industry**

— C —

Campaigns, political

Are the Results of Polls Misleading? *MM,* Issue 12

Did the Election of 1828 Represent a Democratic Revolt of the People? *AH1,* Issue 10

Do Political Action Committees Undermine Democracy? *Pol,* Issue 3

Do Presidential TV Ads Manipulate Voters? *MM,* Issue 10

Has Party Reform Succeeded? *Pol,* Issue 2

Cancer

Can a Positive Mental Attitude Overcome Disease? *Hea,* Issue 6

Can Large Doses of Vitamins Improve Health? *Hea,* Issue 13

Does Exercise Increase Longevity? *Hea,* Issue 14

Has the Federal Government Spent Enough on AIDS Research? *HS,* Issue 17

Is AIDS Getting More Than Its Share of Resources and Media Attention? *Hea,* Issue 4

Should Doctors Ever Help Terminally Ill Patients Commit Suicide? *Hea,* Issue 2

Should Medical Patients Be Permitted to Use Marijuana? *Dru,* Issue 2

Will Practicing Positive Health Behaviors and Emphasizing Prevention Improve Health? *Hea,* Issue 5

Capitalism

Are the Poor Being Harmed by Welfare? *Pol,* Issue 14

Did Capitalist Values Motivate the American Colonists? *AH1,* Issue 4

Do Employees Have a Moral Right to Meaningful Work? *BE,* Issue 4

Does the Breakup of Communism Show the Success of Capitalism? *Soc,* Issue 15

Is Advertising Ethical? *MM,* Issue 14

Is Capitalism Viable for the Future? *BE,* Issue 1; *Mor,* Issue 5

Is There an Ethnic Revolt Against the Melting Pot? *RER,* Issue 16

Should Eastern European Nations Be Encouraged to Develop Free Market Institutions? *BE,* Issue 18

Was the New Deal an Effective Answer to the Great Depression? *AH2,* Issue 10

Will Democracy Survive in Russia? *WP,* Issue 2

Capital punishment. *See* **Death penalty; Punishment**

Carcinogen. *See* **Cancer**

Cardiovascular disease

Can Caffeine Be Bad for Your Health? *Dru,* Issue 9

Can Large Doses of Vitamins Improve Health? *Hea,* Issue 13

Does Exercise Increase Longevity? *Hea,* Issue 14

Has the Federal Government Spent Enough on AIDS Research? *HS,* Issue 17

Is AIDS Getting More Than Its Share of Resources and Media Attention? *Hea,* Issue 4

Is Cholesterol Reduction an Important Health Priority? *Hea,* Issue 12

Checks and balances

Does Congress Need to Be Radically Reformed? *Pol,* Issue 5

The Presidency Versus Congress: Should Divided Government Be Ended? *Pol,* Issue 6

Chemicals, toxic. *See* **Toxic chemicals**

Child development

Are Children of Divorced Parents at Greater Risk? *Psy,* Issue 12

Children of Divorce: Are They at Greater Risk? *Fam,* Issue 15

Do Drug Education Programs Prevent Drug Abuse? *Dru,* Issue 11

Do Stepchildren Need Special Policies and Programs on Their Behalf? *Fam,* Issue 16

Have Men's Family Roles Changed? *Fam,* Issue 3

Is Day Care Harmful? *Psy,* Issue 11

Is Television Harmful for Children? *MM,* Issue 3

Should All Children Be Immunized Against Childhood Diseases? *Hea,* Issue 17

Church, Roman Catholic

Abortion and the "Pro-Life" *v.* "Pro-Choice" Debate: Should the Human Fetus Be Considered a Person? *HS,* Issue 9

Is Euthanasia Immoral? *Mor,* Issue 15

Church and state, Separation of

Do Prayers at Public School Graduation Ceremonies Violate the Constitution? *Leg,* Issue 6

Is Church-State Separation Being Threatened? *Edu,* Issue 5

Is Islamic Fundamentalism a Threat to Political Stability? *WP,* Issue 6

Should There Be a "Wall of Separation" Between Church and State? *Pol,* Issue 18

Civil rights. *See also* **Bill of Rights; Constitution, U.S.**

Are Global Standards of Human Rights Desirable? *WP,* Issue 18

Are Hispanics Making Significant Progress? *RER,* Issue 13

Are Human Rights Basic to Justice? *CR,* Issue 18; *Mor,* Issue 18

Are Programs of Preferential Treatment Unjustifiable? *BE,* Issue 5

Did the Great Society Fail? *AH2,* Issue 14

Does Caller ID Invade Privacy? *Leg,* Issue 16

Does Drug Testing Violate Civil Rights? *Dru,* Issue 3

Do Speech Codes Suppress Freedom of Expression? *MM,* Issue 11

Has Individualism Become Excessive? *Soc,* Issue 3

Is Affirmative Action Reverse Discrimination? *RER,* Issue 12; *Soc,* Issue 11

Is Drug Testing an Unwarranted Invasion of Employee Privacy? *BE,* Issue 8

Is Drug Use Testing Permitted Under the Fourth Amendment? *Leg,* Issue 4

Is "Hate Speech" Fully Protected by the Constitution? *Leg,* Issue 5

Is the Victims' Rights Movement Succeeding? *CR,* Issue 16

Should Gays and Lesbians Fight for the Right to Marry? *Fam,* Issue 5

Should HIV-Infected Health Care Workers Be Restricted from Performing Some Procedures? *Bio,* Issue 10

Should Lawyers Be Prohibited from Presenting a False Case? *Leg,* Issue 2

Should Minorities Continue to Demand More Rights? *RER,* Issue 10

Should Pornography Be Protected as Free Speech? *MM,* Issue 9

Should Pornography Be Protected by the First Amendment? *Leg,* Issue 8

Should the Content of Records Be Censored? *MM,* Issue 5

Should the Exclusionary Rule Be Abolished? *Leg,* Issue 13

Should the Names of Rape Victims Be Published? *MM,* Issue 6

Should Tobacco Advertising Be Banned? *BE,* Issue 12

Should Tobacco Advertising Be Prohibited? *Dru,* Issue 12

Should We Call Ourselves African Americans? *RER,* Issue 5

Was Martin Luther King, Jr.'s Leadership Essential to the Success of the Civil Rights Movement? *AH2,* Issue 16

Civil War

Was Abraham Lincoln America's Greatest President? *AH1,* Issue 16

Was the Confederacy Defeated Because of Its "Loss of Will"? *AH1,* Issue 15

Climate

Are Aggressive International Efforts Needed to Slow Global Warming? *Env,* Issue 16

Does Wilderness Have Intrinsic Value? *Env,* Issue 2

Cognitive processes

Are Gender Differences Rooted in the Brain? *HS,* Issue 1

Can Computers Help Us Understand the Human Mind? *Psy,* Issue 8

Can Intelligence Be Increased? *Psy,* Issue 9

Do Alcoholics Have to Maintain a Lifetime of Abstinence? *Dru,* Issue 16

Is Television Harmful for Children? *MM,* Issue 3

Should Psychologists Study Memory Through Controlled Laboratory Experiments? *Psy,* Issue 2

Should Values Be Developed Rather Than Transmitted? *Edu,* Issue 4

Colonialism

Is Morality Relative to Culture? *Mor,* Issue 2

Was Colonial Culture Uniquely American? *AH1,* Issue 1

Communism

Does the Breakup of Communism Show the Success of Capitalism? *Soc,* Issue 15

Should Eastern European Nations Be Encouraged to Develop Free Market Institutions? *BE,* Issue 18

Will China Become an Asian Superpower? *WP,* Issue 7

Computers

Can Computers Help Us Understand the Human Mind? *Psy,* Issue 8

Can Modern Mass Communication Promote a Better World? *MM,* Issue 18

Does Technology Transfer by Multinational Firms Benefit the Development of Third World Nations? *MM,* Issue 17

Congress

Are the Effects of Acid Rain Serious Enough to Justify Strict Enforcement of Clean Air Legislation? *Env,* Issue 9

Does Congress Need to Be Radically Reformed? *Pol,* Issue 5

Should the Endangered Species Act Be Reauthorized? *Env,* Issue 3

The Presidency Versus Congress: Should Divided Government Be Ended? *Pol,* Issue 6

Conservation

Can Incentives Devised by Industrial Nations Combat Tropical Deforestation? *Env,* Issue 14

Does Wilderness Have Intrinsic Value? *Env,* Issue 2

Should Energy Policy Focus on Reducing the Use of Fossil Fuels? *Env,* Issue 7

Should the Endangered Species Act Be Reauthorized? *Env,* Issue 3

Will the "Greening" of Multinational Corporations Lead to Environmental Improvements? *Env,* Issue 6

Conservatism

Are Liberal Values Propagated by the News Media? *Soc,* Issue 2

Did Reaganomics Fail? *Eco,* Issue 9

Do the News Media Have a Liberal Bias? *Pol,* Issue 4

Is It Possible to Be Pro-Life and Pro-Choice? *Fam,* Issue 6

Was the American Revolution a Conservative Movement? *AH1,* Issue 7

Constitution, U.S. *See also* **Bill of Rights**

Abortion and the "Pro-Life" v. "Pro-Choice" Debate: Should the Human Fetus Be Considered a Person? *HS,* Issue 9

Does Government Have a Constitutional Right to Prohibit Certain Kinds of Sexual Conduct? *HS,* Issue 11

Do Prayers at Public School Graduation Ceremonies Violate the Constitution? *Leg,* Issue 6

Do Speech Codes Suppress Freedom of Expression? *MM,* Issue 11

Is Abortion Protected by the Constitution? *Leg*, Issue 7

Is Affirmative Action Constitutional? *Leg*, Issue 9

Is Affirmative Action Reverse Discrimination? *Pol*, Issue 11; *RER*, Issue 12; *Soc*, Issue 11

Is Capital Punishment Justified? *Pol*, Issue 10

Is Church-State Separation Being Threatened? *Edu*, Issue 5

Is "Hate Speech" Fully Protected by the Constitution? *Leg*, Issue 5

Should the Death Penalty Be Abolished? *Leg*, Issue 12

Should the Federal Courts Be Bound by the "Original Intent" of the Framers? *Pol*, Issue 8

Were the Founding Fathers Democratic Reformers? *AH1*, Issue 8

Consumer health. *See* **Health care**

Consumerism. *See* **Advertising; Health care**

Corporations, U.S. *See* **Industry**

Corrections system

Are Private Prisons a Good Idea? *CR*, Issue 15

Is Criminal Justice Free of Systemic Racism? *CR*, Issue 6

Is Incapacitation the Answer to the Crime Problem? *Soc*, Issue 18

Is Punishment Good Crime Control? *CR*, Issue 5

Should Elderly Offenders Get Lighter Sentences? *CR*, Issue 13

Should Plea Bargaining Continue to Be an Accepted Practice? *CR*, Issue 8

Will Tougher Sentencing Reduce Crime? *Pol*, Issue 9

Counseling. *See* **Psychotherapy**

Court system. *See* **Judicial system; Supreme Court**

Crime. *See also* **Corrections system; Crime prevention; Criminal behavior; Criminal justice system; Death penalty; Juvenile crime**

Are General Theories of Crime Possible? *CR*, Issue 2

Are There Limits to Confidentiality? *Bio*, Issue 8

Can Traditional Criminology Make Sense Out of Domestic Violence? *CR*, Issue 11

Does Insider Trading Serve a Useful Purpose? *BE*, Issue 15

Is Crime Functional? *CR*, Issue 1

Is Criminal Behavior Biologically Determined? *CR*, Issue 3

Is Criminal Justice Free of Systemic Racism? *CR*, Issue 6

Is Incapacitation the Answer to the Crime Problem? *Soc*, Issue 18

Is Pornography Immoral? *Mor*, Issue 12

Is Punishment Good Crime Control? *CR*, Issue 5

Is Research on Criminal Careers Helpful? *CR*, Issue 10

Is Street Crime More Harmful Than White-Collar Crime? *Soc*, Issue 16

Is Street Crime More Serious Than White-Collar Crime? *CR*, Issue 4

Is There a Date Rape Crisis on College Campuses? *HS*, Issue 10

Is the Victims' Rights Movement Succeeding? *CR*, Issue 16

Juvenile Justice: Are Kids "Getting Away With Murder"? *CR*, Issue 7

Should "Battered Wife Syndrome" Be Barred as a Defense in a Murder Case? *Leg*, Issue 14

Should Capital Punishment Be Abolished? *CR*, Issue 9

Should Drugs Be Legalized? *Dru*, Issue 1; *Hea*, Issue 9; *Mor*, Issue 8; *Pol*, Issue 13; *Soc*, Issue 17

Should Elderly Offenders Get Lighter Sentences? *CR*, Issue 13

Should Plea Bargaining Continue to Be an Accepted Practice? *CR*, Issue 8

Should the Government Establish Special Programs and Policies for Black Youths and Their Families? *Fam*, Issue 12

Was City Government in Late Nineteenth-Century America a "Conspicuous Failure"? *AH2*, Issue 6

Will Drug Legalization Help the Criminal Justice System? *CR*, Issue 17

Will Gun Control Reduce Crime? *CR*, Issue 14

Will Tougher Sentencing Reduce Crime? *Pol*, Issue 9

Would Legalizing Drugs Have Beneficial Effects on Society? *Psy*, Issue 19

Crime prevention. *See also* **Crime; Police**

Did the Great Society Fail? *AH2*, Issue 14

Do Ignition Interlocks Reduce Drunk Driving Arrests? *CR*, Issue 12

Is Incapacitation the Answer to the Crime Problem? *Soc*, Issue 18

Juvenile Justice: Are Kids "Getting Away With Murder"? *CR*, Issue 7

Should Capital Punishment Be Abolished? *CR*, Issue 9

Should Drugs Be Legalized? *Dru*, Issue 1; *Hea*, Issue 9; *Mor*, Issue 8; *Pol*, Issue 13; *Soc*, Issue 17

Should the Drinking Age Remain at 21? *Dru*, Issue 4

Will Drug Legalization Help the Criminal Justice System? *CR*, Issue 17

Will Gun Control Reduce Crime? *CR*, Issue 14

Will Tougher Sentencing Reduce Crime? *Pol*, Issue 9

Would Legalizing Drugs Have Beneficial Effects on Society? *Psy*, Issue 19

Criminal behavior. *See also* **Crime**

Are General Theories of Crime Possible? *CR*, Issue 2

Can Traditional Criminology Make Sense Out of Domestic Violence? *CR*, Issue 11

Is Crime Functional? *CR*, Issue 1

Is Criminal Behavior Biologically Determined? *CR*, Issue 3

Is Research on Criminal Careers Helpful? *CR*, Issue 10

Is Street Crime More Harmful Than White-Collar Crime? *Soc*, Issue 16

Is Street Crime More Serious Than White-Collar Crime? *CR*, Issue 4

Is Terrorism Ever Justified? *Mor*, Issue 17

Is There a Date Rape Crisis on College Campuses? *HS*, Issue 10

Juvenile Justice: Are Kids "Getting Away With Murder"? *CR*, Issue 7

Should Drugs Be Legalized? *Soc*, Issue 17

Should the Insanity Defense Be Abolished? *Leg*, Issue 17

Will Gun Control Reduce Crime? *CR*, Issue 14

Criminal justice system. *See also* **Corrections system; Crime; Law enforcement; Police**

Are Global Standards of Human Rights Desirable? *WP*, Issue 18

Are Human Rights Basic to Justice? *CR*, Issue 18; *Mor*, Issue 18

Are Private Prisons a Good Idea? *CR*, Issue 15

Does Arrest Reduce Domestic Violence? *Fam*, Issue 10

Does Drug Testing Violate Civil Rights? *Dru*, Issue 3

Is Capital Punishment Justified? *Pol*, Issue 10

Is Criminal Justice Free of Systemic Racism? *CR*, Issue 6

Is Incapacitation the Answer to the Crime Problem? *Soc*, Issue 18

Is Punishment Good Crime Control? *CR*, Issue 5

Is Systemic Racism in Criminal Justice a Myth? *RER*, Issue 14

Is the Kidnapping of Criminal Suspects from Foreign Countries Justifiable? *WP*, Issue 16

Is the Victims' Rights Movement Succeeding? *CR*, Issue 16

Is the War on Drugs Misdirected? *Dru*, Issue 5

Should "Battered Wife Syndrome" Be Barred as a Defense in a Murder Case? *Leg*, Issue 14

Should Capital Punishment Be Abolished? *CR*, Issue 9

Should Courts Be Permitted to Order Women to Use Long-Acting Contraceptives? *Bio*, Issue 1

Should Drugs Be Legalized? *Dru*, Issue 1; *Hea*, Issue 9; *Mor*, Issue 8; *Pol*, Issue 13; *Soc*, Issue 17

Should Elderly Offenders Get Lighter Sentences? *CR*, Issue 13

Should Lawyers Be Prohibited from Presenting a False Case? *Leg*, Issue 2

Should Plea Bargaining Be Abolished? *Leg*, Issue 3

Should Plea Bargaining Continue to Be an Accepted Practice? *CR*, Issue 8

Should Prostitution Be Decriminalized? *HS*, Issue 14

Should the Insanity Defense Be Abolished? *Leg*, Issue 17

Will Drug Legalization Help the Criminal Justice System? *CR*, Issue 17

Will Tougher Sentencing Reduce Crime? *Pol*, Issue 9

Criminals. *See* **Crime; Criminal behavior; Criminal justice system**

Cultural relativism

Does "Multiculturalism" Debase the Curriculum? *Soc*, Issue 1

Do Gender Differences Originate from Biological Factors? *Psy*, Issue 10

Is Morality Grounded in Religion? *Mor*, Issue 4

Is Morality Relative to Culture? *Mor*, Issue 2

Is Morality Subjective? *Mor*, Issue 3

Should Animals Be Liberated? *Mor*, Issue 6

Culture, American

Are American Values Shaped by the Mass Media? *MM*, Issue 1

Are Extramarital Relationships Becoming More Frequent? *Fam*, Issue 14

Are Media Messages About Women Improving? *MM*, Issue 4

Are the Poor Being Harmed by Welfare? *Pol*, Issue 14

Can Computers Help Us Understand the Human Mind? *Psy*, Issue 8

Did American Slaves Develop a Distinct African American Culture in the Eighteenth Century? *AH1*, Issue 5

Did Slaves Exercise Religious Autonomy? *AH1*, Issue 12

Did the Progressives Fail? *AH2*, Issue 7

Does "Lower-Class" Culture Perpetuate Poverty? *Soc*, Issue 9

Does "Lower-Class" Culture Perpetuate Poverty Among Urban Minorities? *RER*, Issue 11

Does "Multiculturalism" Debase the Curriculum? *Soc*, Issue 1

Does Sexual Infidelity Destroy a Relationship? *HS*, Issue 4

Do Italian Americans Reject Assimilation? *RER*, Issue 4

Do Ratings Serve the Viewing Public's Interest? *MM*, Issue 13

Is Bribery Ever Justified? *BE*, Issue 20

Is Cholesterol Reduction an Important Health Priority? *Hea*, Issue 12

Is Feminism a Positive Value for Society? *Mor*, Issue 7

Is Morality Relative to Culture? *Mor*, Issue 2

Is Objectivity Still a Criterion for Journalism? *MM*, Issue 7

Is There an Ethnic Revolt Against the Melting Pot? *RER*, Issue 16

Must Contemporary Moral Disagreements End in Deadlock? *Mor*, Issue 1

Should Drugs Be Legalized? *Soc*, Issue 17

Should Literacy Be Based on Traditional Culture? *Edu*, Issue 13

Should Values Be Developed Rather Than Transmitted? *Edu*, Issue 4

Should We Call Ourselves African Americans? *RER*, Issue 5

Was Colonial Culture Uniquely American? *AH1*, Issue 1

Was Race a Central Factor in the Colonists' Attitudes Toward Native Americans? *AH1*, Issue 2

Were Southern Slaveholding Women Covert Abolitionists? *AH1*, Issue 14

Were the Immigrants' Old World Cultures Destroyed as They Adjusted to American Life? *AH2*, Issue 4

— D —

Death and dying. *See also* **Euthanasia; Suicide**
Can States Restrict the Right to Die? *Leg,* Issue 10
Is Euthanasia Immoral? *Mor,* Issue 15
Is It Ethical to Withhold the Truth from Dying Patients? *Bio,* Issue 5
Is It Ever Morally Right to Withhold Food and Water from Dying Patients? *Bio,* Issue 7
Is Physician-Assisted Suicide Ethical? *Bio,* Issue 6
Should Capital Punishment Be Abolished? *Mor,* Issue 14
Should Doctors Ever Help Terminally Ill Patients Commit Suicide? *Hea,* Issue 2
Should Newborns Without Brains Be Used as Organ Donors? *Bio,* Issue 16
Should Psychotherapists Allow Suicide? *Psy,* Issue 14

Death penalty
Should Capital Punishment Be Abolished? *CR,* Issue 9; *Mor,* Issue 14
Should the Death Penalty Be Abolished? *Leg,* Issue 12

Democracy
Are the Results of Polls Misleading? *MM,* Issue 12
Did the Election of 1828 Represent a Democratic Revolt of the People? *AH1,* Issue 10
Does the Breakup of Communism Show the Success of Capitalism? *Soc,* Issue 15
Do Political Action Committees Undermine Democracy? *Pol,* Issue 3
Has Individualism Become Excessive? *Soc,* Issue 3
Is America Declining? *Pol,* Issue 20
Is It Possible to Drastically Reduce Defense Expenditures and Remain Secure? *WP,* Issue 13

Should National Self-Interest Be the Basis of American Foreign Policy? *Pol,* Issue 19
Was Reconstruction a "Splendid Failure"? *AH1,* Issue 17; *AH2,* Issue 1
Was the American Revolution a Conservative Movement? *AH1,* Issue 7
Was the Confederacy Defeated Because of Its "Loss of Will"? *AH1,* Issue 15
Were the Founding Fathers Democratic Reformers? *AH1,* Issue 8
Will Democracy Survive in Russia? *WP,* Issue 2

Deregulation. *See* **Government regulation**

Desegregation. *See* **Racial discrimination**

Deviant behavior. *See* **Behavior disorders**

Diet
Can Large Doses of Vitamins Improve Health? *Hea,* Issue 13
Did Nestlé Act Irresponsibly in Marketing Infant Formula to the Third World? *BE,* Issue 19
Is Cholesterol Reduction an Important Health Priority? *Hea,* Issue 12
Will Practicing Positive Health Behaviors and Emphasizing Prevention Improve Health? *Hea,* Issue 5

Discrimination. *See* **Ethnic discrimination; Racial discrimination; Sex discrimination**

Disease. *See also* **specific diseases**
Are Chiropractors Legitimate Health Providers? *Hea,* Issue 18
Are There Limits to Confidentiality? *Bio,* Issue 8
Can a Positive Mental Attitude Overcome Disease? *Hea,* Issue 6
Does Exercise Increase Longevity? *Hea,* Issue 14
Do Physicians Have an Ethical Duty to Treat AIDS Patients? *Bio,* Issue 9
Do Smokers Have a Right to Smoke in Public Places? *Hea,* Issue 7
Has the Federal Government Spent Enough on AIDS Research? *HS,* Issue 17

Is AIDS Getting More Than Its Share of Resources and Media Attention? *Hea,* Issue 4

Is It Ethical to Withhold the Truth from Dying Patients? *Bio,* Issue 5

Is Litigation the Best Way to Compensate Asbestos Workers for Disease and Risk? *BE,* Issue 9

Is the "Disease" of Alcoholism a Myth? *Dru,* Issue 13; *Psy,* Issue 5

Should Alcoholism Be Treated as a Disease? *Hea,* Issue 8

Should All Children Be Immunized Against Childhood Diseases? *Hea,* Issue 17

Should Doctors Be Able to Refuse Demands for "Futile" Treatment? *Bio,* Issue 11

Should Doctors Ever Help Terminally Ill Patients Commit Suicide? *Hea,* Issue 2

Should Needle Exchange Programs Be Promoted? *Dru,* Issue 6

Divorce

Are Children of Divorced Parents at Greater Risk? *Psy,* Issue 12

Children of Divorce: Are They at Greater Risk? *Fam,* Issue 15

Does Sexual Infidelity Destroy a Relationship? *HS,* Issue 4

Do Stepchildren Need Special Policies and Programs on Their Behalf? *Fam,* Issue 16

Is the Success of Remarriage Doomed? *Fam,* Issue 17

DNA. *See* **Genetics**

Drug abuse

Are Drug Addicts Always in Control of Their Addiction? *Dru,* Issue 15

Are Rent Controls the Cause of America's Homelessness? *Eco,* Issue 5

Are the Dangers of Steroids Exaggerated? *Dru,* Issue 17

Can Caffeine Be Bad for Your Health? *Dru,* Issue 9

Do Alcoholics Have to Maintain a Lifetime of Abstinence? *Dru,* Issue 16

Do Drug Education Programs Prevent Drug Abuse? *Dru,* Issue 11

Does Drug Testing Violate Civil Rights? *Dru,* Issue 3

Do Ignition Interlocks Reduce Drunk Driving Arrests? *CR,* Issue 12

Is Alcoholism Hereditary? *Dru,* Issue 10

Is Drug Testing an Unwarranted Invasion of Employee Privacy? *BE,* Issue 8

Is Drug Use Testing Permitted Under the Fourth Amendment? *Leg,* Issue 4

Is Passive Smoking Harmful to Nonsmokers? *Dru,* Issue 8

Is the "Disease" of Alcoholism a Myth? *Dru,* Issue 13; *Psy,* Issue 5

Is the War on Drugs Misdirected? *Dru,* Issue 5

Should Alcohol Advertising Be Limited? *Dru,* Issue 14

Should Alcoholism Be Treated as a Disease? *Hea,* Issue 8

Should Courts Be Permitted to Order Women to Use Long-Acting Contraceptives? *Bio,* Issue 1

Should Drugs Be Legalized? *Dru,* Issue 1; *Hea,* Issue 9; *Mor,* Issue 8; *Pol,* Issue 13; *Soc,* Issue 17

Should Drug Use by Pregnant Women Be Considered Child Abuse? *Dru,* Issue 7

Should Needle Exchange Programs Be Promoted? *Dru,* Issue 6

Should the Drinking Age Remain at 21? *Dru,* Issue 4

Should Tobacco Advertising Be Banned? *BE,* Issue 12

Will Drug Legalization Help the Criminal Justice System? *CR,* Issue 17

Would Legalizing Drugs Have Beneficial Effects on Society? *Psy,* Issue 19

Drug education

Do Drug Education Programs Prevent Drug Abuse? *Dru,* Issue 11

Should Drugs Be Legalized? *Dru,* Issue 1; *Hea,* Issue 9; *Mor,* Issue 8; *Pol,* Issue 13

Should Drug Use by Pregnant Women Be Considered Child Abuse? *Dru,* Issue 7

Should Needle Exchange Programs Be Promoted? *Dru,* Issue 6

Should the Drinking Age Remain at 21? *Dru*, Issue 4

Drugs, as medication
Are the Dangers of Steroids Exaggerated? *Dru*, Issue 17
Can Caffeine Be Bad for Your Health? *Dru*, Issue 9
Is It Unethical to Implant Animal Parts in Humans? *Bio*, Issue 13
Should Medical Patients Be Permitted to Use Marijuana? *Dru*, Issue 2
Should Psychologists Be Allowed to Prescribe Drugs? *Psy*, Issue 18

Dumping
Hazardous Waste: Are Cleanup and Control Efforts Succeeding? *Env*, Issue 11
Municipal Waste: Should Recycling Be Promoted as the Key to Refuse Management? *Env*, Issue 12
Nuclear Waste: Is Yucca Mountain an Appropriate Site for Permanent Waste Disposal? *Env*, Issue 13

Dying. *See* **Death and dying**

— E —

Earth Summit (1992)
Did the United Nations Earth Summit Produce Useful Results? *Env*, Issue 1
Does the Global Environmental Movement Threaten Economic Prosperity? *WP*, Issue 12
Is Population Control the Key to Preventing Environmental Deterioration? *Env*, Issue 4

Economic growth
Did Reaganomics Fail? *Eco*, Issue 9
Does Japan Represent a Worldwide Economic Threat? *WP*, Issue 9
Does Population Growth Threaten Humanity? *Soc*, Issue 19
Does Society Have an Obligation to Care for the Less Well Off? *Mor*, Issue 9
Does the Global Environmental Movement Threaten Economic Prosperity? *WP*, Issue 12

Does the Government Regulate Too Much? *Pol*, Issue 7
Is the National Debt a National Liability? *Pol*, Issue 15
Is There a World Population Crisis? *WP*, Issue 19
Should the Capital Gains Tax Be Lowered? *Eco*, Issue 13
Should the Developed North Increase Aid to the Less Developed South? *WP*, Issue 10
Should the Federal Reserve Target Zero Inflation? *Eco*, Issue 11
Should the Global Arms Trade Be Severely Restricted? *WP*, Issue 11
Will the European Community Increase Its Level of Integration? *WP*, Issue 4
Will the North American Free Trade Agreement Benefit All Its Member Countries? *WP*, Issue 5

Economic history, Colonial
Did Capitalist Values Motivate the American Colonists? *AH1*, Issue 4
Was the American Revolution a Conservative Movement? *AH1*, Issue 7

Economic history, Post–Civil War
Was Reconstruction a "Splendid Failure"? *AH1*, Issue 17; *AH2*, Issue 1
Was the American Labor Movement Radical? *AH2*, Issue 3
Were Nineteenth-Century Entrepreneurs Robber Barons? *AH2*, Issue 2
Were the Immigrants' Old World Cultures Destroyed as They Adjusted to American Life? *AH2*, Issue 4

Economic history, Twentieth century
Are Profits the Only Business of Business? *Eco*, Issue 1
Are Women Paid Less Than Men Because Their Working Conditions Are More Favorable? *Eco*, Issue 4
Can Corporate Codes of Ethics Promote Ethical Behavior? *BE*, Issue 2
Did Reaganomics Fail? *Eco*, Issue 9
Did the Great Society Fail? *AH2*, Issue 14
Does Japan Represent a Worldwide Economic Threat? *WP*, Issue 9

Does "Lower-Class" Culture Perpetuate Poverty? *Soc,* Issue 9

Does "Lower-Class" Culture Perpetuate Poverty Among Urban Minorities? *RER,* Issue 11

Does the Government Regulate Too Much? *Pol,* Issue 7

Does the United States Save Enough? *Eco,* Issue 12

Do Federal Budget Deficits Matter? *Eco,* Issue 10

Do Hostile Takeovers Harm Society? *Eco,* Issue 6

Is America Declining? *Pol,* Issue 20

Is America's Socioeconomic System Breaking Down? *Soc,* Issue 20

Is Capitalism Viable for the Future? *BE,* Issue 1; *Mor,* Issue 5

Is Japan a Threat to America's Economic and National Security? *Eco,* Issue 16

Is Mass Transit the Answer to Improving U.S. Energy Efficiency? *Eco,* Issue 7

Is the National Debt a National Liability? *Pol,* Issue 15

Is Workfare a Good Substitute for Welfare? *Eco,* Issue 14

Should American Farmers Be Forced to Face Market Competition? *Eco,* Issue 2

Should the Capital Gains Tax Be Lowered? *Eco,* Issue 13

Should the Global Arms Trade Be Severely Restricted? *WP,* Issue 11

Should the United States Abandon Its Superpower Role? *WP,* Issue 3

Was Dwight Eisenhower a Great President? *AH2,* Issue 13

Was Early Twentieth-Century American Foreign Policy in the Caribbean Basin Dominated by Economic Concerns? *AH2,* Issue 8

Was the New Deal an Effective Answer to the Great Depression? *AH2,* Issue 10

Will the European Community Increase Its Level of Integration? *WP,* Issue 4

Economic philosophy

Are Profits the Only Business of Business? *Eco,* Issue 1

Did Reaganomics Fail? *Eco,* Issue 9

Is America Declining? *Pol,* Issue 20

Is America's Socioeconomic System Breaking Down? *Soc,* Issue 20

Is Capitalism Viable for the Future? *BE,* Issue 1; *Mor,* Issue 5

Is Japan a Threat to America's Economic and National Security? *Eco,* Issue 16

Should the Capital Gains Tax Be Lowered? *Eco,* Issue 13

Should the Federal Reserve Target Zero Inflation? *Eco,* Issue 11

Should the "Pay-for-Performance" System Be Overhauled? *BE,* Issue 3

Will the European Community Increase Its Level of Integration? *WP,* Issue 4

Education. *See* **Cognitive processes; Intelligence; Learning; School curriculum; School reform; Schools**

Education alternatives

Can "Choice" Lead the Way to Educational Reform? *Edu,* Issue 9

Can Schools Prevent Urban Dropouts? *Edu,* Issue 12

Is Home Schooling a Viable Alternative? *Edu,* Issue 11

Is Mainstreaming Beneficial to All? *Edu,* Issue 17

Should Bilingual Education Programs Be Abandoned? *Edu,* Issue 15

Should Bilingual Education Programs Be Stopped? *RER,* Issue 7

Will the "Edison Project" Prompt Major Reforms? *Edu,* Issue 10

Elections

Are the Results of Polls Misleading? *MM,* Issue 12

Did the Election of 1828 Represent a Democratic Revolt of the People? *AH1,* Issue 10

Do Political Action Committees Undermine Democracy? *Pol,* Issue 3

Do Presidential TV Ads Manipulate Voters? *MM,* Issue 10

Has Party Reform Succeeded? *Pol,* Issue 2

The Presidency Versus Congress: Should Divided Government Be Ended? *Pol,* Issue 6

Elite

Does Wilderness Have Intrinsic Value? *Env*, Issue 2

Do the News Media Have a Liberal Bias? *Pol*, Issue 4

Is American Government Dominated by Big Business? *Pol*, Issue 1

Is Punishment Good Crime Control? *CR*, Issue 5

Media Monopolies: Does Concentration of Ownership Jeopardize Media Content? *MM*, Issue 15

Should the "Pay-for-Performance" System Be Overhauled? *BE*, Issue 3

Were the Founding Fathers Democratic Reformers? *AH1*, Issue 8

Employment

Are Hispanics Making Significant Progress? *RER*, Issue 13

Are Women Only Victims in Their Roles as Social Support Providers? *Fam*, Issue 2

Are Women Paid Less Than Men Because Their Working Conditions Are More Favorable? *Eco*, Issue 4

Can Corporate Codes of Ethics Promote Ethical Behavior? *BE*, Issue 2

Can Hostile Takeovers Be Justified? *BE*, Issue 14

Can Whistle-Blowing Be Clearly Justified? *BE*, Issue 7

Did Reaganomics Fail? *Eco*, Issue 9

Do Employees Have a Moral Right to Meaningful Work? *BE*, Issue 4

Do Employers Have an Obligation to Provide Parental Leave Policies for Their Employees? *BE*, Issue 6

Is Drug Testing an Unwarranted Invasion of Employee Privacy? *BE*, Issue 8

Is Drug Use Testing Permitted Under the Fourth Amendment? *Leg*, Issue 4

Is Economic Inequality Beneficial to Society? *Soc*, Issue 8

Is Litigation the Best Way to Compensate Asbestos Workers for Disease and Risk? *BE*, Issue 9

Is Workfare a Good Substitute for Welfare? *Eco*, Issue 14

Was the American Labor Movement Radical? *AH2*, Issue 3

Will the North American Free Trade Agreement Benefit All Its Member Countries? *WP*, Issue 5

Would a "Mommy Track" Benefit Employed Women? *Fam*, Issue 11; *Soc*, Issue 5

Endangered species. *See* **Wildlife**

Energy issues. *See also* **specific fuels and energies**

Are Abundant Resources and an Improved Environment Likely Future Prospects for the World's People? *Env*, Issue 17

Can Current Pollution Strategies Improve Air Quality? *BE*, Issue 17; *Env*, Issue 8

Is Mass Transit the Answer to Improving U.S. Energy Efficiency? *Eco*, Issue 7

Should Energy Policy Focus on Reducing the Use of Fossil Fuels? *Env*, Issue 7

Will the North American Free Trade Agreement Benefit All Its Member Countries? *WP*, Issue 5

Environment. *See also* **Conservation; Environmental laws**

Are Abundant Resources and an Improved Environment Likely Future Prospects for the World's People? *Env*, Issue 17

Can Current Pollution Strategies Improve Air Quality? *BE*, Issue 17; *Env*, Issue 8

Does Global Warming Require Immediate Government Action? *Eco*, Issue 17

Does Population Growth Threaten Humanity? *Soc*, Issue 19

Does the Global Environmental Movement Threaten Economic Prosperity? *WP*, Issue 12

Does the Government Regulate Too Much? *Pol*, Issue 7

Do Smokers Have a Right to Smoke in Public Places? *Hea*, Issue 7

Is Acid Rain a Serious Environmental Problem? *Hea*, Issue 16

Is Alcoholism Hereditary? *Dru*, Issue 10

Is Day Care Harmful? *Psy*, Issue 11

Is Mass Transit the Answer to Improving U.S. Energy Efficiency? *Eco*, Issue 7

Is Population Control the Key to Preventing Environmental Deterioration? *Env*, Issue 4

Nuclear Waste: Is Yucca Mountain an Appropriate Site for Permanent Waste Disposal? *Env*, Issue 13

Should Industry Be Held Accountable for Acid Rain? *BE*, Issue 16

Should the Phaseout of Chlorofluorocarbons Be Accelerated to Protect the Ozone Layer from Further Depletion? *Env*, Issue 15

Was Dwight Eisenhower a Great President? *AH2*, Issue 13

Will Environmental Degradation Be a Feature of International Conflicts in the Future? *Env*, Issue 18

Environmental laws

Are Aggressive International Efforts Needed to Slow Global Warming? *Env*, Issue 16

Are the Effects of Acid Rain Serious Enough to Justify Strict Enforcement of Clean Air Legislation? *Env*, Issue 9

Can Current Pollution Strategies Improve Air Quality? *BE*, Issue 17; *Env*, Issue 8

Did the United Nations Earth Summit Produce Useful Results? *Env*, Issue 1

Does the Global Environmental Movement Threaten Economic Prosperity? *WP*, Issue 12

Hazardous Waste: Are Cleanup and Control Efforts Succeeding? *Env*, Issue 11

Is the Widespread Use of Pesticides Required to Feed the World's People? *Env*, Issue 10

Should American Farmers Be Forced to Face Market Competition? *Eco*, Issue 2

Should Industry Be Held Accountable for Acid Rain? *BE*, Issue 16

Should Risk Assessment Methods Be Used to Set Environmental Priorities? *Env*, Issue 5

Should the Endangered Species Act Be Reauthorized? *Env*, Issue 3

Should the Phaseout of Chlorofluorocarbons Be Accelerated to Protect the Ozone Layer from Further Depletion? *Env*, Issue 15

Will the "Greening" of Multinational Corporations Lead to Environmental Improvements? *Env*, Issue 6

Equality. *See* **African Americans; Ethnic discrimination; Inequality; Minorities; Racial discrimination; Sex discrimination; Women's issues**

ERA. *See* **Bill of Rights; Constitution, U.S.; Sex discrimination; Women's issues**

Ethical issues

Are Current Sex Education Programs Lacking in Moral Guidance? *Edu*, Issue 19

Are Extramarital Relationships Becoming More Frequent? *Fam*, Issue 14

Are Federal "Marketing Orders" Unfair? *BE*, Issue 13

Are There Limits to Confidentiality? *Bio*, Issue 8

Can Abortion Be a Morally Acceptable Choice? *Hea*, Issue 11

Can Corporate Codes of Ethics Promote Ethical Behavior? *BE*, Issue 2

Can Deception in Research Be Justified? *Psy*, Issue 1

Can Experiments Using Animals Be Justified? *Psy*, Issue 3

Can Hostile Takeovers Be Justified? *BE*, Issue 14

Can Modern War Be Just? *WP*, Issue 20

Can Whistle-Blowing Be Clearly Justified? *BE*, Issue 7

Did Nestlé Act Irresponsibly in Marketing Infant Formula to the Third World? *BE*, Issue 19

Do Employees Have a Moral Right to Meaningful Work? *BE*, Issue 4

Does Insider Trading Serve a Useful Purpose? *BE*, Issue 15

Does Society Have an Obligation to Care for the Less Well Off? *Mor*, Issue 9

Do Hostile Takeovers Harm Society? *Eco,* Issue 6

Do Physicians Have an Ethical Duty to Treat AIDS Patients? *Bio,* Issue 9

Do Smokers Have a Right to Smoke in Public Places? *Hea,* Issue 7

Is Abortion Immoral? *Mor,* Issue 13

Is Advertising Ethical? *MM,* Issue 14

Is Advertising Fundamentally Deceptive? *BE,* Issue 10

Is Affirmative Action Morally Justifiable? *Mor,* Issue 16

Is Bribery Ever Justified? *BE,* Issue 20

Is Capitalism Viable for the Future? *BE,* Issue 1; *Mor,* Issue 5

Is Capital Punishment Justified? *Pol,* Issue 10

Is Crime Functional? *CR,* Issue 1

Is Drug Testing an Unwarranted Invasion of Employee Privacy? *BE,* Issue 8

Is Economic Inequality Beneficial to Society? *Soc,* Issue 8

Is Euthanasia Immoral? *Mor,* Issue 15

Is It Ethical for Scientists to Use Data from the Nazi Experiments? *Bio,* Issue 14

Is It Ethical to Withhold the Truth from Dying Patients? *Bio,* Issue 5

Is It Ever Morally Right to Withhold Food and Water from Dying Patients? *Bio,* Issue 7

Is It Possible to Be Pro-Life and Pro-Choice? *Fam,* Issue 6

Is It Unethical to Implant Animal Parts in Humans? *Bio,* Issue 13

Is Morality Grounded in Religion? *Mor,* Issue 4

Is Morality Subjective? *Mor,* Issue 3

Is Patriotism a Virtue? *Mor,* Issue 19

Is Physician-Assisted Suicide Ethical? *Bio,* Issue 6

Is Pornography Immoral? *Mor,* Issue 12

Is Terrorism Ever Justified? *Mor,* Issue 17

Is There a Moral Right to Abortion? *Bio,* Issue 2

Must Contemporary Moral Disagreements End in Deadlock? *Mor,* Issue 1

Product Liability: Was Ford to Blame in the Pinto Case? *BE,* Issue 11

Should Animal Experimentation Be Permitted? *Bio,* Issue 12

Should Animals Be Liberated? *Mor,* Issue 6

Should Capital Punishment Be Abolished? *Mor,* Issue 14

Should Commercial Surrogate Motherhood Be Banned? *Bio,* Issue 4

Should Courts Be Permitted to Order Women to Use Long-Acting Contraceptives? *Bio,* Issue 1

Should Doctors Be Able to Refuse Demands for "Futile" Treatment? *Bio,* Issue 11

Should Drugs Be Legalized? *Soc,* Issue 17

Should Health Care for the Elderly Be Limited? *Bio,* Issue 18

Should HIV-Infected Health Care Workers Be Restricted from Performing Some Procedures? *Bio,* Issue 10

Should Homosexuality Be Accepted by Society? *Mor,* Issue 11

Should Lawyers Be Prohibited from Presenting a False Case? *Leg,* Issue 2

Should Morality and Human Rights Strongly Influence Foreign Policy-Making? *WP,* Issue 17

Should Newborns Without Brains Be Used as Organ Donors? *Bio,* Issue 16

Should Prostitution Be Decriminalized? *HS,* Issue 14

Should Psychotherapy Include Religious Values? *Psy,* Issue 16

Should Research With Aborted Fetal Tissue Be Banned? *Bio,* Issue 15

Should Risk Assessment Methods Be Used to Set Environmental Priorities? *Env,* Issue 5

Should Schools Distribute Condoms? *HS,* Issue 7

Should Surrogate Parenting Be Permitted for Infertile Couples? *Fam,* Issue 8

Should Thawing Unused Frozen Embryos Be Permitted? *Bio,* Issue 3

Should the Death Penalty Be Abolished? *Leg,* Issue 12

Should the Insanity Defense Be Abolished? *Leg*, Issue 17

Should There Be a Market in Body Parts? *Bio*, Issue 17

Should Tobacco Advertising Be Banned? *BE*, Issue 12

Should Values Be Developed Rather Than Transmitted? *Edu*, Issue 4

Was City Government in Late Nineteenth-Century America a "Conspicuous Failure"? *AH2*, Issue 6

Was Dwight Eisenhower a Great President? *AH2*, Issue 13

Was the Ku Klux Klan of the 1920s an Extremist Movement? *AH2*, Issue 9

Were Nineteenth-Century Entrepreneurs Robber Barons? *AH2*, Issue 2

Will the Human Genome Project Lead to Abuses in Genetic Engineering? *Bio*, Issue 20

Ethnic discrimination

Are Nonethnic Scholars Able to Successfully Research Minorities? *RER*, Issue 1

Do Italian Americans Reject Assimilation? *RER*, Issue 4

Is Affirmative Action Constitutional? *Leg*, Issue 9

Is There an Ethnic Revolt Against the Melting Pot? *RER*, Issue 16

Was the Ku Klux Klan of the 1920s an Extremist Movement? *AH2*, Issue 9

Euthanasia

Can States Restrict the Right to Die? *Leg*, Issue 10

Is Euthanasia Immoral? *Mor*, Issue 15

Is Physician-Assisted Suicide Ethical? *Bio*, Issue 6

Should Doctors Ever Help Terminally Ill Patients Commit Suicide? *Hea*, Issue 2

— F —

Family structure

Are Asian Americans a "Model Minority"? *RER*, Issue 3

Are Children of Divorced Parents at Greater Risk? *Psy*, Issue 12

Are the Poor Being Harmed by Welfare? *Pol*, Issue 14

Are Women Only Victims in Their Roles as Social Support Providers? *Fam*, Issue 2

Children of Divorce: Are They at Greater Risk? *Fam*, Issue 15

Did American Slaves Develop a Distinct African American Culture in the Eighteenth Century? *AH1*, Issue 5

Did Capitalist Values Motivate the American Colonists? *AH1*, Issue 4

Do Cultural Differences Between Home and School Explain the High Dropout Rates for American Indian Students? *RER*, Issue 6

Does Sex Education Prevent Teen Pregnancy? *Hea*, Issue 10

Does Sexual Infidelity Destroy a Relationship? *HS*, Issue 4

Do Italian Americans Reject Assimilation? *RER*, Issue 4

Do Stepchildren Need Special Policies and Programs on Their Behalf? *Fam*, Issue 16

Have Men's Family Roles Changed? *Fam*, Issue 3

Is Day Care Harmful? *Psy*, Issue 11

Is Feminism a Harmful Ideology? *Soc*, Issue 4

Is Feminism a Positive Value for Society? *Mor*, Issue 7

Is the Success of Remarriage Doomed? *Fam*, Issue 17

Should Doctors Be Able to Refuse Demands for "Futile" Treatment? *Bio*, Issue 11

Should Homosexuality Bar a Parent from Being Awarded Custody of a Child? *Leg*, Issue 11

Should Surrogate Parenting Be Permitted for Infertile Couples? *Fam*, Issue 8

Should Traditional Families Be Preserved? *Soc*, Issue 7

Should We Call Ourselves African Americans? *RER*, Issue 5

Were the Immigrants' Old World Cultures Destroyed as They Adjusted to American Life? *AH2*, Issue 4

Would a "Mommy Track" Benefit Employed Women? *Fam*, Issue 11; *Soc*, Issue 5

Far East

Does Japan Represent a Worldwide Economic Threat? *WP*, Issue 9

Is Japan a Threat to America's Economic and National Security? *Eco*, Issue 16

Should Morality and Human Rights Strongly Influence Foreign Policy-Making? *WP*, Issue 17

Will China Become an Asian Superpower? *WP*, Issue 7

Farming. *See* **Agriculture**

Fathering. *See also* **Mothering; Parenting; Surrogate parenting**

Have Men's Family Roles Changed? *Fam*, Issue 3

Should Pregnant Teens Marry the Fathers of Their Babies? *Fam*, Issue 9

Should Surrogate Parenting Be Permitted for Infertile Couples? *Fam*, Issue 8

Federal budget

Are the Poor Being Harmed by Welfare? *Pol*, Issue 14

Does the United States Need Socialized Medicine? *Pol*, Issue 16

Does the United States Save Enough? *Eco*, Issue 12

Do Federal Budget Deficits Matter? *Eco*, Issue 10

Is It Possible to Drastically Reduce Defense Expenditures and Remain Secure? *WP*, Issue 13

Is the National Debt a National Liability? *Pol*, Issue 15

Should a New Military-Industrial Complex Be Developed? *Eco*, Issue 18

Should the Federal Reserve Target Zero Inflation? *Eco*, Issue 11

Federal government

Are Federal "Marketing Orders" Unfair? *BE*, Issue 13

Does Congress Need to Be Radically Reformed? *Pol*, Issue 5

Does Global Warming Require Immediate Government Action? *Eco*, Issue 17

Does the Government Regulate Too Much? *Pol*, Issue 7

Does the United States Need Socialized Medicine? *Pol*, Issue 16

Helping the Homeless: Do We Need More Government Regulation? *Soc*, Issue 12

Is American Government Dominated by Big Business? *Pol*, Issue 1

Is Drug Use Testing Permitted Under the Fourth Amendment? *Leg*, Issue 4

Is Government Dominated by Big Business? *Soc*, Issue 13

Is National Service at Odds With American National Interest? *Eco*, Issue 3

Should a National Gun Control Policy Be Established? *Leg*, Issue 15

Should National Goals Guide School Performance? *Edu*, Issue 8

Should the Federal Courts Be Bound by the "Original Intent" of the Framers? *Pol*, Issue 8

Should There Be a "Wall of Separation" Between Church and State? *Pol*, Issue 18

Should the United States Adopt a National Health Insurance Program? *Hea*, Issue 1

Was the New Deal an Effective Answer to the Great Depression? *AH2*, Issue 10

Feminism. *See* **Women's issues**

Food supply

Are Pesticides in Foods Harmful to Human Health? *Hea*, Issue 15

Is the Widespread Use of Pesticides Required to Feed the World's People? *Env*, Issue 10

Foreign policy, American

Could the United States Have Prevented the Fall of South Vietnam? *AH2*, Issue 15

Did the United Nations Earth Summit Produce Useful Results? *Env*, Issue 1

Does Japan Represent a Worldwide Economic Threat? *WP*, Issue 9

Is America Declining? *Pol*, Issue 20

Is a "New World Order" a Realistic Possibility for International Politics? *WP*, Issue 1

Is the Kidnapping of Criminal Suspects from Foreign Countries Justifiable? *WP*, Issue 16

Should Morality and Human Rights Strongly Influence Foreign Policy-Making? *WP*, Issue 17

Should National Self-Interest Be the Basis of American Foreign Policy? *Pol*, Issue 19

Should the Developed North Increase Aid to the Less Developed South? *WP*, Issue 10

Should the Global Arms Trade Be Severely Restricted? *WP*, Issue 11

Should the United States Abandon Its Superpower Role? *WP*, Issue 3

Was Dwight Eisenhower a Great President? *AH2*, Issue 13

Was Early Twentieth-Century American Foreign Policy in the Caribbean Basin Dominated by Economic Concerns? *AH2*, Issue 8

Was Intervention in Somalia Strictly for Humanitarian Purposes? *WP*, Issue 8

Was It Necessary to Drop the Atomic Bomb to End World War II? *AH2*, Issue 12

Was U.S. Foreign Policy in the Early Nineteenth Century Imperialistic? *AH1*, Issue 13

Fuel. *See* **specific sources of fuel**

Future

Are Abundant Resources and an Improved Environment Likely Future Prospects for the World's People? *Env*, Issue 17

Can Hostile Takeovers Be Justified? *BE*, Issue 14

Can Modern Mass Communication Promote a Better World? *MM*, Issue 18

Can Modern War Be Just? *WP*, Issue 20

Does Global Warming Require Immediate Government Action? *Eco*, Issue 17

Does Population Growth Threaten Humanity? *Soc*, Issue 19

Do Ratings Serve the Viewing Public's Interest? *MM*, Issue 13

Do Rich Nations Have an Obligation to Help Poor Nations? *Mor*, Issue 20

Is America's Socioeconomic System Breaking Down? *Soc*, Issue 20

Is a "New World Order" a Realistic Possibility for International Politics? *WP*, Issue 1

Is Capitalism Viable for the Future? *BE*, Issue 1; *Mor*, Issue 5

Is It Possible to Drastically Reduce Defense Expenditures and Remain Secure? *WP*, Issue 13

Is the National Debt a National Liability? *Pol*, Issue 15

Should a New Military-Industrial Complex Be Developed? *Eco*, Issue 18

Should Elderly Offenders Get Lighter Sentences? *CR*, Issue 13

Should National Goals Guide School Performance? *Edu*, Issue 8

Should the United Nations Take on Greater Military Capabilities and Roles? *WP*, Issue 14

Will China Become an Asian Superpower? *WP*, Issue 7

Will Environmental Degradation Be a Feature of International Conflicts in the Future? *Env*, Issue 18

Will the Human Genome Project Lead to Abuses in Genetic Engineering? *Bio*, Issue 20

— G —

Genetics

Are Gender Differences Present at Birth? *Fam*, Issue 1

Are Gender Differences Rooted in the Brain? *HS*, Issue 1

Is Alcoholism Hereditary? *Dru*, Issue 10

Is the "Disease" of Alcoholism a Myth?
Dru, Issue 13; *Psy*, Issue 5

Should Alcoholism Be Treated as a
Disease? *Hea*, Issue 8

Will the Human Genome Project Lead to
Abuses in Genetic Engineering? *Bio*,
Issue 20

Government regulation

Are Federal "Marketing Orders" Unfair?
BE, Issue 13

Are Pesticides in Foods Harmful to
Human Health? *Hea*, Issue 15

Are Private Prisons a Good Idea? *CR*,
Issue 15

Can Abortion Be a Morally Acceptable
Choice? *Hea*, Issue 11

Does Caller ID Invade Privacy? *Leg*,
Issue 16

Does Government Have a Constitutional
Right to Prohibit Certain Kinds of
Sexual Conduct? *HS*, Issue 11

Does the Government Regulate Too
Much? *Pol*, Issue 7

Does the United States Need Socialized
Medicine? *Pol*, Issue 16

Does Welfare Do More Harm Than
Good? *Soc*, Issue 14

Do Smokers Have a Right to Smoke in
Public Places? *Hea*, Issue 7

Hazardous Waste: Are Cleanup and
Control Efforts Succeeding? *Env*,
Issue 11

Helping the Homeless: Do We Need
More Government Regulation? *Soc*,
Issue 12

Is Abortion Protected by the
Constitution? *Leg*, Issue 7

Is Black Self-Help the Solution to Racial
Inequality? *Soc*, Issue 10

Is the Public Best Served by a
Marketplace Approach to Regulation?
MM, Issue 8

Nuclear Waste: Is Yucca Mountain an
Appropriate Site for Permanent Waste
Disposal? *Env*, Issue 13

Product Liability: Was Ford to Blame in
the Pinto Case? *BE*, Issue 11

Should American Farmers Be Forced to
Face Market Competition? *Eco*, Issue 2

Should Eastern European Nations Be
Encouraged to Develop Free Market
Institutions? *BE*, Issue 18

Should Energy Policy Focus on Reducing
the Use of Fossil Fuels? *Env*, Issue 7

Should Pornography Be Protected as Free
Speech? *MM*, Issue 9

Should Pornography Be Protected by the
First Amendment? *Leg*, Issue 8

Should Prostitution Be Decriminalized?
HS, Issue 14

Should Surrogate Motherhood Be
Outlawed? *HS*, Issue 8

Should the Content of Records Be
Censored? *MM*, Issue 5

Should the Government Establish Special
Programs and Policies for Black Youths
and Their Families? *Fam*, Issue 12

Should the Policy Banning Gays from the
Military Be Lifted? *HS*, Issue 13

Should the United States Adopt a
National Health Insurance Program?
Hea, Issue 1

Should the United States Follow the
Canadian Model of a National Health
Program? *Bio*, Issue 19

Was the New Deal an Effective Answer
to the Great Depression? *AH2*, Issue 10

Government spending

Can "Choice" Lead the Way to
Educational Reform? *Edu*, Issue 9

Does the United States Save Enough?
Eco, Issue 12

Do Federal Budget Deficits Matter? *Eco*,
Issue 10

Has the Federal Government Spent
Enough on AIDS Research? *HS*,
Issue 17

Helping the Homeless: Do We Need
More Government Regulation? *Soc*,
Issue 12

Is AIDS Getting More Than Its Share of
Resources and Media Attention? *Hea*
Issue 4

Is America's Socioeconomic System
Breaking Down? *Soc*, Issue 20

Is Incapacitation the Answer to the Crime Problem? *Soc*, Issue 18

Is the National Debt a National Liability? *Pol*, Issue 15

Should American Farmers Be Forced to Face Market Competition? *Eco*, Issue 2

Should a New Military-Industrial Complex Be Developed? *Eco*, Issue 18

Should Bilingual Education Programs Be Abandoned? *Edu*, Issue 15

Should Bilingual Education Programs Be Stopped? *RER*, Issue 7

Should Drugs Be Legalized? *Hea*, Issue 9

Should Health Care for the Elderly Be Limited? *Hea*, Issue 3

Should the Phaseout of Chlorofluorocarbons Be Accelerated to Protect the Ozone Layer from Further Depletion? *Env*, Issue 15

Will Practicing Positive Health Behaviors and Emphasizing Prevention Improve Health? *Hea*, Issue 5

Will the "Edison Project" Prompt Major Reforms? *Edu*, Issue 10

Would Legalizing Drugs Have Beneficial Effects on Society? *Psy*, Issue 19

Groundwater. *See* **Water pollution**

Growth rate. *See* **Economic growth**

Gun control

Should a National Gun Control Policy Be Established? *Leg*, Issue 15

Will Gun Control Reduce Crime? *CR*, Issue 14

— H —

Handguns. *See* **Gun control**

Hazardous waste

Hazardous Waste: Are Cleanup and Control Efforts Succeeding? *Env*, Issue 11

Municipal Waste: Should Recycling Be Promoted as the Key to Refuse Management? *Env*, Issue 12

Nuclear Waste: Is Yucca Mountain an Appropriate Site for Permanent Waste Disposal? *Env*, Issue 13

Health care

Are Chiropractors Legitimate Health Providers? *Hea*, Issue 18

Are Pesticides in Foods Harmful to Human Health? *Hea*, Issue 15

Are the Dangers of Steroids Exaggerated? *Dru*, Issue 17

Are There Limits to Confidentiality? *Bio*, Issue 8

Can Caffeine Be Bad for Your Health? *Dru*, Issue 9

Children of Divorce: Are They at Greater Risk? *Fam*, Issue 15

Did Nestlé Act Irresponsibly in Marketing Infant Formula to the Third World? *BE*, Issue 19

Did the Great Society Fail? *AH2*, Issue 14

Does Exercise Increase Longevity? *Hea*, Issue 14

Does the United States Need Socialized Medicine? *Pol*, Issue 16

Do Physicians Have an Ethical Duty to Treat AIDS Patients? *Bio*, Issue 9

Has the Federal Government Spent Enough on AIDS Research? *HS*, Issue 17

Is Acid Rain a Serious Environmental Problem? *Hea*, Issue 16

Is AIDS Getting More Than Its Share of Resources and Media Attention? *Hea*, Issue 4

Is Cholesterol Reduction an Important Health Priority? *Hea*, Issue 12

Is Litigation the Best Way to Compensate Asbestos Workers for Disease and Risk? *BE*, Issue 9

Is Marriage Good for You? *Fam*, Issue 4

Is Our State of Mind Responsible for Our State of Health? *Psy*, Issue 6

Is Passive Smoking Harmful to Nonsmokers? *Dru*, Issue 8

Is Street Crime More Serious Than White-Collar Crime? *CR*, Issue 4

Is the War on Drugs Misdirected? *Dru*, Issue 5

Should All Children Be Immunized Against Childhood Diseases? *Hea*, Issue 17

Should Doctors Be Able to Refuse Demands for "Futile" Treatment? *Bio*, Issue 11

Should Drug Use by Pregnant Women Be Considered Child Abuse? *Dru*, Issue 7

Should Health Care for the Elderly Be Limited? *Bio*, Issue 18; *Hea*, Issue 3

Should HIV-Infected Health Care Workers Be Restricted from Performing Some Procedures? *Bio*, Issue 10

Should Medical Patients Be Permitted to Use Marijuana? *Dru*, Issue 2

Should Needle Exchange Programs Be Promoted? *Dru*, Issue 6

Should RU 486 Be Legalized? *HS*, Issue 6

Should Schools Distribute Condoms? *HS*, Issue 7

Should the United States Adopt a National Health Insurance Program? *Hea*, Issue 1

Should the United States Follow the Canadian Model of a National Health Program? *Bio*, Issue 19

Should Tobacco Advertising Be Banned? *BE*, Issue 12

Should Tobacco Advertising Be Prohibited? *Dru*, Issue 12

Will Practicing Positive Health Behaviors and Emphasizing Prevention Improve Health? *Hea*, Issue 5

Health insurance

Are Chiropractors Legitimate Health Providers? *Hea*, Issue 18

Does the United States Need Socialized Medicine? *Pol*, Issue 16

Is Marriage Good for You? *Fam*, Issue 4

Should Health Care for the Elderly Be Limited? *Bio*, Issue 18; *Hea*, Issue 3

Should the United States Adopt a National Health Insurance Program? *Hea*, Issue 1

Should the United States Follow the Canadian Model of a National Health Program? *Bio*, Issue 19

Herbicides. *See* **Toxic chemicals**

Heredity. *See* **Genetics**

Homosexuality

Does Government Have a Constitutional Right to Prohibit Certain Kinds of Sexual Conduct? *HS*, Issue 11

Should Gays and Lesbians Fight for the Right to Marry? *Fam*, Issue 5

Should Homosexuality Bar a Parent from Being Awarded Custody of a Child? *Leg*, Issue 11

Should Homosexuality Be Accepted by Society? *Mor*, Issue 11

Should Society Recognize Gay Marriages? *HS*, Issue 15

Should the Policy Banning Gays from the Military Be Lifted? *HS*, Issue 13

Human development

Abortion and the "Pro-Life" v. "Pro-Choice" Debate: Should the Human Fetus Be Considered a Person? *HS*, Issue 9

Is Abortion Immoral? *Mor*, Issue 13

Is Day Care Harmful? *Psy*, Issue 11

Is Mainstreaming Beneficial to All? *Edu*, Issue 17

Is Morality Relative to Culture? *Mor*, Issue 2

Is Morality Subjective? *Mor*, Issue 3

Is Parenthood Necessary for a Good Marriage? *Fam*, Issue 7

Is There a World Population Crisis? *WP*, Issue 19

Should Homosexuality Be Accepted by Society? *Mor*, Issue 11

Will the Human Genome Project Lead to Abuses in Genetic Engineering? *Bio*, Issue 20

Human rights. *See also* **Bill of Rights; Civil rights**

Abortion and the "Pro-Life" v. "Pro-Choice" Debate: Should the Human Fetus Be Considered a Person? *HS*, Issue 9

Are Global Standards of Human Rights Desirable? *WP*, Issue 18

Are Human Rights Basic to Justice? *CR*, Issue 18; *Mor*, Issue 18

Can Abortion Be a Morally Acceptable Choice? *Hea*, Issue 11

Did Capitalist Values Motivate the American Colonists? *AH1*, Issue 4

Does Arrest Reduce Domestic Violence? *Fam*, Issue 10

Does Government Have a Constitutional Right to Prohibit Certain Kinds of Sexual Conduct? *HS*, Issue 11

Does Society Have an Obligation to Care for the Less Well Off? *Mor*, Issue 9

Is It Ethical for Scientists to Use Data from the Nazi Experiments? *Bio*, Issue 14

Is It Ever Morally Right to Withhold Food and Water from Dying Patients? *Bio*, Issue 7

Is Patriotism a Virtue? *Mor*, Issue 19

Is Terrorism Ever Justified? *Mor*, Issue 17

Is There an Ethnic Revolt Against the Melting Pot? *RER*, Issue 16

Should Animals Be Liberated? *Mor*, Issue 6

Should Eastern European Nations Be Encouraged to Develop Free Market Institutions? *BE*, Issue 18

Should Morality and Human Rights Strongly Influence Foreign Policy-Making? *WP*, Issue 17

Should National Self-Interest Be the Basis of American Foreign Policy? *Pol*, Issue 19

Should Psychotherapists Allow Suicide? *Psy*, Issue 14

Should Research With Aborted Fetal Tissue Be Banned? *Bio*, Issue 15

Should Schools Determine What Is Learned? *Edu*, Issue 2

Should Society Recognize Gay Marriages? *HS*, Issue 15

Should Thawing Unused Frozen Embryos Be Permitted? *Bio*, Issue 3

Should There Be a Market in Body Parts? *Bio*, Issue 17

Will the Human Genome Project Lead to Abuses in Genetic Engineering? *Bio*, Issue 20

—I—

Immigration

Are Asian Americans a "Model Minority"? *RER*, Issue 3

Do Italian Americans Reject Assimilation? *RER*, Issue 4

Is Italy Solving Its Immigration Problem? *RER*, Issue 15

Should Bilingual Education Programs Be Abandoned? *Edu*, Issue 15

Should Bilingual Education Programs Be Stopped? *RER*, Issue 7

Should Literacy Be Based on Traditional Culture? *Edu*, Issue 13

Was Colonial Culture Uniquely American? *AH1*, Issue 1

Were the Immigrants' Old World Cultures Destroyed as They Adjusted to American Life? *AH2*, Issue 4

Income taxes. *See* **Tax structure**

Indians, American. *See* **Native Americans**

Industrial policy

Are Programs of Preferential Treatment Unjustifiable? *BE*, Issue 5

Can Corporate Codes of Ethics Promote Ethical Behavior? *BE*, Issue 2

Can Whistle-Blowing Be Clearly Justified? *BE*, Issue 7

Do Employees Have a Moral Right to Meaningful Work? *BE*, Issue 4

Is Drug Testing an Unwarranted Invasion of Employee Privacy? *BE*, Issue 8

Is Street Crime More Serious Than White-Collar Crime? *CR*, Issue 4

Should the "Pay-for-Performance" System Be Overhauled? *BE*, Issue 3

Was the American Labor Movement Radical? *AH2*, Issue 3

Industry. *See also* **specific industry**

Are Federal "Marketing Orders" Unfair? *BE*, Issue 13

Are Profits the Only Business of Business? *Eco*, Issue 1

Are Programs of Preferential Treatment Unjustifiable? *BE*, Issue 5

Can Corporate Codes of Ethics Promote Ethical Behavior? *BE*, Issue 2

Can Current Pollution Strategies Improve Air Quality? *BE*, Issue 17; *Env*, Issue 8

Can Hostile Takeovers Be Justified? *BE*, Issue 14

Can Incentives Devised by Industrial Nations Combat Tropical Deforestation? *Env*, Issue 14

Can Network News Survive? *MM*, Issue 16

Can Whistle-Blowing Be Clearly Justified? *BE*, Issue 7

Did Nestlé Act Irresponsibly in Marketing Infant Formula to the Third World? *BE*, Issue 19

Did the Progressives Fail? *AH2*, Issue 7

Did the United Nations Earth Summit Produce Useful Results? *Env*, Issue 1

Did World War II Liberate American Women? *AH2*, Issue 11

Do Employees Have a Moral Right to Meaningful Work? *BE*, Issue 4

Do Employers Have an Obligation to Provide Parental Leave Policies for Their Employees? *BE*, Issue 6

Does Drug Testing Violate Civil Rights? *Dru*, Issue 3

Does Global Warming Require Immediate Government Action? *Eco*, Issue 17

Does Insider Trading Serve a Useful Purpose? *BE*, Issue 15

Does Technology Transfer by Multinational Firms Benefit the Development of Third World Nations? *MM*, Issue 17

Does the Global Environmental Movement Threaten Economic Prosperity? *WP*, Issue 12

Do Hostile Takeovers Harm Society? *Eco*, Issue 6

Do the News Media Have a Liberal Bias? *Pol*, Issue 4

Hazardous Waste: Are Cleanup and Control Efforts Succeeding? *Env*, Issue 11

Is Advertising Fundamentally Deceptive? *BE*, Issue 10

Is Affirmative Action Morally Justifiable? *Mor*, Issue 16

Is Affirmative Action Reverse Discrimination? *Pol*, Issue 11

Is American Government Dominated by Big Business? *Pol*, Issue 1

Is Bribery Ever Justified? *BE*, Issue 20

Is Capitalism Viable for the Future? *BE*, Issue 1; *Mor*, Issue 5

Is Drug Testing an Unwarranted Invasion of Employee Privacy? *BE*, Issue 8

Is Economic Inequality Beneficial to Society? *Soc*, Issue 8

Is Government Dominated by Big Business? *Soc*, Issue 13

Is Japan a Threat to America's Economic and National Security? *Eco*, Issue 16

Is Litigation the Best Way to Compensate Asbestos Workers for Disease and Risk? *BE*, Issue 9

Is Mass Transit the Answer to Improving U.S. Energy Efficiency? *Eco*, Issue 7

Is Population Control the Key to Preventing Environmental Deterioration? *Env*, Issue 4

Is Sexual Harassment a Pervasive Problem? *HS*, Issue 16

Is Sexual Harassment a Pervasive Problem in America? *Soc*, Issue 6

Is Street Crime More Harmful Than White-Collar Crime? *Soc*, Issue 16

Is Street Crime More Serious Than White-Collar Crime? *CR*, Issue 4

Is the Legal System Damaging the American Economy? *Leg*, Issue 1

Is the Widespread Use of Pesticides Required to Feed the World's People? *Env*, Issue 10

Media Monopolies: Does Concentration of Ownership Jeopardize Media Content? *MM*, Issue 15

Product Liability: Was Ford to Blame in the Pinto Case? *BE*, Issue 11

Should a New Military-Industrial Complex Be Developed? *Eco*, Issue 18

Should Industry Be Held Accountable for Acid Rain? *BE*, Issue 16

Should the Federal Reserve Target Zero Inflation? *Eco*, Issue 11

Should the "Pay-for-Performance" System Be Overhauled? *BE*, Issue 3

Should the Phaseout of Chlorofluorocarbons Be Accelerated to Protect the Ozone Layer from Further Depletion? *Env*, Issue 15

Should the United States Protect Domestic Industries from Foreign Competition? *Eco*, Issue 15

Should Tobacco Advertising Be Banned? *BE*, Issue 12

Should Traditional Families Be Preserved? *Soc*, Issue 7

Was City Government in Late Nineteenth-Century America a "Conspicuous Failure"? *AH2*, Issue 6

Was the American Labor Movement Radical? *AH2*, Issue 3

Were Nineteenth-Century Entrepreneurs Robber Barons? *AH2*, Issue 2

Were the Immigrants' Old World Cultures Destroyed as They Adjusted to American Life? *AH2*, Issue 4

Will the "Edison Project" Prompt Major Reforms? *Edu*, Issue 10

Will the "Greening" of Multinational Corporations Lead to Environmental Improvements? *Env*, Issue 6

Would a "Mommy Track" Benefit Employed Women? *Fam*, Issue 11; *Soc*, Issue 5

Inequality

Are Extramarital Relationships Becoming More Frequent? *Fam*, Issue 14

Are Media Messages About Women Improving? *MM*, Issue 4

Are Positive Images of African Americans Increasing in the Media? *MM*, Issue 2; *RER*, Issue 9

Are Programs of Preferential Treatment Unjustifiable? *BE*, Issue 5

Are Women Paid Less Than Men Because Their Working Conditions Are More Favorable? *Eco*, Issue 4

Did the Progressives Fail? *AH2*, Issue 7

Does a Common Curriculum Promote Equality? *Edu*, Issue 6

Does Technology Transfer by Multinational Firms Benefit the Development of Third World Nations? *MM*, Issue 17

Does Tracking Create Educational Inequality? *Edu*, Issue 16

Has Individualism Become Excessive? *Soc*, Issue 3

Is Affirmative Action Reverse Discrimination? *RER*, Issue 12; *Soc*, Issue 11

Is Black Self-Help the Solution to Racial Inequality? *Soc*, Issue 10

Is Economic Inequality Beneficial to Society? *Soc*, Issue 8

Is Feminism a Harmful Ideology? *Soc*, Issue 4

Is Punishment Good Crime Control? *CR*, Issue 5

Should Animals Be Liberated? *Mor*, Issue 6

Should Homosexuality Be Accepted by Society? *Mor*, Issue 11

Should Minorities Continue to Demand More Rights? *RER*, Issue 10

Should the Federal Reserve Target Zero Inflation? *Eco*, Issue 11

Will Reforming School Funding Remove "Savage Inequalities"? *Edu*, Issue 7

Would a "Mommy Track" Benefit Employed Women? *Fam*, Issue 11; *Soc*, Issue 5

Would Women in Combat Weaken National Security? *WP*, Issue 15

Insanity. *See* **Mental illness**

Insanity defense. *See* **Criminal behavior**

Intelligence. *See also* **Learning**

Can Computers Help Us Understand the Human Mind? *Psy*, Issue 8

Can Intelligence Be Increased? *Psy*, Issue 9

Intelligence Quotient (IQ). *See*
Intelligence
Interest groups
Does Congress Need to Be Radically
Reformed? *Pol*, Issue 5
Do Political Action Committees
Undermine Democracy? *Pol*, Issue 3
Is American Government Dominated by
Big Business? *Pol*, Issue 1
International economy
Are Aggressive International Efforts
Needed to Slow Global Warming? *Env*,
Issue 16
Does Japan Represent a Worldwide
Economic Threat? *WP*, Issue 9
Is America Declining? *Pol*, Issue 20
Is America's Socioeconomic System
Breaking Down? *Soc*, Issue 20
Is Japan a Threat to America's Economic
and National Security? *Eco*, Issue 16
Is Mass Transit the Answer to Improving
U.S. Energy Efficiency? *Eco*, Issue 7
Is the Legal System Damaging the
American Economy? *Leg*, Issue 1
Should National Self-Interest Be the Basis
of American Foreign Policy? *Pol*,
Issue 19
Should the Developed North Increase
Aid to the Less Developed South? *WP*,
Issue 10
Should the United States Protect
Domestic Industries from Foreign
Competition? *Eco*, Issue 15
Will the European Community Increase
Its Level of Integration? *WP*, Issue 4
Will the North American Free Trade
Agreement Benefit All Its Member
Countries? *WP*, Issue 5
International law
Are Aggressive International Efforts
Needed to Slow Global Warming? *Env*,
Issue 16
Is a "New World Order" a Realistic
Possibility for International Politics?
WP, Issue 1
Is the Kidnapping of Criminal Suspects
from Foreign Countries Justifiable? *WP*,
Issue 16

International relations
Can Modern Mass Communication
Promote a Better World? *MM*, Issue 18
Did President Reagan Win the Cold War?
AH2, Issue 17
Did the United Nations Earth Summit
Produce Useful Results? *Env*, Issue 1
Is a "New World Order" a Realistic
Possibility for International Politics?
WP, Issue 1
Is Bribery Ever Justified? *BE*, Issue 20
Should Morality and Human Rights
Strongly Influence Foreign
Policy-Making? *WP*, Issue 17
Should National Self-Interest Be the Basis
of American Foreign Policy? *Pol*,
Issue 19
Should the United States Abandon Its
Superpower Role? *WP*, Issue 3
Was Intervention in Somalia Strictly for
Humanitarian Purposes? *WP*, Issue 8
Will China Become an Asian
Superpower? *WP*, Issue 7
Will the European Community Increase
Its Level of Integration? *WP*, Issue 4
International trade. *See* Trade

—J—

Jobs. *See* Employment; Unemployment
Journalism
Are Liberal Values Propagated by the
News Media? *Soc*, Issue 2
Can Network News Survive? *MM*,
Issue 16
Is Objectivity Still a Criterion for
Journalism? *MM*, Issue 7
Media Monopolies: Does Concentration
of Ownership Jeopardize Media
Content? *MM*, Issue 15
Should the Names of Rape Victims Be
Published? *MM*, Issue 6
Judicial system
Can States Restrict the Right to Die? *Leg*,
Issue 10
Is Capital Punishment Justified? *Pol*,
Issue 10

Is Criminal Justice Free of Systemic Racism? *CR*, Issue 6

Is Litigation the Best Way to Compensate Asbestos Workers for Disease and Risk? *BE*, Issue 9

Is the Legal System Damaging the American Economy? *Leg*, Issue 1

Product Liability: Was Ford to Blame in the Pinto Case? *BE*, Issue 11

Should Homosexuality Bar a Parent from Being Awarded Custody of a Child? *Leg*, Issue 11

Should Homosexuality Be Accepted by Society? *Mor*, Issue 11

Should Plea Bargaining Be Abolished? *Leg*, Issue 3

Should Plea Bargaining Continue to Be an Accepted Practice? *CR*, Issue 8

Should the Drinking Age Remain at 21? *Dru*, Issue 4

Should the Exclusionary Rule Be Abolished? *Leg*, Issue 13

Should the Federal Courts Be Bound by the "Original Intent" of the Framers? *Pol*, Issue 8

Will Tougher Sentencing Reduce Crime? *Pol*, Issue 9

Juvenile crime

Are Private Prisons a Good Idea? *CR*, Issue 15

Juvenile Justice: Are Kids "Getting Away With Murder"? *CR*, Issue 7

— K —

Kinship. *See* **Family structure; Marriage**

— L —

Labor force

Are Hispanics Making Significant Progress? *RER*, Issue 13

Are Women Paid Less Than Men Because Their Working Conditions Are More Favorable? *Eco*, Issue 4

Can Whistle-Blowing Be Clearly Justified? *BE*, Issue 7

Did World War II Liberate American Women? *AH2*, Issue 11

Do Employees Have a Moral Right to Meaningful Work? *BE*, Issue 4

Do Employers Have an Obligation to Provide Parental Leave Policies for Their Employees? *BE*, Issue 6

Does Technology Transfer by Multinational Firms Benefit the Development of Third World Nations? *MM*, Issue 17

Do Federal Budget Deficits Matter? *Eco*, Issue 10

Is National Service at Odds With American National Interest? *Eco*, Issue 3

Should the "Pay-for-Performance" System Be Overhauled? *BE*, Issue 3

Was the American Labor Movement Radical? *AH2*, Issue 3

Would a "Mommy Track" Benefit Employed Women? *Fam*, Issue 11; *Soc*, Issue 5

Latin America

Was Early Twentieth-Century American Foreign Policy in the Caribbean Basin Dominated by Economic Concerns? *AH2*, Issue 8

Was U.S. Foreign Policy in the Early Nineteenth Century Imperialistic? *AH1*, Issue 13

Law enforcement. *See also* **Crime prevention; Police**

Does Arrest Reduce Domestic Violence? *Fam*, Issue 10

Does Drug Testing Violate Civil Rights? *Dru*, Issue 3

Is It Possible to Be Pro-Life and Pro-Choice? *Fam*, Issue 6

Is the Kidnapping of Criminal Suspects from Foreign Countries Justifiable? *WP*, Issue 16

Is the War on Drugs Misdirected? *Dru*, Issue 5

Should a National Gun Control Policy Be Established? *Leg*, Issue 15

Should "Battered Wife Syndrome" Be Barred as a Defense in a Murder Case? *Leg*, Issue 14

Should Drugs Be Legalized? *Dru*, Issue 1; *Hea*, Issue 9; *Mor*, Issue 8; *Pol*, Issue 13; *Soc*, Issue 17

Should Prostitution Be Decriminalized? *HS*, Issue 14

Should the Exclusionary Rule Be Abolished? *Leg*, Issue 13

Will Drug Legalization Help the Criminal Justice System? *CR*, Issue 17

Would Legalizing Drugs Have Beneficial Effects on Society? *Psy*, Issue 19

Law enforcement officers. *See* **Police**

Law of the Sea. *See* **International law**

Lawyers
Is Litigation the Best Way to Compensate Asbestos Workers for Disease and Risk? *BE*, Issue 9

Is the Legal System Damaging the American Economy? *Leg*, Issue 1

Product Liability: Was Ford to Blame in the Pinto Case? *BE*, Issue 11

Should Lawyers Be Prohibited from Presenting a False Case? *Leg*, Issue 2

Should Plea Bargaining Be Abolished? *Leg*, Issue 3

Should Plea Bargaining Continue to Be an Accepted Practice? *CR*, Issue 8

Learning
Can Intelligence Be Increased? *Psy*, Issue 9

Do Black Students Need an Afrocentric Curriculum? *Edu*, Issue 14

Does a Common Curriculum Promote Equality? *Edu*, Issue 6

Does Tracking Create Educational Inequality? *Edu*, Issue 16

Do Gender Differences Originate from Biological Factors? *Psy*, Issue 10

Is Home Schooling a Viable Alternative? *Edu*, Issue 11

Is Mainstreaming Beneficial to All? *Edu*, Issue 17

Is Workfare a Good Substitute for Welfare? *Eco*, Issue 14

Should Behaviorism Shape Educational Practices? *Edu*, Issue 3

Should Literacy Be Based on Traditional Culture? *Edu*, Issue 13

Should National Goals Guide School Performance? *Edu*, Issue 8

Should Schooling Be Based on Social Experiences? *Edu*, Issue 1

Should Schools Determine What Is Learned? *Edu*, Issue 2

Should Schools of Education Be Abolished? *Edu*, Issue 20

Legislation
Are Women Paid Less Than Men Because Their Working Conditions Are More Favorable? *Eco*, Issue 4

Can Experiments Using Animals Be Justified? *Psy*, Issue 3

Does Caller ID Invade Privacy? *Leg*, Issue 16

Do Hostile Takeovers Harm Society? *Eco*, Issue 6

Do Parental Notification Laws Benefit Minors Seeking Abortions? *HS*, Issue 12

Do Physicians Have an Ethical Duty to Treat AIDS Patients? *Bio*, Issue 9

Is Mainstreaming Beneficial to All? *Edu*, Issue 17

Is National Service at Odds With American National Interest? *Eco*, Issue 3

Is the Public Best Served by a Marketplace Approach to Regulation? *MM*, Issue 8

Should American Farmers Be Forced to Face Market Competition? *Eco*, Issue 2

Should a National Gun Control Policy Be Established? *Leg*, Issue 15

Should Pornography Be Protected as Free Speech? *MM*, Issue 9

Should Prostitution Be Decriminalized? *HS*, Issue 14

Should Risk Assessment Methods Be Used to Set Environmental Priorities? *Env*, Issue 5

Should Society Recognize Gay Marriages? *HS*, Issue 15

Should the Capital Gains Tax Be Lowered? *Eco,* Issue 13

Should the Endangered Species Act Be Reauthorized? *Env,* Issue 3

Should the Federal Reserve Target Zero Inflation? *Eco,* Issue 11

Should the Policy Banning Gays from the Military Be Lifted? *HS,* Issue 13

Less developed countries

Are Global Standards of Human Rights Desirable? *WP,* Issue 18

Are Human Rights Basic to Justice? *CR,* Issue 18; *Mor,* Issue 18

Can Incentives Devised by Industrial Nations Combat Tropical Deforestation? *Env,* Issue 14

Did Nestlé Act Irresponsibly in Marketing Infant Formula to the Third World? *BE,* Issue 19

Does "Multiculturalism" Debase the Curriculum? *Soc,* Issue 1

Does Technology Transfer by Multinational Firms Benefit the Development of Third World Nations? *MM,* Issue 17

Do Rich Nations Have an Obligation to Help Poor Nations? *Mor,* Issue 20

Is Italy Solving Its Immigration Problem? *RER,* Issue 15

Should the Developed North Increase Aid to the Less Developed South? *WP,* Issue 10

Should the United Nations Take on Greater Military Capabilities and Roles? *WP,* Issue 14

Liberalism

Are Liberal Values Propagated by the News Media? *Soc,* Issue 2

Do the News Media Have a Liberal Bias? *Pol,* Issue 4

Life expectancy

Can Large Doses of Vitamins Improve Health? *Hea,* Issue 13

Does Exercise Increase Longevity? *Hea,* Issue 14

Does Population Growth Threaten Humanity? *Soc,* Issue 19

Is Cholesterol Reduction an Important Health Priority? *Hea,* Issue 12

Should Health Care for the Elderly Be Limited? *Bio,* Issue 18

Lobbyists. *See* **Interest groups**

Lobotomy. *See* **Mental illness**

Local government

Is Choice a Panacea for the Ills of Public Education? *Eco,* Issue 8

Is "Hate Speech" Fully Protected by the Constitution? *Leg,* Issue 5

Should Bilingual Education Programs Be Abandoned? *Edu,* Issue 15

Should Bilingual Education Programs Be Stopped? *RER,* Issue 7

Should National Goals Guide School Performance? *Edu,* Issue 8

Was City Government in Late Nineteenth-Century America a "Conspicuous Failure"? *AH2,* Issue 6

— M —

Marriage

Are Children of Divorced Parents at Greater Risk? *Psy,* Issue 12

Are Extramarital Relationships Becoming More Frequent? *Fam,* Issue 14

Children of Divorce: Are They at Greater Risk? *Fam,* Issue 15

Did the Westward Movement Transform the Traditional Roles of Women in the Late Nineteenth Century? *AH2,* Issue 5

Does Arrest Reduce Domestic Violence? *Fam,* Issue 10

Does Sexual Infidelity Destroy a Relationship? *HS,* Issue 4

Do Stepchildren Need Special Policies and Programs on Their Behalf? *Fam,* Issue 16

Husband Battering: Is It a Social Problem? *Fam,* Issue 13

Is Feminism a Positive Value for Society? *Mor,* Issue 7

Is Marriage Good for You? *Fam,* Issue 4

Is Parenthood Necessary for a Good Marriage? *Fam,* Issue 7

Is the Success of Remarriage Doomed?
Fam, Issue 17

Should "Battered Wife Syndrome" Be
Barred as a Defense in a Murder Case?
Leg, Issue 14

Should Gays and Lesbians Fight for the
Right to Marry? *Fam*, Issue 5

Should Pregnant Teens Marry the Fathers
of Their Babies? *Fam*, Issue 9

Should Society Recognize Gay
Marriages? *HS*, Issue 15

Should Surrogate Parenting Be Permitted
for Infertile Couples? *Fam*, Issue 8

Media. *See also* **Journalism; Newspapers;
Television**

Are American Values Shaped by the
Mass Media? *MM*, Issue 1

Are Liberal Values Propagated by the
News Media? *Soc*, Issue 2

Are Media Messages About Women
Improving? *MM*, Issue 4

Are Positive Images of African
Americans Increasing in the Media?
MM, Issue 2; *RER*, Issue 9

Are the Results of Polls Misleading?
MM, Issue 12

Can Modern Mass Communication
Promote a Better World? *MM*, Issue 18

Can Network News Survive? *MM*,
Issue 16

Do Presidential TV Ads Manipulate
Voters? *MM*, Issue 10

Do Ratings Serve the Viewing Public's
Interest? *MM*, Issue 13

Do Speech Codes Suppress Freedom of
Expression? *MM*, Issue 11

Do the News Media Have a Liberal Bias?
Pol, Issue 4

Is Acid Rain a Serious Environmental
Problem? *Hea*, Issue 16

Is Advertising Ethical? *MM*, Issue 14

Is Advertising Fundamentally Deceptive?
BE, Issue 10

Is Objectivity Still a Criterion for
Journalism? *MM*, Issue 7

Is Pornography Harmful? *HS*, Issue 5

Is Television Harmful for Children? *MM*,
Issue 3

Is the Public Best Served by a
Marketplace Approach to Regulation?
MM, Issue 8

Media Monopolies: Does Concentration
of Ownership Jeopardize Media
Content? *MM*, Issue 15

Should Alcohol Advertising Be Limited?
Dru, Issue 14

Should the Content of Records Be
Censored? *MM*, Issue 5

Should the Names of Rape Victims Be
Published? *MM*, Issue 6

Should Tobacco Advertising Be Banned?
BE, Issue 12

Should Tobacco Advertising Be
Prohibited? *Dru*, Issue 12

Was Intervention in Somalia Strictly for
Humanitarian Purposes? *WP*, Issue 8

Medical care. *See* **Health care**

Medical costs

Is Marriage Good for You? *Fam*, Issue 4

Should All Children Be Immunized
Against Childhood Diseases? *Hea*,
Issue 17

Should Doctors Be Able to Refuse
Demands for "Futile" Treatment? *Bio*,
Issue 11

Should Health Care for the Elderly Be
Limited? *Bio*, Issue 18; *Hea*, Issue 3

Should the United States Follow the
Canadian Model of a National Health
Program? *Bio*, Issue 19

Medicine

Are Chiropractors Legitimate Health
Providers? *Hea*, Issue 18

Are There Limits to Confidentiality? *Bio*,
Issue 8

Can a Positive Mental Attitude
Overcome Disease? *Hea*, Issue 6

Can States Restrict the Right to Die? *Leg*,
Issue 10

Do Diagnostic Labels Hinder the
Effective Treatment of Persons With
Mental Disorders? *Psy*, Issue 15

Does Exercise Increase Longevity? *Hea*,
Issue 14

Does the United States Need Socialized
Medicine? *Pol*, Issue 16

Do Physicians Have an Ethical Duty to Treat AIDS Patients? *Bio*, Issue 9

Is Criminal Behavior Biologically Determined? *CR*, Issue 3

Is Electroconvulsive Therapy Safe? *Psy*, Issue 17

Is Euthanasia Immoral? *Mor*, Issue 15

Is It Ethical for Scientists to Use Data from the Nazi Experiments? *Bio*, Issue 14

Is It Ethical to Withhold the Truth from Dying Patients? *Bio*, Issue 5

Is It Ever Morally Right to Withhold Food and Water from Dying Patients? *Bio*, Issue 7

Is It Possible to Be Pro-Life and Pro-Choice? *Fam*, Issue 6

Is It Unethical to Implant Animal Parts in Humans? *Bio*, Issue 13

Is Our State of Mind Responsible for Our State of Health? *Psy*, Issue 6

Is Physician-Assisted Suicide Ethical? *Bio*, Issue 6

Should All Children Be Immunized Against Childhood Diseases? *Hea*, Issue 17

Should Animal Experimentation Be Permitted? *Bio*, Issue 12

Should Doctors Be Able to Refuse Demands for "Futile" Treatment? *Bio*, Issue 11

Should Doctors Ever Help Terminally Ill Patients Commit Suicide? *Hea*, Issue 2

Should Health Care for the Elderly Be Limited? *Bio*, Issue 18; *Hea*, Issue 3

Should HIV-Infected Health Care Workers Be Restricted from Performing Some Procedures? *Bio*, Issue 10

Should Medical Patients Be Permitted to Use Marijuana? *Dru*, Issue 2

Should Psychologists Be Allowed to Prescribe Drugs? *Psy*, Issue 18

Should Psychotherapy Include Religious Values? *Psy*, Issue 16

Should RU 486 Be Legalized? *HS*, Issue 6

Should There Be a Market in Body Parts? *Bio*, Issue 17

Should the United States Adopt a National Health Insurance Program? *Hea*, Issue 1

Will Practicing Positive Health Behaviors and Emphasizing Prevention Improve Health? *Hea*, Issue 5

Mental functions

Can Computers Help Us Understand the Human Mind? *Psy*, Issue 8

Has Science Discredited ESP? *Psy*, Issue 7

Is Our Behavior Primarily Determined by Biological Processes? *Psy*, Issue 4

Is Our State of Mind Responsible for Our State of Health? *Psy*, Issue 6

Should Psychologists Study Memory Through Controlled Laboratory Experiments? *Psy*, Issue 2

Mental health

Can a Positive Mental Attitude Overcome Disease? *Hea*, Issue 6

Mental illness

Are Children of Divorced Parents at Greater Risk? *Psy*, Issue 12

Are Rent Controls the Cause of America's Homelessness? *Eco*, Issue 5

Children of Divorce: Are They at Greater Risk? *Fam*, Issue 15

Do Diagnostic Labels Hinder the Effective Treatment of Persons With Mental Disorders? *Psy*, Issue 15

Is Electroconvulsive Therapy Safe? *Psy*, Issue 17

Should Psychologists Be Allowed to Prescribe Drugs? *Psy*, Issue 18

Should Psychotherapists Allow Suicide? *Psy*, Issue 14

Should Psychotherapy Include Religious Values? *Psy*, Issue 16

Middle class

Are Hispanics Making Significant Progress? *RER*, Issue 13

Did President Jefferson Outfederalize the Federalists? *AH1*, Issue 9

Should the Insanity Defense Be Abolished? *Leg*, Issue 17

Was Antebellum Reform Motivated Primarily by Humanitarian Goals? *AH1*, Issue 11

Was the Ku Klux Klan of the 1920s an Extremist Movement? *AH2*, Issue 9

Migration. *See* **Immigration**

Military

Can Modern War Be Just? *WP*, Issue 20

Could the United States Have Prevented the Fall of South Vietnam? *AH2*, Issue 15

Is It Possible to Drastically Reduce Defense Expenditures and Remain Secure? *WP*, Issue 13

Is National Service at Odds With American National Interest? *Eco*, Issue 3

Should a New Military-Industrial Complex Be Developed? *Eco*, Issue 18

Should the Policy Banning Gays from the Military Be Lifted? *HS*, Issue 13

Should the United Nations Take on Greater Military Capabilities and Roles? *WP*, Issue 14

Was Early Twentieth-Century American Foreign Policy in the Caribbean Basin Dominated by Economic Concerns? *AH2*, Issue 8

Was Intervention in Somalia Strictly for Humanitarian Purposes? *WP*, Issue 8

Was It Necessary to Drop the Atomic Bomb to End World War II? *AH2*, Issue 12

Will Environmental Degradation Be a Feature of International Conflicts in the Future? *Env*, Issue 18

Would Women in Combat Weaken National Security? *WP*, Issue 15

Minorities

Are Asian Americans a "Model Minority"? *RER*, Issue 3

Are Hispanics Making Significant Progress? *RER*, Issue 13

Are Nonethnic Scholars Able to Successfully Research Minorities? *RER*, Issue 1

Are Positive Images of African Americans Increasing in the Media? *MM*, Issue 2; *RER*, Issue 9

Are Programs of Preferential Treatment Unjustifiable? *BE*, Issue 5

Can Schools Prevent Urban Dropouts? *Edu*, Issue 12

Do Cultural Differences Between Home and School Explain the High Dropout Rates for American Indian Students? *RER*, Issue 6

Do Employers Have an Obligation to Provide Parental Leave Policies for Their Employees? *BE*, Issue 6

Does "Multiculturalism" Debase the Curriculum? *Soc*, Issue 1

Is Affirmative Action Reverse Discrimination? *Pol*, Issue 11

Is Criminal Behavior Biologically Determined? *CR*, Issue 3

Is Research on Criminal Careers Helpful? *CR*, Issue 10

Is Systemic Racism in Criminal Justice a Myth? *RER*, Issue 14

Is the Concept of the Underclass Useful for Studying Race and Ethnic Relations? *RER*, Issue 2

Should Alcohol Advertising Be Limited? *Dru*, Issue 14

Should Bilingual Education Programs Be Abandoned? *Edu*, Issue 15

Should Bilingual Education Programs Be Stopped? *RER*, Issue 7

Should Black Women Join the Feminist Movement? *RER*, Issue 8

Should Drug Use by Pregnant Women Be Considered Child Abuse? *Dru*, Issue 7

Should "Hate Speech" Be Protected? *Pol*, Issue 12

Should "Hate Speech" Be Tolerated? *Mor*, Issue 10

Should Minorities Continue to Demand More Rights? *RER*, Issue 10

Should the Government Establish Special Programs and Policies for Black Youths and Their Families? *Fam*, Issue 12

Should We Call Ourselves African Americans? *RER*, Issue 5

Were Southern Slaveholding Women Covert Abolitionists? *AH1*, Issue 14

Moral issues. *See* **Ethical issues**

Mothering. *See also* **Fathering; Parenting; Surrogate parenting**
Are Women Only Victims in Their Roles as Social Support Providers? *Fam*, Issue 2
Is Day Care Harmful? *Psy*, Issue 11
Should Commercial Surrogate Motherhood Be Banned? *Bio*, Issue 4
Should Pregnant Teens Marry the Fathers of Their Babies? *Fam*, Issue 9
Should Surrogate Motherhood Be Outlawed? *HS*, Issue 8
Should Surrogate Parenting Be Permitted for Infertile Couples? *Fam*, Issue 8
Would a "Mommy Track" Benefit Employed Women? *Fam*, Issue 11; *Soc*, Issue 5

— N —

Native Americans
Do Cultural Differences Between Home and School Explain the High Dropout Rates for American Indian Students? *RER*, Issue 6
Is There an Ethnic Revolt Against the Melting Pot? *RER*, Issue 16
Was Colonial Culture Uniquely American? *AH1*, Issue 1
Was Race a Central Factor in the Colonists' Attitudes Toward Native Americans? *AH1*, Issue 2

Natural resources
Are Abundant Resources and an Improved Environment Likely Future Prospects for the World's People? *Env*, Issue 17
Can Current Pollution Strategies Improve Air Quality? *BE*, Issue 17; *Env*, Issue 8
Can Incentives Devised by Industrial Nations Combat Tropical Deforestation? *Env*, Issue 14
Does Population Growth Threaten Humanity? *Soc*, Issue 19

Does Wilderness Have Intrinsic Value? *Env*, Issue 2
Is Patriotism a Virtue? *Mor*, Issue 19
Is Population Control the Key to Preventing Environmental Deterioration? *Env*, Issue 4
Is There a World Population Crisis? *WP*, Issue 19
Municipal Waste: Should Recycling Be Promoted as the Key to Refuse Management? *Env*, Issue 12
Should the Endangered Species Act Be Reauthorized? *Env*, Issue 3
Was Early Twentieth-Century American Foreign Policy in the Caribbean Basin Dominated by Economic Concerns? *AH2*, Issue 8
Will Environmental Degradation Be a Feature of International Conflicts in the Future? *Env*, Issue 18
Will the "Greening" of Multinational Corporations Lead to Environmental Improvements? *Env*, Issue 6

Neurosis. *See* **Mental illness**

News media. *See* **Journalism; Media; Newspapers**

Newspapers
Are Liberal Values Propagated by the News Media? *Soc*, Issue 2
Is Advertising Fundamentally Deceptive? *BE*, Issue 10
Is Objectivity Still a Criterion for Journalism? *MM*, Issue 7
Media Monopolies: Does Concentration of Ownership Jeopardize Media Content? *MM*, Issue 15
Should the Names of Rape Victims Be Published? *MM*, Issue 6

Nuclear arms race. *See* **Nuclear weapons**

Nuclear waste. *See* **Hazardous waste**

Nuclear weapons
Is It Possible to Drastically Reduce Defense Expenditures and Remain Secure? *WP*, Issue 13
Should the Global Arms Trade Be Severely Restricted? *WP*, Issue 11

Was Dwight Eisenhower a Great President? *AH2*, Issue 13

Was It Necessary to Drop the Atomic Bomb to End World War II? *AH2*, Issue 12

Will China Become an Asian Superpower? *WP*, Issue 7

—O—

Oil

Can Current Pollution Strategies Improve Air Quality? *BE*, Issue 17; *Env*, Issue 8

Is Mass Transit the Answer to Improving U.S. Energy Efficiency? *Eco*, Issue 7

Should Energy Policy Focus on Reducing the Use of Fossil Fuels? *Env*, Issue 7

Will the "Greening" of Multinational Corporations Lead to Environmental Improvements? *Env*, Issue 6

Overpopulation. *See* **Population growth**

Ozone

Are Aggressive International Efforts Needed to Slow Global Warming? *Env*, Issue 16

Does Global Warming Require Immediate Government Action? *Eco*, Issue 17

Should Industry Be Held Accountable for Acid Rain? *BE*, Issue 16

Should the Phaseout of Chlorofluorocarbons Be Accelerated to Protect the Ozone Layer from Further Depletion? *Env*, Issue 15

—P—

PACs. *See also* **Interest groups**

Do Political Action Committees Undermine Democracy? *Pol*, Issue 3

Is American Government Dominated by Big Business? *Pol*, Issue 1

Parenting. *See also* **Fathering; Mothering; Surrogate parenting**

Are Women Only Victims in Their Roles as Social Support Providers? *Fam*, Issue 2

Do Employers Have an Obligation to Provide Parental Leave Policies for Their Employees? *BE*, Issue 6

Do Parental Notification Laws Benefit Minors Seeking Abortions? *HS*, Issue 12

Have Men's Family Roles Changed? *Fam*, Issue 3

Is Feminism a Positive Value for Society? *Mor*, Issue 7

Is Home Schooling a Viable Alternative? *Edu*, Issue 11

Is Parenthood Necessary for a Good Marriage? *Fam*, Issue 7

Should Adolescents Be Allowed to Make Decisions About Abortion Without Parental Involvement? *Psy*, Issue 13

Should All Children Be Immunized Against Childhood Diseases? *Hea*, Issue 17

Should Homosexuality Bar a Parent from Being Awarded Custody of a Child? *Leg*, Issue 11

Should Pregnant Teens Marry the Fathers of Their Babies? *Fam*, Issue 9

Should Surrogate Parenting Be Permitted for Infertile Couples? *Fam*, Issue 8

Should the Content of Records Be Censored? *MM*, Issue 5

Should Traditional Families Be Preserved? *Soc*, Issue 7

Would a "Mommy Track" Benefit Employed Women? *Fam*, Issue 11; *Soc*, Issue 5

Passivity

Do Ratings Serve the Viewing Public's Interest? *MM*, Issue 13

Is Advertising Ethical? *MM*, Issue 14

Is Television Harmful for Children? *MM*, Issue 3

Pesticides. *See* **Toxic chemicals**

Police. *See also* **Crime; Crime prevention; Law enforcement**

Do Ignition Interlocks Reduce Drunk Driving Arrests? *CR*, Issue 12

Is Criminal Justice Free of Systemic Racism? *CR*, Issue 6

Is Systemic Racism in Criminal Justice a Myth? *RER*, Issue 14

Should the Exclusionary Rule Be Abolished? *Leg*, Issue 13

Political Action Committees. *See* **PACs**

Political campaigns. *See* **Campaigns, political**

Political history, Post–Civil War

Did the Progressives Fail? *AH2*, Issue 7

Was City Government in Late Nineteenth-Century America a "Conspicuous Failure"? *AH2*, Issue 6

Was the American Labor Movement Radical? *AH2*, Issue 3

Political history, Pre–Civil War

Did President Jefferson Outfederalize the Federalists? *AH1*, Issue 9

Did the Election of 1828 Represent a Democratic Revolt of the People? *AH1*, Issue 10

Were the Founding Fathers Democratic Reformers? *AH1*, Issue 8

Political history, Twentieth century

Could the United States Have Prevented the Fall of South Vietnam? *AH2*, Issue 15

Has Party Reform Succeeded? *Pol*, Issue 2

Is Government Dominated by Big Business? *Soc*, Issue 13

Is Terrorism Ever Justified? *Mor*, Issue 17

Was Early Twentieth-Century American Foreign Policy in the Caribbean Basin Dominated by Economic Concerns? *AH2*, Issue 8

Was It Necessary to Drop the Atomic Bomb to End World War II? *AH2*, Issue 12

Will Democracy Survive in Russia? *WP*, Issue 2

Political parties

Did the Election of 1828 Represent a Democratic Revolt of the People? *AH1*, Issue 10

Has Party Reform Succeeded? *Pol*, Issue 2

Is American Government Dominated by Big Business? *Pol*, Issue 1

Is Government Dominated by Big Business? *Soc*, Issue 13

The Presidency Versus Congress: Should Divided Government Be Ended? *Pol*, Issue 6

Was Reconstruction a "Splendid Failure"? *AH1*, Issue 17; *AH2*, Issue 1

Political philosophy

Did President Jefferson Outfederalize the Federalists? *AH1*, Issue 9

Did the Progressives Fail? *AH2*, Issue 7

Is a "New World Order" a Realistic Possibility for International Politics? *WP*, Issue 1

Is Islamic Fundamentalism a Threat to Political Stability? *WP*, Issue 6

Was Abraham Lincoln America's Greatest President? *AH1*, Issue 16

Was the American Revolution a Conservative Movement? *AH1*, Issue 7

Was the Great Awakening a Key to the American Revolution? *AH1*, Issue 6

Were Southern Slaveholding Women Covert Abolitionists? *AH1*, Issue 14

Political systems

Does Congress Need to Be Radically Reformed? *Pol*, Issue 5

Does the Breakup of Communism Show the Success of Capitalism? *Soc*, Issue 15

Do Political Action Committees Undermine Democracy? *Pol*, Issue 3

Is American Government Dominated by Big Business? *Pol*, Issue 1

Is Government Dominated by Big Business? *Soc*, Issue 13

Is Islamic Fundamentalism a Threat to Political Stability? *WP*, Issue 6

Should the United States Abandon Its Superpower Role? *WP*, Issue 3

The Presidency Versus Congress: Should Divided Government Be Ended? *Pol*, Issue 6

Will Democracy Survive in Russia? *WP*, Issue 2

Pollution. *See also* Acid rain; Hazardous waste; Toxic chemicals; Water pollution

Are Abundant Resources and an Improved Environment Likely Future Prospects for the World's People? *Env,* Issue 17

Are the Effects of Acid Rain Serious Enough to Justify Strict Enforcement of Clean Air Legislation? *Env,* Issue 9

Can Current Pollution Strategies Improve Air Quality? *BE,* Issue 17; *Env,* Issue 8

Does Population Growth Threaten Humanity? *Soc,* Issue 19

Is Street Crime More Serious Than White-Collar Crime? *CR,* Issue 4

Municipal Waste: Should Recycling Be Promoted as the Key to Refuse Management? *Env,* Issue 12

Should Industry Be Held Accountable for Acid Rain? *BE,* Issue 16

Will Environmental Degradation Be a Feature of International Conflicts in the Future? *Env,* Issue 18

Poor. *See* **Poverty**

Population growth

Are Abundant Resources and an Improved Environment Likely Future Prospects for the World's People? *Env,* Issue 17

Does Population Growth Threaten Humanity? *Soc,* Issue 19

Does Wilderness Have Intrinsic Value? *Env,* Issue 2

Do Rich Nations Have an Obligation to Help Poor Nations? *Mor,* Issue 20

Is Population Control the Key to Preventing Environmental Deterioration? *Env,* Issue 4

Is There a World Population Crisis? *WP,* Issue 19

Pornography

Can Sex Be an Addiction? *HS,* Issue 2

Is Pornography Harmful? *HS,* Issue 5

Is Pornography Immoral? *Mor,* Issue 12

Should Pornography Be Protected as Free Speech? *MM,* Issue 9

Should Pornography Be Protected by the First Amendment? *Leg,* Issue 8

Poverty

Are Hispanics Making Significant Progress? *RER,* Issue 13

Are Rent Controls the Cause of America's Homelessness? *Eco,* Issue 5

Are the Poor Being Harmed by Welfare? *Pol,* Issue 14

Does "Lower-Class" Culture Perpetuate Poverty? *Soc,* Issue 9

Does "Lower-Class" Culture Perpetuate Poverty Among Urban Minorities? *RER,* Issue 11

Does Society Have an Obligation to Care for the Less Well Off? *Mor,* Issue 9

Does Welfare Do More Harm Than Good? *Soc,* Issue 14

Do Rich Nations Have an Obligation to Help Poor Nations? *Mor,* Issue 20

Helping the Homeless: Do We Need More Government Regulation? *Soc,* Issue 12

Is Black Self-Help the Solution to Racial Inequality? *Soc,* Issue 10

Is Criminal Behavior Biologically Determined? *CR,* Issue 3

Is Economic Inequality Beneficial to Society? *Soc,* Issue 8

Is Italy Solving Its Immigration Problem? *RER,* Issue 15

Is Research on Criminal Careers Helpful? *CR,* Issue 10

Is Street Crime More Harmful Than White-Collar Crime? *Soc,* Issue 16

Is the Concept of the Underclass Useful for Studying Race and Ethnic Relations? *RER,* Issue 2

Is Workfare a Good Substitute for Welfare? *Eco,* Issue 14

Should Drug Use by Pregnant Women Be Considered Child Abuse? *Dru,* Issue 7

Should Plea Bargaining Be Abolished? *Leg,* Issue 3

Should Surrogate Motherhood Be Outlawed? *HS,* Issue 8

Should the Developed North Increase Aid to the Less Developed South? *WP,* Issue 10

Should the Government Establish Special Programs and Policies for Black Youths and Their Families? *Fam*, Issue 12

Should the United States Follow the Canadian Model of a National Health Program? *Bio*, Issue 19

Will Reforming School Funding Remove "Savage Inequalities"? *Edu*, Issue 7

Pregnancy

Abortion and the "Pro-Life" v. "Pro-Choice" Debate: Should the Human Fetus Be Considered a Person? *HS*, Issue 9

Can Abortion Be a Morally Acceptable Choice? *Hea*, Issue 11

Does Sex Education Prevent Teen Pregnancy? *Hea*, Issue 10

Do Parental Notification Laws Benefit Minors Seeking Abortions? *HS*, Issue 12

Is Abortion Immoral? *Mor*, Issue 13

Is Parenthood Necessary for a Good Marriage? *Fam*, Issue 7

Is There a Moral Right to Abortion? *Bio*, Issue 2

Should Adolescents Be Allowed to Make Decisions About Abortion Without Parental Involvement? *Psy*, Issue 13

Should Commercial Surrogate Motherhood Be Banned? *Bio*, Issue 4

Should Drug Use by Pregnant Women Be Considered Child Abuse? *Dru*, Issue 7

Should Pregnant Teens Marry the Fathers of Their Babies? *Fam*, Issue 9

Should RU 486 Be Legalized? *HS*, Issue 6

Should Schools Distribute Condoms? *HS*, Issue 7

Should Surrogate Motherhood Be Outlawed? *HS*, Issue 8

Was *Roe v. Wade* a Mistake? *Pol*, Issue 17

Prejudice. *See* **Minorities; Racial discrimination; Sex discrimination; Women's issues**

Presidency

Could the United States Have Prevented the Fall of South Vietnam? *AH2*, Issue 15

Did President Jefferson Outfederalize the Federalists? *AH1*, Issue 9

Did President Reagan Win the Cold War? *AH2*, Issue 17

Did the Election of 1828 Represent a Democratic Revolt of the People? *AH1*, Issue 10

Did the Great Society Fail? *AH2*, Issue 14

Do Presidential TV Ads Manipulate Voters? *MM*, Issue 10

Has Party Reform Succeeded? *Pol*, Issue 2

The Presidency Versus Congress: Should Divided Government Be Ended? *Pol*, Issue 6

Was Abraham Lincoln America's Greatest President? *AH1*, Issue 16

Was Dwight Eisenhower a Great President? *AH2*, Issue 13

Was the New Deal an Effective Answer to the Great Depression? *AH2*, Issue 10

Press, The. *See* **Journalism; Media; Newspapers; Television**

Psychological research

Are Drug Addicts Always in Control of Their Addiction? *Dru*, Issue 15

Can a Positive Mental Attitude Overcome Disease? *Hea*, Issue 6

Can Deception in Research Be Justified? *Psy*, Issue 1

Can Experiments Using Animals Be Justified? *Psy*, Issue 3

Does Sexual Infidelity Destroy a Relationship? *HS*, Issue 4

Has Science Discredited ESP? *Psy*, Issue 7

Is Electroconvulsive Therapy Safe? *Psy*, Issue 17

Is Our State of Mind Responsible for Our State of Health? *Psy*, Issue 6

Should Adolescents Be Allowed to Make Decisions About Abortion Without Parental Involvement? *Psy*, Issue 13

Should Behaviorism Shape Educational Practices? *Edu*, Issue 3

Should Psychologists Study Memory Through Controlled Laboratory Experiments? *Psy*, Issue 2

Psychosis. *See* Mental illness

Psychotherapy

Are Children of Divorced Parents at Greater Risk? *Psy*, Issue 12

Can Sex Be an Addiction? *HS*, Issue 2

Is Electroconvulsive Therapy Safe? *Psy*, Issue 17

Should Psychologists Be Allowed to Prescribe Drugs? *Psy*, Issue 18

Should Psychotherapists Allow Suicide? *Psy*, Issue 14

Should Psychotherapy Include Religious Values? *Psy*, Issue 16

Punishment. *See also* Corrections system; Death penalty

Are Private Prisons a Good Idea? *CR*, Issue 15

Do Ignition Interlocks Reduce Drunk Driving Arrests? *CR*, Issue 12

Is Capital Punishment Justified? *Pol*, Issue 10

Is Incapacitation the Answer to the Crime Problem? *Soc*, Issue 18

Is Punishment Good Crime Control? *CR*, Issue 5

Juvenile Justice: Are Kids "Getting Away With Murder"? *CR*, Issue 7

Should Capital Punishment Be Abolished? *CR*, Issue 9; *Mor*, Issue 14

Should Elderly Offenders Get Lighter Sentences? *CR*, Issue 13

Should Plea Bargaining Continue to Be an Accepted Practice? *CR*, Issue 8

Will Tougher Sentencing Reduce Crime? *Pol*, Issue 9

— R —

Racial discrimination

Are Asian Americans a "Model Minority"? *RER*, Issue 3

Are Nonethnic Scholars Able to Successfully Research Minorities? *RER*, Issue 1

Are Positive Images of African Americans Increasing in the Media? *MM*, Issue 2; *RER*, Issue 9

Is Affirmative Action Constitutional? *Leg*, Issue 9

Is Affirmative Action Morally Justifiable? *Mor*, Issue 16

Is Affirmative Action Reverse Discrimination? *Pol*, Issue 11; *RER*, Issue 12; *Soc*, Issue 11

Is Black Self-Help the Solution to Racial Inequality? *Soc*, Issue 10

Is Criminal Justice Free of Systemic Racism? *CR*, Issue 6

Is Italy Solving Its Immigration Problem? *RER*, Issue 15

Is Patriotism a Virtue? *Mor*, Issue 19

Is Systemic Racism in Criminal Justice a Myth? *RER*, Issue 14

Is the Concept of the Underclass Useful for Studying Race and Ethnic Relations? *RER*, Issue 2

Is There an Ethnic Revolt Against the Melting Pot? *RER*, Issue 16

Should Black Women Join the Feminist Movement? *RER*, Issue 8

Should "Hate Speech" Be Protected? *Pol*, Issue 12

Should "Hate Speech" Be Tolerated? *Mor*, Issue 10

Should Minorities Continue to Demand More Rights? *RER*, Issue 10

Should the Death Penalty Be Abolished? *Leg*, Issue 12

Was Early Twentieth-Century American Foreign Policy in the Caribbean Basin Dominated by Economic Concerns? *AH2*, Issue 8

Was Martin Luther King, Jr.'s Leadership Essential to the Success of the Civil Rights Movement? *AH2*, Issue 16

Was Race a Central Factor in the Colonists' Attitudes Toward Native Americans? *AH1*, Issue 2

Was the Ku Klux Klan of the 1920s an Extremist Movement? *AH2*, Issue 9

Was U.S. Foreign Policy in the Early Nineteenth Century Imperialistic? *AH1*, Issue 13

Radioactive waste. *See* **Hazardous waste**

Rape

Does Arrest Reduce Domestic Violence? *Fam*, Issue 10

Is Pornography Harmful? *HS*, Issue 5

Is Rape Motivated by Aggression Instead of Sex? *HS*, Issue 3

Is There a Date Rape Crisis on College Campuses? *HS*, Issue 10

Is the Victims' Rights Movement Succeeding? *CR*, Issue 16

Should the Names of Rape Victims Be Published? *MM*, Issue 6

Reagan administration

Did President Reagan Win the Cold War? *AH2*, Issue 17

Did Reaganomics Fail? *Eco*, Issue 9

Refugees. *See* **Immigration**

Regional geography

Is There a World Population Crisis? *WP*, Issue 19

Was the Confederacy Defeated Because of Its "Loss of Will"? *AH1*, Issue 15

Regulation. *See* **Government regulation**

Rehabilitation

Juvenile Justice: Are Kids "Getting Away With Murder"? *CR*, Issue 7

Will Tougher Sentencing Reduce Crime? *Pol*, Issue 9

Religion. *See also* **Church, Roman Catholic; Church and state, Separation of**

Did Capitalist Values Motivate the American Colonists? *AH1*, Issue 4

Did Slaves Exercise Religious Autonomy? *AH1*, Issue 12

Do Prayers at Public School Graduation Ceremonies Violate the Constitution? *Leg*, Issue 6

Is Church-State Separation Being Threatened? *Edu*, Issue 5

Is Islamic Fundamentalism a Threat to Political Stability? *WP*, Issue 6

Is It Ever Morally Right to Withhold Food and Water from Dying Patients? *Bio*, Issue 7

Is It Possible to Be Pro-Life and Pro-Choice? *Fam*, Issue 6

Is Morality Grounded in Religion? *Mor*, Issue 4

Is Morality Relative to Culture? *Mor*, Issue 2

Must Contemporary Moral Disagreements End in Deadlock? *Mor*, Issue 1

Should Psychotherapy Include Religious Values? *Psy*, Issue 16

Should Research With Aborted Fetal Tissue Be Banned? *Bio*, Issue 15

Should Society Recognize Gay Marriages? *HS*, Issue 15

Should There Be a "Wall of Separation" Between Church and State? *Pol*, Issue 18

Should Values Be Developed Rather Than Transmitted? *Edu*, Issue 4

Was Antebellum Reform Motivated Primarily by Humanitarian Goals? *AH1*, Issue 11

Was Race a Central Factor in the Colonists' Attitudes Toward Native Americans? *AH1*, Issue 2

Was the Great Awakening a Key to the American Revolution? *AH1*, Issue 6

Was the Ku Klux Klan of the 1920s an Extremist Movement? *AH2*, Issue 9

Was the Salem Witchcraft Hysteria Caused by a Fear of Women? *AH1*, Issue 3

Reproduction. *See also* **Pregnancy**

Is There a Moral Right to Abortion? *Bio*, Issue 2

Should Commercial Surrogate Motherhood Be Banned? *Bio*, Issue 4

Should Courts Be Permitted to Order Women to Use Long-Acting Contraceptives? *Bio*, Issue 1

Should RU 486 Be Legalized? *HS*, Issue 6

Should Surrogate Motherhood Be Outlawed? *HS*, Issue 8

Should Thawing Unused Frozen Embryos Be Permitted? *Bio*, Issue 3

Republic of South Africa. *See* **South Africa, Republic of**

Revolution. *See* **American Revolution**

Roman Catholic Church. *See* **Church, Roman Catholic**

Russia. *See* **Soviet Union**

— S —

School curriculum

Are Current Sex Education Programs Lacking in Moral Guidance? *Edu,* Issue 19

Do Black Students Need an Afrocentric Curriculum? *Edu,* Issue 14

Do Cultural Differences Between Home and School Explain the High Dropout Rates for American Indian Students? *RER,* Issue 6

Does a Common Curriculum Promote Equality? *Edu,* Issue 6

Does "Multiculturalism" Debase the Curriculum? *Soc,* Issue 1

Does Sex Education Prevent Teen Pregnancy? *Hea,* Issue 10

Does Tracking Create Educational Inequality? *Edu,* Issue 16

Is Church-State Separation Being Threatened? *Edu,* Issue 5

Should Black Women Join the Feminist Movement? *RER,* Issue 8

Should Literacy Be Based on Traditional Culture? *Edu,* Issue 13

Should Schools Determine What Is Learned? *Edu,* Issue 2

Should Schools of Education Be Abolished? *Edu,* Issue 20

School reform

Can "Choice" Lead the Way to Educational Reform? *Edu,* Issue 9

Can Schools Prevent Urban Dropouts? *Edu,* Issue 12

Does a Common Curriculum Promote Equality? *Edu,* Issue 6

Do Stepchildren Need Special Policies and Programs on Their Behalf? *Fam,* Issue 16

Is Choice a Panacea for the Ills of Public Education? *Eco,* Issue 8

Should Behaviorism Shape Educational Practices? *Edu,* Issue 3

Should Literacy Be Based on Traditional Culture? *Edu,* Issue 13

Should National Goals Guide School Performance? *Edu,* Issue 8

Should Schooling Be Based on Social Experiences? *Edu,* Issue 1

Should Schools Determine What Is Learned? *Edu,* Issue 2

Should Schools of Education Be Abolished? *Edu,* Issue 20

Will Reforming School Funding Remove "Savage Inequalities"? *Edu,* Issue 7

Will the "Edison Project" Prompt Major Reforms? *Edu,* Issue 10

Schools. *See also* **Education alternatives; School curriculum; School reform**

Are Current Sex Education Programs Lacking in Moral Guidance? *Edu,* Issue 19

Can "Choice" Lead the Way to Educational Reform? *Edu,* Issue 9

Can Intelligence Be Increased? *Psy,* Issue 9

Can Schools Prevent Urban Dropouts? *Edu,* Issue 12

Do Black Students Need an Afrocentric Curriculum? *Edu,* Issue 14

Do Cultural Differences Between Home and School Explain the High Dropout Rates for American Indian Students? *RER,* Issue 6

Do "Discipline Programs" Promote Ethical Behavior? *Edu,* Issue 18

Do Drug Education Programs Prevent Drug Abuse? *Dru,* Issue 11

Does a Common Curriculum Promote Equality? *Edu,* Issue 6

Does "Multiculturalism" Debase the Curriculum? *Soc,* Issue 1

Does Sex Education Prevent Teen Pregnancy? *Hea,* Issue 10

Does Tracking Create Educational Inequality? *Edu,* Issue 16

Do Prayers at Public School Graduation Ceremonies Violate the Constitution? *Leg*, Issue 6

Do Speech Codes Suppress Freedom of Expression? *MM*, Issue 11

Do Stepchildren Need Special Policies and Programs on Their Behalf? *Fam*, Issue 16

Is Choice a Panacea for the Ills of Public Education? *Eco*, Issue 8

Is Church-State Separation Being Threatened? *Edu*, Issue 5

Is Mainstreaming Beneficial to All? *Edu*, Issue 17

Is National Service at Odds With American National Interest? *Eco*, Issue 3

Is Workfare a Good Substitute for Welfare? *Eco*, Issue 14

Should Behaviorism Shape Educational Practices? *Edu*, Issue 3

Should Bilingual Education Programs Be Abandoned? *Edu*, Issue 15

Should Bilingual Education Programs Be Stopped? *RER*, Issue 7

Should "Hate Speech" Be Protected? *Pol*, Issue 12

Should "Hate Speech" Be Tolerated? *Mor*, Issue 10

Should Literacy Be Based on Traditional Culture? *Edu*, Issue 13

Should National Goals Guide School Performance? *Edu*, Issue 8

Should Pregnant Teens Marry the Fathers of Their Babies? *Fam*, Issue 9

Should Psychologists Be Allowed to Prescribe Drugs? *Psy*, Issue 18

Should Schooling Be Based on Social Experiences? *Edu*, Issue 1

Should Schools Determine What Is Learned? *Edu*, Issue 2

Should Schools Distribute Condoms? *HS*, Issue 7

Should Schools of Education Be Abolished? *Edu*, Issue 20

Should There Be a "Wall of Separation" Between Church and State? *Pol*, Issue 18

Should Values Be Developed Rather Than Transmitted? *Edu*, Issue 4

Will Reforming School Funding Remove "Savage Inequalities"? *Edu*, Issue 7

Will the "Edison Project" Prompt Major Reforms? *Edu*, Issue 10

Scientific research

Are Gender Differences Rooted in the Brain? *HS*, Issue 1

Are General Theories of Crime Possible? *CR*, Issue 2

Are the Dangers of Steroids Exaggerated? *Dru*, Issue 17

Are the Effects of Acid Rain Serious Enough to Justify Strict Enforcement of Clean Air Legislation? *Env*, Issue 9

Can Caffeine Be Bad for Your Health? *Dru*, Issue 9

Can Deception in Research Be Justified? *Psy*, Issue 1

Can Experiments Using Animals Be Justified? *Psy*, Issue 3

Do Gender Differences Originate from Biological Factors? *Psy*, Issue 10

Has Science Discredited ESP? *Psy*, Issue 7

Has the Federal Government Spent Enough on AIDS Research? *HS*, Issue 17

Is AIDS Getting More Than Its Share of Resources and Media Attention? *Hea*, Issue 4

Is Alcoholism Hereditary? *Dru*, Issue 10

Is Cholesterol Reduction an Important Health Priority? *Hea*, Issue 12

Is It Ethical for Scientists to Use Data from the Nazi Experiments? *Bio*, Issue 14

Is It Unethical to Implant Animal Parts in Humans? *Bio*, Issue 13

Is Morality Grounded in Religion? *Mor*, Issue 4

Is Morality Subjective? *Mor*, Issue 3

Is Our State of Mind Responsible for Our State of Health? *Psy*, Issue 6

Is Passive Smoking Harmful to Nonsmokers? *Dru*, Issue 8

Is Research on Criminal Careers Helpful? *CR*, Issue 10

Is the "Disease" of Alcoholism a Myth? *Dru,* Issue 13; *Psy,* Issue 5

Must Contemporary Moral Disagreements End in Deadlock? *Mor,* Issue 1

Should Animal Experimentation Be Permitted? *Bio,* Issue 12

Should Animals Be Liberated? *Mor,* Issue 6

Should Medical Patients Be Permitted to Use Marijuana? *Dru,* Issue 2

Should Newborns Without Brains Be Used as Organ Donors? *Bio,* Issue 16

Should Psychologists Study Memory Through Controlled Laboratory Experiments? *Psy,* Issue 2

Should Research With Aborted Fetal Tissue Be Banned? *Bio,* Issue 15

Should Risk Assessment Methods Be Used to Set Environmental Priorities? *Env,* Issue 5

Should Thawing Unused Frozen Embryos Be Permitted? *Bio,* Issue 3

Should There Be a Market in Body Parts? *Bio,* Issue 17

Will Practicing Positive Health Behaviors and Emphasizing Prevention Improve Health? *Hea,* Issue 5

Will the Human Genome Project Lead to Abuses in Genetic Engineering? *Bio,* Issue 20

Self

Can Deception in Research Be Justified? *Psy,* Issue 1

Can Sex Be an Addiction? *HS,* Issue 2

Do Black Students Need an Afrocentric Curriculum? *Edu,* Issue 14

Do Diagnostic Labels Hinder the Effective Treatment of Persons With Mental Disorders? *Psy,* Issue 15

Does Tracking Create Educational Inequality? *Edu,* Issue 16

Has Individualism Become Excessive? *Soc,* Issue 3

Is Alcoholism Hereditary? *Dru,* Issue 10

Is Black Self-Help the Solution to Racial Inequality? *Soc,* Issue 10

Is the "Disease" of Alcoholism a Myth? *Dru,* Issue 13; *Psy,* Issue 5

Should Schools of Education Be Abolished? *Edu,* Issue 20

Sex discrimination

Are Gender Differences Present at Birth? *Fam,* Issue 1

Are Gender Differences Rooted in the Brain? *HS,* Issue 1

Are Nonethnic Scholars Able to Successfully Research Minorities? *RER,* Issue 1

Are Women Paid Less Than Men Because Their Working Conditions Are More Favorable? *Eco,* Issue 4

Is Affirmative Action Constitutional? *Leg,* Issue 9

Is Affirmative Action Morally Justifiable? *Mor,* Issue 16

Is Feminism a Harmful Ideology? *Soc,* Issue 4

Is Feminism a Positive Value for Society? *Mor,* Issue 7

Is Sexual Harassment a Pervasive Problem? *HS,* Issue 16

Is Sexual Harassment a Pervasive Problem in America? *Soc,* Issue 6

Should Commercial Surrogate Motherhood Be Banned? *Bio,* Issue 4

Should Homosexuality Be Accepted by Society? *Mor,* Issue 11

Should Society Recognize Gay Marriages? *HS,* Issue 15

Would Women in Combat Weaken National Security? *WP,* Issue 15

Sex roles

Are Gender Differences Present at Birth? *Fam,* Issue 1

Are Media Messages About Women Improving? *MM,* Issue 4

Are Women Only Victims in Their Roles as Social Support Providers? *Fam,* Issue 2

Did the Westward Movement Transform the Traditional Roles of Women in the Late Nineteenth Century? *AH2,* Issue 5

Did World War II Liberate American Women? *AH2,* Issue 11

Does Sexual Infidelity Destroy a Relationship? *HS*, Issue 4

Do Gender Differences Originate from Biological Factors? *Psy*, Issue 10

Have Men's Family Roles Changed? *Fam*, Issue 3

Is Feminism a Harmful Ideology? *Soc*, Issue 4

Is Sexual Harassment a Pervasive Problem? *HS*, Issue 16

Is Sexual Harassment a Pervasive Problem in America? *Soc*, Issue 6

Should Gays and Lesbians Fight for the Right to Marry? *Fam*, Issue 5

Should Homosexuality Be Accepted by Society? *Mor*, Issue 11

Would a "Mommy Track" Benefit Employed Women? *Fam*, Issue 11; *Soc*, Issue 5

Would Women in Combat Weaken National Security? *WP*, Issue 15

Sexuality

Are Extramarital Relationships Becoming More Frequent? *Fam*, Issue 14

Can Sex Be an Addiction? *HS*, Issue 2

Does Sex Education Prevent Teen Pregnancy? *Hea*, Issue 10

Is Pornography Harmful? *HS*, Issue 5

Should Homosexuality Be Accepted by Society? *Mor*, Issue 11

Should Schools Distribute Condoms? *HS*, Issue 7

Slavery

Did American Slaves Develop a Distinct African American Culture in the Eighteenth Century? *AH1*, Issue 5

Did Slaves Exercise Religious Autonomy? *AH1*, Issue 12

Was Abraham Lincoln America's Greatest President? *AH1*, Issue 16

Was Reconstruction a "Splendid Failure"? *AH1*, Issue 17; *AH2*, Issue 1

Was the Confederacy Defeated Because of Its "Loss of Will"? *AH1*, Issue 15

Were Southern Slaveholding Women Covert Abolitionists? *AH1*, Issue 14

Social change

Are American Values Shaped by the Mass Media? *MM*, Issue 1

Are Extramarital Relationships Becoming More Frequent? *Fam*, Issue 14

Are Gender Differences Present at Birth? *Fam*, Issue 1

Are Global Standards of Human Rights Desirable? *WP*, Issue 18

Are Human Rights Basic to Justice? *CR*, Issue 18; *Mor*, Issue 18

Are Profits the Only Business of Business? *Eco*, Issue 1

Can "Choice" Lead the Way to Educational Reform? *Edu*, Issue 9

Can Current Pollution Strategies Improve Air Quality? *BE*, Issue 17; *Env*, Issue 8

Did the Westward Movement Transform the Traditional Roles of Women in the Late Nineteenth Century? *AH2*, Issue 5

Does Welfare Do More Harm Than Good? *Soc*, Issue 14

Do Stepchildren Need Special Policies and Programs on Their Behalf? *Fam*, Issue 16

Have Men's Family Roles Changed? *Fam*, Issue 3

Is America's Socioeconomic System Breaking Down? *Soc*, Issue 20

Is Choice a Panacea for the Ills of Public Education? *Eco*, Issue 8

Is Crime Functional? *CR*, Issue 1

Is Euthanasia Immoral? *Mor*, Issue 15

Is Feminism a Harmful Ideology? *Soc*, Issue 4

Is Italy Solving Its Immigration Problem? *RER*, Issue 15

Is Sexual Harassment a Pervasive Problem? *HS*, Issue 16

Is Sexual Harassment a Pervasive Problem in America? *Soc*, Issue 6

Is the Success of Remarriage Doomed? *Fam*, Issue 17

Should Gays and Lesbians Fight for the Right to Marry? *Fam*, Issue 5

Should Minorities Continue to Demand More Rights? *RER*, Issue 10

Should Traditional Families Be Preserved? *Soc*, Issue 7

Should We Call Ourselves African Americans? *RER*, Issue 5

Was Antebellum Reform Motivated Primarily by Humanitarian Goals? *AH1*, Issue 11

Was the Great Awakening a Key to the American Revolution? *AH1*, Issue 6

Was the Ku Klux Klan of the 1920s an Extremist Movement? *AH2*, Issue 9

Was the Salem Witchcraft Hysteria Caused by a Fear of Women? *AH1*, Issue 3

Social class. *See* **Middle class; Upper class**

Social history, Colonial

Did American Slaves Develop a Distinct African American Culture in the Eighteenth Century? *AH1*, Issue 5

Was the Salem Witchcraft Hysteria Caused by a Fear of Women? *AH1*, Issue 3

Social history, Post–Civil War

Did the Westward Movement Transform the Traditional Roles of Women in the Late Nineteenth Century? *AH2*, Issue 5

Was Antebellum Reform Motivated Primarily by Humanitarian Goals? *AH1*, Issue 11

Were the Immigrants' Old World Cultures Destroyed as They Adjusted to American Life? *AH2*, Issue 4

Social history, Pre–Civil War

Did Slaves Exercise Religious Autonomy? *AH1*, Issue 12

Social history, Twentieth century

Are Programs of Preferential Treatment Unjustifiable? *BE*, Issue 5

Can Corporate Codes of Ethics Promote Ethical Behavior? *BE*, Issue 2

Does Welfare Do More Harm Than Good? *Soc*, Issue 14

Is Capitalism Viable for the Future? *BE*, Issue 1; *Mor*, Issue 5

Is Feminism a Harmful Ideology? *Soc*, Issue 4

Is Government Dominated by Big Business? *Soc*, Issue 13

Is Sexual Harassment a Pervasive Problem? *HS*, Issue 16

Is Sexual Harassment a Pervasive Problem in America? *Soc*, Issue 6

Was Martin Luther King, Jr.'s Leadership Essential to the Success of the Civil Rights Movement? *AH2*, Issue 16

Social interaction

Do Stepchildren Need Special Policies and Programs on Their Behalf? *Fam*, Issue 16

Is Marriage Good for You? *Fam*, Issue 4

Is Parenthood Necessary for a Good Marriage? *Fam*, Issue 7

Is the Success of Remarriage Doomed? *Fam*, Issue 17

Should Gays and Lesbians Fight for the Right to Marry? *Fam*, Issue 5

Should Schools Determine What Is Learned? *Edu*, Issue 2

Socialization

Are American Values Shaped by the Mass Media? *MM*, Issue 1

Is Television Harmful for Children? *MM*, Issue 3

Should Traditional Families Be Preserved? *Soc*, Issue 7

Social stratification

Are Gender Differences Present at Birth? *Fam*, Issue 1

Are Nonethnic Scholars Able to Successfully Research Minorities? *RER*, Issue 1

Do Italian Americans Reject Assimilation? *RER*, Issue 4

Is the Concept of the Underclass Useful for Studying Race and Ethnic Relations? *RER*, Issue 2

Should Black Women Join the Feminist Movement? *RER*, Issue 8

Social welfare programs

Are Rent Controls the Cause of America's Homelessness? *Eco*, Issue 5

Are the Poor Being Harmed by Welfare? *Pol*, Issue 14

Did the Great Society Fail? *AH2*, Issue 14

Does Sex Education Prevent Teen
Pregnancy? *Hea*, Issue 10

Does Society Have an Obligation to Care
for the Less Well Off? *Mor*, Issue 9

Does Welfare Do More Harm Than
Good? *Soc*, Issue 14

Helping the Homeless: Do We Need
More Government Regulation? *Soc*,
Issue 12

Is Workfare a Good Substitute for
Welfare? *Eco*, Issue 14

South Africa, Republic of
Should Morality and Human Rights
Strongly Influence Foreign
Policy-Making? *WP*, Issue 17

South America. *See* **Latin America**

Soviet-American relations. *See* **United
States–Soviet Union relations**

Soviet Union
Did President Reagan Win the Cold War?
AH2, Issue 17

Does the Breakup of Communism Show
the Success of Capitalism? *Soc*,
Issue 15

Will Democracy Survive in Russia? *WP*,
Issue 2

Special interest groups. *See* **Interest
groups; PACs**

State government
Can States Restrict the Right to Die? *Leg*,
Issue 10

Do Parental Notification Laws Benefit
Minors Seeking Abortions? *HS*,
Issue 12

Is Capital Punishment Justified? *Pol*,
Issue 10

Is Choice a Panacea for the Ills of Public
Education? *Eco*, Issue 8

Is "Hate Speech" Fully Protected by the
Constitution? *Leg*, Issue 5

Should Lawyers Be Prohibited from
Presenting a False Case? *Leg*, Issue 2

Was *Roe v. Wade* a Mistake? *Pol*, Issue 17

Was the Confederacy Defeated Because
of Its "Loss of Will"? *AH1*, Issue 15

Will Reforming School Funding Remove
"Savage Inequalities"? *Edu*, Issue 7

Stock market
Can Hostile Takeovers Be Justified? *BE*,
Issue 14

Does Insider Trading Serve a Useful
Purpose? *BE*, Issue 15

Do Federal Budget Deficits Matter? *Eco*,
Issue 10

Do Hostile Takeovers Harm Society? *Eco*,
Issue 6

Should the "Pay-for-Performance"
System Be Overhauled? *BE*, Issue 3

Suicide. *See also* **Death and dying;
Euthanasia**
Is Physician-Assisted Suicide Ethical? *Bio*,
Issue 6

Should Doctors Ever Help Terminally Ill
Patients Commit Suicide? *Hea*, Issue 2

Should Psychotherapists Allow Suicide?
Psy, Issue 14

Will Gun Control Reduce Crime? *CR*,
Issue 14

Supreme Court
Can States Restrict the Right to Die? *Leg*,
Issue 10

Does Government Have a Constitutional
Right to Prohibit Certain Kinds of
Sexual Conduct? *HS*, Issue 11

Do Parental Notification Laws Benefit
Minors Seeking Abortions? *HS*,
Issue 12

Do Prayers at Public School Graduation
Ceremonies Violate the Constitution?
Leg, Issue 6

Is Abortion Immoral? *Mor*, Issue 13

Is Abortion Protected by the
Constitution? *Leg*, Issue 7

Is Affirmative Action Constitutional? *Leg*,
Issue 9

Is Capital Punishment Justified? *Pol*,
Issue 10

Is Drug Use Testing Permitted Under the
Fourth Amendment? *Leg*, Issue 4

Is "Hate Speech" Fully Protected by the
Constitution? *Leg*, Issue 5

Is It Possible to Be Pro-Life and
Pro-Choice? *Fam*, Issue 6

Should Capital Punishment Be
Abolished? *CR*, Issue 9

Should the Death Penalty Be Abolished? *Leg*, Issue 12

Should the Exclusionary Rule Be Abolished? *Leg*, Issue 13

Should the Federal Courts Be Bound by the "Original Intent" of the Framers? *Pol*, Issue 8

Was *Roe v. Wade* a Mistake? *Pol*, Issue 17

Surrogate parenting

Should Commercial Surrogate Motherhood Be Banned? *Bio*, Issue 4

Should Surrogate Motherhood Be Outlawed? *HS*, Issue 8

Should Surrogate Parenting Be Permitted for Infertile Couples? *Fam*, Issue 8

— T —

Tax structure

Can Hostile Takeovers Be Justified? *BE*, Issue 14

Does the Government Regulate Too Much? *Pol*, Issue 7

Is Economic Inequality Beneficial to Society? *Soc*, Issue 8

Is the National Debt a National Liability? *Pol*, Issue 15

Should the Capital Gains Tax Be Lowered? *Eco*, Issue 13

Will Reforming School Funding Remove "Savage Inequalities"? *Edu*, Issue 7

Teaching

Are Current Sex Education Programs Lacking in Moral Guidance? *Edu*, Issue 19

Can "Choice" Lead the Way to Educational Reform? *Edu*, Issue 9

Can Schools Prevent Urban Dropouts? *Edu*, Issue 12

Do Cultural Differences Between Home and School Explain the High Dropout Rates for American Indian Students? *RER*, Issue 6

Do "Discipline Programs" Promote Ethical Behavior? *Edu*, Issue 18

Does a Common Curriculum Promote Equality? *Edu*, Issue 6

Does Sex Education Prevent Teen Pregnancy? *Hea*, Issue 10

Is Home Schooling a Viable Alternative? *Edu*, Issue 11

Should Schooling Be Based on Social Experiences? *Edu*, Issue 1

Should Schools of Education Be Abolished? *Edu*, Issue 20

Should There Be a "Wall of Separation" Between Church and State? *Pol*, Issue 18

Should Values Be Developed Rather Than Transmitted? *Edu*, Issue 4

Will the "Edison Project" Prompt Major Reforms? *Edu*, Issue 10

Technological innovation

Can Current Pollution Strategies Improve Air Quality? *BE*, Issue 17; *Env*, Issue 8

Can Modern Mass Communication Promote a Better World? *MM*, Issue 18

Does Caller ID Invade Privacy? *Leg*, Issue 16

Does Technology Transfer by Multinational Firms Benefit the Development of Third World Nations? *MM*, Issue 17

Do Ignition Interlocks Reduce Drunk Driving Arrests? *CR*, Issue 12

Is Population Control the Key to Preventing Environmental Deterioration? *Env*, Issue 4

Is the Legal System Damaging the American Economy? *Leg*, Issue 1

Media Monopolies: Does Concentration of Ownership Jeopardize Media Content? *MM*, Issue 15

Should Health Care for the Elderly Be Limited? *Hea*, Issue 3

Should Risk Assessment Methods Be Used to Set Environmental Priorities? *Env*, Issue 5

Television. *See also* **Media**

Are American Values Shaped by the Mass Media? *MM*, Issue 1

Are Liberal Values Propagated by the News Media? *Soc*, Issue 2

Are Positive Images of African Americans Increasing in the Media? *MM*, Issue 2; *RER*, Issue 9

Can Modern Mass Communication Promote a Better World? *MM*, Issue 18

Can Network News Survive? *MM*, Issue 16

Do Presidential TV Ads Manipulate Voters? *MM*, Issue 10

Do Ratings Serve the Viewing Public's Interest? *MM*, Issue 13

Is Advertising Fundamentally Deceptive? *BE*, Issue 10

Is Television Harmful for Children? *MM*, Issue 3

Is the Public Best Served by a Marketplace Approach to Regulation? *MM*, Issue 8

Should the Names of Rape Victims Be Published? *MM*, Issue 6

Terrorism

Is Islamic Fundamentalism a Threat to Political Stability? *WP*, Issue 6

Is Terrorism Ever Justified? *Mor*, Issue 17

Is the Kidnapping of Criminal Suspects from Foreign Countries Justifiable? *WP*, Issue 16

Therapy. *See* **Psychotherapy**

Third World. *See* **Less developed countries**

Tobacco

Do Smokers Have a Right to Smoke in Public Places? *Hea*, Issue 7

Is Passive Smoking Harmful to Nonsmokers? *Dru*, Issue 8

Is the War on Drugs Misdirected? *Dru*, Issue 5

Should Tobacco Advertising Be Banned? *BE*, Issue 12

Should Tobacco Advertising Be Prohibited? *Dru*, Issue 12

Will Practicing Positive Health Behaviors and Emphasizing Prevention Improve Health? *Hea*, Issue 5

Toxic chemicals

Are Pesticides in Foods Harmful to Human Health? *Hea*, Issue 15

Can Incentives Devised by Industrial Nations Combat Tropical Deforestation? *Env*, Issue 14

Can Large Doses of Vitamins Improve Health? *Hea*, Issue 13

Does Global Warming Require Immediate Government Action? *Eco*, Issue 17

Do Smokers Have a Right to Smoke in Public Places? *Hea*, Issue 7

Hazardous Waste: Are Cleanup and Control Efforts Succeeding? *Env*, Issue 11

Is Acid Rain a Serious Environmental Problem? *Hea*, Issue 16

Is the Widespread Use of Pesticides Required to Feed the World's People? *Env*, Issue 10

Municipal Waste: Should Recycling Be Promoted as the Key to Refuse Management? *Env*, Issue 12

Nuclear Waste: Is Yucca Mountain an Appropriate Site for Permanent Waste Disposal? *Env*, Issue 13

Should the Phaseout of Chlorofluorocarbons Be Accelerated to Protect the Ozone Layer from Further Depletion? *Env*, Issue 15

Will the "Greening" of Multinational Corporations Lead to Environmental Improvements? *Env*, Issue 6

Toxic waste. *See* **Hazardous waste; Toxic chemicals**

Trade

Does Technology Transfer by Multinational Firms Benefit the Development of Third World Nations? *MM*, Issue 17

Is America Declining? *Pol*, Issue 20

Is Japan a Threat to America's Economic and National Security? *Eco*, Issue 16

Should a New Military-Industrial Complex Be Developed? *Eco*, Issue 18

Should Eastern European Nations Be Encouraged to Develop Free Market Institutions? *BE*, Issue 18

Should the Global Arms Trade Be Severely Restricted? *WP*, Issue 11

Should the United States Protect Domestic Industries from Foreign Competition? *Eco*, Issue 15

Will the European Community Increase Its Level of Integration? *WP*, Issue 4

Will the North American Free Trade Agreement Benefit All Its Member Countries? *WP*, Issue 5

— U —

Underdeveloped countries. *See* Less developed countries

Unemployment

Are Rent Controls the Cause of America's Homelessness? *Eco*, Issue 5

Can Whistle-Blowing Be Clearly Justified? *BE*, Issue 7

Is Italy Solving Its Immigration Problem? *RER*, Issue 15

Is the Concept of the Underclass Useful for Studying Race and Ethnic Relations? *RER*, Issue 2

Should the Government Establish Special Programs and Policies for Black Youths and Their Families? *Fam*, Issue 12

Will the North American Free Trade Agreement Benefit All Its Member Countries? *WP*, Issue 5

Unions. *See* **Labor force**

United Nations

Did the United Nations Earth Summit Produce Useful Results? *Env*, Issue 1

Does the Global Environmental Movement Threaten Economic Prosperity? *WP*, Issue 12

Is There a World Population Crisis? *WP*, Issue 19

Should the United Nations Take on Greater Military Capabilities and Roles? *WP*, Issue 14

Was Intervention in Somalia Strictly for Humanitarian Purposes? *WP*, Issue 8

United States–Less developed countries relations. *See also* **Less developed countries**

Did Nestlé Act Irresponsibly in Marketing Infant Formula to the Third World? *BE*, Issue 19

Did the United Nations Earth Summit Produce Useful Results? *Env*, Issue 1

Should the United States Abandon Its Superpower Role? *WP*, Issue 3

United States military. *See* **Military**

United States–Soviet Union relations

Did President Reagan Win the Cold War? *AH2*, Issue 17

Upper class

Should Surrogate Motherhood Be Outlawed? *HS*, Issue 8

Should the Insanity Defense Be Abolished? *Leg*, Issue 17

Was Antebellum Reform Motivated Primarily by Humanitarian Goals? *AH1*, Issue 11

Urbanization

Can Schools Prevent Urban Dropouts? *Edu*, Issue 12

Did the Progressives Fail? *AH2*, Issue 7

Is Mass Transit the Answer to Improving U.S. Energy Efficiency? *Eco*, Issue 7

Is Street Crime More Harmful Than White-Collar Crime? *Soc*, Issue 16

Was City Government in Late Nineteenth-Century America a "Conspicuous Failure"? *AH2*, Issue 6

Were Nineteenth-Century Entrepreneurs Robber Barons? *AH2*, Issue 2

— V —

Victims

Are Women Only Victims in Their Roles as Social Support Providers? *Fam*, Issue 2

Can Traditional Criminology Make Sense Out of Domestic Violence? *CR*, Issue 11

Does Arrest Reduce Domestic Violence? *Fam*, Issue 10

Does "Lower-Class" Culture Perpetuate Poverty? *Soc,* Issue 9

Does "Lower-Class" Culture Perpetuate Poverty Among Urban Minorities? *RER,* Issue 11

Husband Battering: Is It a Social Problem? *Fam,* Issue 13

Is Affirmative Action Reverse Discrimination? *RER,* Issue 12; *Soc,* Issue 11

Is Rape Motivated by Aggression Instead of Sex? *HS,* Issue 3

Is Street Crime More Serious Than White-Collar Crime? *CR,* Issue 4

Is There a Date Rape Crisis on College Campuses? *HS,* Issue 10

Is the Victims' Rights Movement Succeeding? *CR,* Issue 16

Should "Battered Wife Syndrome" Be Barred as a Defense in a Murder Case? *Leg,* Issue 14

Should Pornography Be Protected as Free Speech? *MM,* Issue 9

Should the Names of Rape Victims Be Published? *MM,* Issue 6

Violence

Are Asian Americans a "Model Minority"? *RER,* Issue 3

Can Traditional Criminology Make Sense Out of Domestic Violence? *CR,* Issue 11

Does Arrest Reduce Domestic Violence? *Fam,* Issue 10

Husband Battering: Is It a Social Problem? *Fam,* Issue 13

Is Pornography Harmful? *HS,* Issue 5

Is Pornography Immoral? *Mor,* Issue 12

Is Rape Motivated by Aggression Instead of Sex? *HS,* Issue 3

Is Street Crime More Serious Than White-Collar Crime? *CR,* Issue 4

Is Terrorism Ever Justified? *Mor,* Issue 17

Is There a Date Rape Crisis on College Campuses? *HS,* Issue 10

Should a National Gun Control Policy Be Established? *Leg,* Issue 15

Should "Battered Wife Syndrome" Be Barred as a Defense in a Murder Case? *Leg,* Issue 14

Should Drugs Be Legalized? *Hea,* Issue 9

Should the Content of Records Be Censored? *MM,* Issue 5

Was Race a Central Factor in the Colonists' Attitudes Toward Native Americans? *AH1,* Issue 2

Would Legalizing Drugs Have Beneficial Effects on Society? *Psy,* Issue 19

Voting. *See* **Elections**

— W —

War

Can Modern War Be Just? *WP,* Issue 20

Can Network News Survive? *MM,* Issue 16

Could the United States Have Prevented the Fall of South Vietnam? *AH2,* Issue 15

Did World War II Liberate American Women? *AH2,* Issue 11

Is Patriotism a Virtue? *Mor,* Issue 19

Should the Policy Banning Gays from the Military Be Lifted? *HS,* Issue 13

Was It Necessary to Drop the Atomic Bomb to End World War II? *AH2,* Issue 12

Was U.S. Foreign Policy in the Early Nineteenth Century Imperialistic? *AH1,* Issue 13

Will Environmental Degradation Be a Feature of International Conflicts in the Future? *Env,* Issue 18

Would Women in Combat Weaken National Security? *WP,* Issue 15

Waste disposal. *See* **Hazardous waste**

Water pollution. *See also* **Pollution**

Hazardous Waste: Are Cleanup and Control Efforts Succeeding? *Env,* Issue 11

Is Acid Rain a Serious Environmental Problem? *Hea,* Issue 16

Municipal Waste: Should Recycling Be Promoted as the Key to Refuse Management? *Env,* Issue 12

Will Environmental Degradation Be a Feature of International Conflicts in the Future? *Env,* Issue 18

Wealth

Are Liberal Values Propagated by the News Media? *Soc,* Issue 2

Does Insider Trading Serve a Useful Purpose? *BE,* Issue 15

Does Society Have an Obligation to Care for the Less Well Off? *Mor,* Issue 9

Do Rich Nations Have an Obligation to Help Poor Nations? *Mor,* Issue 20

Do the News Media Have a Liberal Bias? *Pol,* Issue 4

Is America Declining? *Pol,* Issue 20

Is Crime Functional? *CR,* Issue 1

Should the Capital Gains Tax Be Lowered? *Eco,* Issue 13

Were Nineteenth-Century Entrepreneurs Robber Barons? *AH2,* Issue 2

Were the Founding Fathers Democratic Reformers? *AH1,* Issue 8

Welfare. *See* **Social welfare programs**

Wildlife

Can Experiments Using Animals Be Justified? *Psy,* Issue 3

Is It Unethical to Implant Animal Parts in Humans? *Bio,* Issue 13

Should Animal Experimentation Be Permitted? *Bio,* Issue 12

Should Animals Be Liberated? *Mor,* Issue 6

Should the Endangered Species Act Be Reauthorized? *Env,* Issue 3

Women's issues

Are Gender Differences Present at Birth? *Fam,* Issue 1

Are Media Messages About Women Improving? *MM,* Issue 4

Are Women Only Victims in Their Roles as Social Support Providers? *Fam,* Issue 2

Are Women Paid Less Than Men Because Their Working Conditions Are More Favorable? *Eco,* Issue 4

Can Traditional Criminology Make Sense Out of Domestic Violence? *CR,* Issue 11

Did the Westward Movement Transform the Traditional Roles of Women in the Late Nineteenth Century? *AH2,* Issue 5

Did World War II Liberate American Women? *AH2,* Issue 11

Do Employers Have an Obligation to Provide Parental Leave Policies for Their Employees? *BE,* Issue 6

Does Arrest Reduce Domestic Violence? *Fam,* Issue 10

Do Gender Differences Originate from Biological Factors? *Psy,* Issue 10

Husband Battering: Is It a Social Problem? *Fam,* Issue 13

Is Abortion Protected by the Constitution? *Leg,* Issue 7

Is Day Care Harmful? *Psy,* Issue 11

Is Feminism a Harmful Ideology? *Soc,* Issue 4

Is Feminism a Positive Value for Society? *Mor,* Issue 7

Is Pornography Harmful? *HS,* Issue 5

Is Pornography Immoral? *Mor,* Issue 12

Is Rape Motivated by Aggression Instead of Sex? *HS,* Issue 3

Is There a Date Rape Crisis on College Campuses? *HS,* Issue 10

Is There a Moral Right to Abortion? *Bio,* Issue 2

Is the Victims' Rights Movement Succeeding? *CR,* Issue 16

Should Black Women Join the Feminist Movement? *RER,* Issue 8

Should Commercial Surrogate Motherhood Be Banned? *Bio,* Issue 4

Should Courts Be Permitted to Order Women to Use Long-Acting Contraceptives? *Bio,* Issue 1

Should Pornography Be Protected by the First Amendment? *Leg,* Issue 8

Should Prostitution Be Decriminalized? *HS,* Issue 14

Should RU 486 Be Legalized? *HS,* Issue 6

Should Surrogate Motherhood Be Outlawed? *HS*, Issue 8

Should Traditional Families Be Preserved? *Soc*, Issue 7

Was *Roe v. Wade* a Mistake? *Pol*, Issue 17

Was the Salem Witchcraft Hysteria Caused by a Fear of Women? *AH1*, Issue 3

Were Southern Slaveholding Women Covert Abolitionists? *AH1*, Issue 14

Would a "Mommy Track" Benefit Employed Women? *Fam*, Issue 11; *Soc*, Issue 5

Would Women in Combat Weaken National Security? *WP*, Issue 15

Working women. *See* **Women's issues**

— Y —

Youth

Do Drug Education Programs Prevent Drug Abuse? *Dru*, Issue 11

Does Sex Education Prevent Teen Pregnancy? *Hea*, Issue 10

Is Home Schooling a Viable Alternative? *Edu*, Issue 11

Is National Service at Odds With American National Interest? *Eco*, Issue 3

Should Adolescents Be Allowed to Make Decisions About Abortion Without Parental Involvement? *Psy*, Issue 13

Should Alcohol Advertising Be Limited? *Dru*, Issue 14

Should Pregnant Teens Marry the Fathers of Their Babies? *Fam*, Issue 9

Should Schooling Be Based on Social Experiences? *Edu*, Issue 1

Should the Content of Records Be Censored? *MM*, Issue 5

Should the Drinking Age Remain at 21? *Dru*, Issue 4

Should the Government Establish Special Programs and Policies for Black Youths and Their Families? *Fam*, Issue 12

Will Gun Control Reduce Crime? *CR*, Issue 14

— Z —

Zero population growth. *See* **Population growth**